GOOD HOUSEKEEPING
Complete Book of
Home Preserving

GOOD HOUSEKEEPING
Complete Book of
Home Preserving

Good Housekeeping Institute

EBURY PRESS
London

Published by
Ebury Press
National Magazine House
72 Broadwick Street
London W1V 2BP

First impression 1981

ISBN 0 85223 198 9

Designed by Mike Rose and Robert Lamb

Home economist Susanna Tee

Line drawings by
John Woodcock, Sally Holmes
and Ken Stott

Colour photography by Roger
Phillips except pages 38, 66 and
96 by Melvin Grey

The publishers would like to
thank the Long Ashton Research
Station; Carewell Fruit Farm,
Lingfield, Surrey; Boots The
Chemists; David Mellor; Dickins
& Jones Ltd and Habitat Designs Ltd
for their help in the production of
this book.

Typeset by Advanced Filmsetters (Glasgow) Limited
Printed and bound by New Interlitho s.p.a., Milan

Contents

Notes on Metrication

It is important to follow either the metric or imperial measures when using the recipes in this book as they are not exact conversions and are not interchangeable. Some metric measures have been rounded up or down from the exact conversion for simplicity when buying or weighing large quantities of ingredients. Metric quantities of other ingredients in a recipe have therefore been adjusted to ensure good results. Using the metric measures for a recipe will result in a slightly larger quantity of preserve.

An Introduction to Home Preserving

The making of preserves was once an important and regular feature of family life. Every household had a cupboard or shelf stacked with jars full of preserved foods and families were often dependent on them during the winter months. Nowadays, the increasing availability of fresh foods and of commercially-produced preserves has meant that the art of home preserving is practised much less frequently.

Why Preserve?
The object of preserving has always been to take fresh foods in prime condition and to store or prepare them in such a way that they will remain in this condition for long periods of time.

In the days before refrigeration and easily obtainable canned, dried and frozen foods, it was vital to be able to preserve fresh foods to feed the family when food was scarce. In country areas, each family kept a pig to fatten up during the summer and slaughter at the beginning of winter. Some meat was eaten fresh but the bulk of it had to be preserved in various ways so that it would last throughout the winter. Fresh fruits and vegetables were made into preserves both to prevent wastage and to enable people to enjoy their flavour when they were not available.

Although the necessity for preserving does not exist in quite the same way today, one of the most important benefits is still that of saving money. Jams, jellies and marmalades are best made when fruits are plentiful, cheap and in perfect condition.

Despite their high cost, the quality of commercially-produced preserves is rarely as good as that of home-made preserves. For example, fruits and vegetables certainly lose more of their nutritive value during commercial processing. Making preserves at home enables you to experiment with unusual combinations of flavours and to enjoy the satisfaction of serving foods that are the produce of your own kitchen. An added bonus is that some preserves, such as candied or crystallised fruits, make very acceptable gifts, particularly when decoratively packed.

Like any activity that is worthwhile, home preserving demands time and patience. Most people will find, however, that the end result is always worth any extra work involved. When you are able to enjoy delicious new potatoes at Christmas time or the flavour of cherries in autumn, you will undoubtedly be glad you made the effort.

How Preserving Works
Foods contain enzymes which are responsible for their growth, development and eventual breaking down and rotting. The action of these enzymes is what causes the cut surface of a piece of fruit to turn brown, and allows for the growth of micro-organisms in the form of bacteria, yeasts and moulds. Bacteria in foods can lead to food poisoning, yeasts cause foods to ferment, and moulds spoil the appearance and flavour of foods. Moulds themselves are not harmful, but are often an indication of the presence of bacteria.

Traditional forms of preserving aim to keep out and prevent the growth of micro-organisms and so maintain the foods in prime condition. The first methods of preservation were probably the result of experimentation and a fair amount of luck, but nowadays we know how and why these methods worked. They made use of natural facilities—sun, wind, smoke and salt.

Drying It was discovered that when foods were spread out in the sun or hung in the wind to dry, they did not perish. This is because micro-organisms can only survive where there is moisture and the drying effects of sunshine and wind prevent the growth of micro-organisms. Nowadays, fruits, vegetables and herbs can easily be dried at home in a very cool oven, airing cupboard or some other warm place. Of course, it is always important to store dried foods carefully to prevent the re-absorption of moisture.

Smoking When houses had huge fireplaces and chimneys, meat and fish could be hung in the chimneys until well dried out and 'smoked'. Again, it was the drying process that prevented the growth of bacteria. The flavour of the smoked foods would depend on the type of wood burned in the fire. Nowadays, such facilities for smoking are hard to find and smoking is rarely done in the home. It can also be dangerous if not carried out properly and if the growth of bacteria is not completely eliminated. Commercially-smoked foods are of good quality, if rather expensive, and some, such as smoked salmon, are even preferred to the fresh variety. Because of the facilities needed, the risk of food poisoning and the availability of commercially-produced smoked foods, we do not recommend smoking as a method of home preserving.

Salting In early days, sea salt was obtained by evaporation and rubbed into fish, meat and vegetables. The salt drew moisture out of the food and prevented the growth of micro-organisms. The salting of meat, however, is another method of preservation that can be dangerous if not carried out correctly. As fresh meat is now available all year round and can be preserved in other safer and more efficient ways, such as by freezing, we have not included instructions for salting or curing meat. Small fish and vegetables such as beans can, however, be salted in the home without too much trouble.

These original methods of preservation were used long before it was discovered that sugar, vinegar, alcohol and temperature could also play a part in food preservation.

Sugar A high concentration of sugar prevents the growth of micro-organisms and it is the sugar, combined with cooking to a high temperature, that preserves the fruits in jams, jellies, marmalades, conserves, butters and cheeses. Sugar also acts as the preservative when bottling fruits in a sugar syrup. Again, however, it is necessary to heat the filled bottles to a high temperature in order to sterilise the contents and hermetically seal the bottles to prevent further attack from micro-organisms (see below).

Vinegar and alcohol Vinegar and alcohol also prevent the growth of micro-organisms. Vinegar is used for pickling fruits and vegetables, and in chutneys, sauces and relishes; alcohol is used to preserve fruits.

Sterilisation Extremely high temperatures stop enzyme activity and prevent growth of micro-organisms. Sauces, ketchups and bottled fruits and vegetables all need to be sterilised by heat. This has to be done after the bottles have been filled and covered so that the sterilising process can form a seal to keep out micro-organisms in the air. Milk is commercially sterilised by heat treatment during the pasteurisation process and some milk is heated to a higher temperature ('long-life' or UHT—ultra-high temperature) and can be kept for long periods of time without being refrigerated.

Refrigeration and freezing The discovery that low temperatures slow down or stop enzyme activity in foods has made a major difference to life in the home. Nowadays, almost every household has a refrigerator and many also own a freezer. Frozen foods are kept at a sufficiently low temperature to stop the action of enzymes as long as the food is frozen. Once the food is allowed to thaw, enzyme activity starts up again and micro-organisms will be produced in the food even more quickly than before, so frozen foods, especially fruits and vegetables, will deteriorate rapidly once thawed. Vegetables are first blanched in boiling water in order to destroy the enzymes present before freezing.

Although freezing is a method of home preserving, it is not one of the traditional home skills, so we have included it only as an *alternative* method of preserving fruits and vegetables which are only seasonally available. As fresh meat and fish are now available all the year round, we have not included instructions for freezing them.

How to Use this Book
The traditional skills of home preserving are no longer passed on from generation to generation, and preserving has almost come to be thought of as a mysterious, complicated process. We hope this brief introduction to home preserving will help you understand how the various methods work, and the chapters that follow clearly explain the techniques involved. For each method of preserving, a recipe has been chosen to illustrate, with step-by-step drawings, the simple techniques used. The recipes have all been tested to ensure success with whichever preserves you choose to make.

9

Jams

Jam-making is probably the most popular of all methods of preserving, and most people make their first venture into this specialised kind of cookery with a simple jam, such as plum or gooseberry. If you are lucky enough to have a garden that produces a variety of different fruits, you can not only obtain the produce cheaply, but can also experiment with more unusual and very delicious mixed fruit preserves. If you don't grow your own fruit, look out for the glut seasons for produce like apples, plums, rhubarb and marrow when they are at their cheapest (see charts on pages 181–187), and if you live in or near the countryside, you may be able to harvest such fruits as blackberries and bilberries.

Equipment for Jam-making
Some special utensils and tools, though by no means essential, make jam-making easier.

Preserving pans Choose a preserving pan made from heavy aluminium, stainless steel or tin-lined copper. It should have a fairly thick base to prevent the jam burning, and should be wide enough to allow the jam to boil rapidly without splashing all over the cooker. The best size for you will depend on how much jam you want to make at one time—preferably, the jam should come no more than half-way up the pan.

Old-style preserving pans made from un-lined copper or brass can be used for jams, providing they are perfectly clean. Any discoloration or tarnish should be removed with a patent cleaner and the pan should be thoroughly washed before use. Jams made in copper or brass pans will contain less vitamin C than those made in aluminium or stainless

steel pans so any preserve must not be left standing in a copper or brass pan for any length of time.

If you haven't got a preserving pan, use a large thick-based saucepan, remembering that, since most saucepans are not as wide as a preserving pan, you may need to allow a longer simmering and boiling period for the fruit.

Jam jars   You will need a good supply of jars, which should be free from cracks, chips or other flaws. Jars holding 500 g or 1 kg (1 or 2 lb) are the most useful sizes as you can buy covers for these sizes. Wash them well in warm soapy water and rinse thoroughly in clean, warm water. Dry off the jars in a cool oven, at 140°C (275°F) mark 1, and use while hot so that they do not crack when filled with boiling jam. You will need waxed discs, cellophane covers, rubber bands and labels for covering and labelling the jars. Packets containing all these are available from most stationery shops.

Other equipment
1. A large, long-handled wooden spoon for stirring jam.
2. A slotted spoon is useful for skimming off any scum or fruit stones from the surface of jam.
3. A sugar thermometer, though not essential, is very helpful when testing for a set (see page 12).
4. A funnel with a wide tube for filling jars is useful. Failing this, use a heatproof jug or large cup.
5. A cherry stoner saves time and prevents hands becoming stained with cherry juice.
6. Any sieve that is used in jam-making should be made of nylon, not metal which may discolour the fruit.

Fruit for Jam-making

Fruit should be sound and just ripe. It is better to use slightly under- rather than over-ripe fruit as the pectin (see below) is most readily available at this stage.

Pectin and acid content of fruit   The jam will only set if there are sufficient quantities of pectin, acid and sugar present. Some fruits are rich in pectin and acid and give a good set,

while others do not contain so much (see chart below).

Pectin Content of Fruits and Vegetables used in Preserving		
Good	*Medium*	*Poor*
Cooking apples	Dessert apples	Bananas
Crab-apples	Apricots	Carrots
Cranberries	Bilberries	Cherries
Currants	Blackberries	Elderberries
(red and black)	Cranberries	Figs
Damsons	Greengages	Grapes
Gooseberries	Loganberries	Japonica
Lemons	Mulberries	Marrows
Limes	Plums	Medlars
Seville oranges	Raspberries	Melons
Plums		Nectarines
(some varieties)		Peaches
Quinces		Pineapple
		Rhubarb
		Strawberries

Test for pectin content   If you are not sure of the setting qualities of the fruit you are using, the following test can be made: When fruit has been cooked until soft and before you add the sugar (see page 12), take 5 ml (1 tsp) juice, as free as possible from seeds and skin, put it in a glass and, when cool, add 15 ml (1 tbsp) methylated spirits. Shake the glass and then leave for 1 minute. If the mixture forms a jelly-like clot, the fruit has a good pectin content. If it does not form a single, firm clot, the pectin content is low and some form of extra pectin will be needed.

Fruits that lack acid and pectin require the addition of a fruit or fruit juice that is rich in these substances. Lemon juice is most often used for this purpose, since it aids the set and often brings out the flavour of the fruit. Allow 30 ml (2 tbsp) lemon juice to 2 kg (4 lb) of a fruit with poor setting properties. Alternatively, use some home-made pectin extract (see page 12) or add the whole fruit, making a mixed fruit jam. Yet another method is to use a commercially bottled pectin according to the manufacturer's instructions.

Sometimes an acid only is added, such as citric or tartaric acid. These contain no pectin but help to extract the natural pectin from the tissues of the fruit and improve the flavour of fruits lacking in acid. Allow 2.5 ml ($\frac{1}{2}$ level tsp) to 2 kg (4 lb) of a fruit with poor setting properties.

Home-made pectin extracts Apple pectin extract can be made from any sour cooking apples or crab-apples as well as from apple peelings and cores and windfalls. Wash 1 kg (2 lb) fruit and chop it roughly, without peeling or coring. Cover with 600–900 ml (1–1$\frac{1}{2}$ pints) water and stew gently for about 45 minutes, until well pulped. Strain through a jelly bag or muslin cloth (see page 34). Carry out the pectin test (see page 11) to ensure that the extract has a high pectin content. Allow 150–300 ml ($\frac{1}{4}$–$\frac{1}{2}$ pint) of this extract to 2 kg (4 lb) fruit that is low in pectin. Pectin extract can be made from redcurrants or gooseberries in the same way.

Sugar

The presence of sugar in jam is very important as it acts as a preservative and affects the setting quality. The exact amount of sugar to be used depends on the pectin strength of the fruit, so always use the amount specified in the recipe. Too little sugar will result in a poor set and the jam may go mouldy on storing. Too much sugar will produce a dark and sticky jam, the flavour will be lost and it may crystallise. Granulated sugar is suitable and the most economical for jam-making but less scum is formed when lump sugar or preserving crystals are used. The finished preserve will also be slightly clearer and brighter, but this does not really justify the extra cost unless you intend to show your preserves. Caster sugar or brown sugar can also be used, but brown sugar is, of course, more expensive than white sugars and produces much darker jam with a changed flavour.

There is no completely satisfactory substitute for sugar in jam-making. If honey or treacle is used, its flavour is usually distinctly noticeable and the jam will not set easily. Glucose and glycerine do not have the same sweetening power as cane sugar. If one of these alternatives must be used, not more than half the amount of sugar specified in the recipe should be replaced.

Preparing the Fruit and Cooking the Jam

Pick over the fruit, prepare it according to variety, and wash it quickly. Put the fruit into a preserving pan or large, strong saucepan, add water as directed in the recipe and then simmer gently until it is quite tender. The time will vary according to the fruit—tough-skinned fruit, such as gooseberries, black-currants or plums, will take 30–45 minutes. This simmering process releases the pectin and acid. If extra acid or pectin is needed, it should be added at this stage (see page 11). Adequate reduction of the fruit before adding the sugar is necessary for a good set. The sugar should only be added when the fruit has been sufficiently softened and reduced as sugar has a hardening effect on the fruit and, once added, the fruit will not soften.

Remove the pan from the heat and add the sugar, stirring well until dissolved. (The sugar will dissolve easily if warmed in the oven before it is added.) Add a knob of butter to reduce foaming, then return the pan to the heat and boil rapidly, stirring constantly, until the jam sets when tested (see below).

Testing for a Set (see drawings opposite)

There are several ways of testing a preserve for setting point, some of which are less accurate than others or require special equipment. The methods given here are the simplest and most accurate.

Temperature test This is the most accurate method of testing for a set. Stir the jam and put in a sugar thermometer. Continue cooking and, when the temperature reaches 105°C (221°F), a set should be obtained. Some fruits may need a degree lower or higher than this, so it is a good idea to combine this test with one of the following.

Saucer test Put a very little of the jam on a cold saucer or plate, allow it to cool, then push a finger gently through the jam. If the surface of the jam wrinkles, setting point has been reached. (The pan should be removed from the heat during the test or the jam may be over-boiled, which weakens the setting property.)

Flake test Lift some jam out of the pan on a wooden spoon, let it cool a little and then allow it to drop back into the pan. If it has been boiled long enough, drops of jam will run together along the edge of the spoon and form flakes which will break off sharply.

Potting, Covering and Storing

The jars used for jam must be clean and free

PLUM JAM
(see page 22)

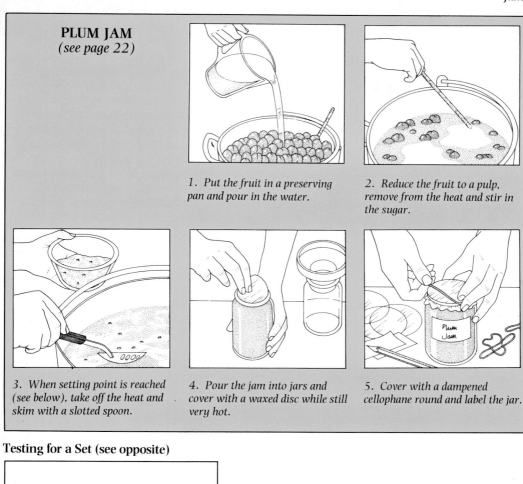

1. Put the fruit in a preserving pan and pour in the water.

2. Reduce the fruit to a pulp, remove from the heat and stir in the sugar.

3. When setting point is reached (see below), take off the heat and skim with a slotted spoon.

4. Pour the jam into jars and cover with a waxed disc while still very hot.

5. Cover with a dampened cellophane round and label the jar.

Testing for a Set (see opposite)

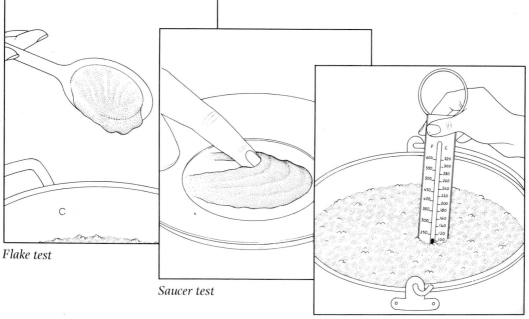

Flake test

Saucer test

Temperature test

from flaws and they must be warmed before the jam is put in them (see page 11). As soon as a set has been reached, remove the pan from the heat, remove any scum with a slotted spoon and pot the jam, filling right to the tops. Exceptions are strawberry and other whole-fruit jams—these should be allowed to cool for about 15 minutes before being potted, to prevent the fruit rising in the jars. Wipe the outside and rims of the pots and cover the jam, while still very hot, with a waxed disc, waxed-side down, making sure it lies flat. Either cover immediately with a dampened cellophane round, securing with a rubber band or string, or leave the jam until quite cold before doing this. Label the jar and store in a cool, dry, dark place.

Most preserves keep well for over a year if properly covered and stored, but their flavour deteriorates if they are kept for too long. The best idea, therefore, is to eat them within the year, thus making room in the store-cupboard for next year's batch of preserves.

Jam-making Problems

Mould This is most often caused by failure to cover the jam with a waxed disc while it is still very hot—this should be done immediately the jam is potted, or it may become infected with mould spores from the air. Alternatively, the pots may have been damp or cold when used, or insufficiently filled, or they may have been stored in a damp or warm place. Other possible causes are insufficient evaporation of water while the fruit is being 'broken down' by the preliminary cooking, and/or too short boiling after the sugar has been added. Mould is not actually harmful to the jam, but it may affect the flavour slightly. To treat the jam, remove the mould, boil the jam up again, re-pot in clean, pre-heated jars and re-cover. Use the jam for cooking purposes.

Bubbles in the jam Bubbles indicate fermentation, which is usually the result of too small a proportion of sugar in relation to fruit; accurate weighing of fruit and sugar is very important. This trouble can also occur, however, when jam is not reduced sufficiently, because this too affects the proportion of sugar in the preserve. Fermentation is harmless enough, but it is apt to spoil both flavour and colour. Fermented jam can be boiled up again but the boiling should only be continued for a short time if the preserve was not reduced enough in the first instance. Then it can be re-potted and sealed in clean, pre-heated jars and used for cooking purposes.

Peel or fruit rising in the jam Strawberry jam is particularly susceptible to this trouble. It helps if the jam is allowed to cool for 15–20 minutes and then given a stir before potting (despite the fact that it is normally advisable to pot all preserves as hot as possible).

Crystallised jam This is usually caused by lack of sufficient acid. You should either use a fruit rich in acid, or make sure that acid is added to the fruit during the preliminary softening process (see page 11). Under- or over-boiling the jam after the sugar has been added can also cause crystallising, as it will upset the proportion of sugar in the finished jam.

Setting problems One cause is the use of over-ripe fruit in which the pectin has deteriorated. Another reason is under-boiling of the fruit, so that the pectin is not fully extracted; there may also be insufficient evaporation of the water before the sugar is added (this can be remedied by further boiling); or over-cooking after adding the sugar, for which there is no remedy.

To ensure a set with fruits deficient in pectin, such as strawberries, it is helpful to add an acid such as lemon juice or citric acid (see page 11); alternatively, mix with a pectin-rich fruit such as redcurrants, or a pectin extract (commercially made or prepared at home from apples—see page 12).

Shrinkage of jam on storage This is caused by inadequate covering, or failure to store the jam in a cool, dark, dry place.

Pressure Cooking Jams

Provided your cooker is one with a three-pressure gauge, it is a good idea to use it for preserving, as it saves quite a bit of time and the fruit retains its flavour and colour.

There are a few points to remember:
1. Always remove the trivet from the pressure pan.
2. Never fill the pan more than half-full.
3. Cook the fruit at medium (10 lb) pressure.
4. Reduce pressure at room temperature.
5. Only the preliminary cooking and softening of the fruit must be done under pressure—never cook a preserve under pressure after adding the sugar (and lemon juice, if used), but boil it up in an open pan.

6. You can adapt any ordinary jam recipe for use with a pressure cooker by using half the stated amount of water and doing the preliminary cooking of the fruit under pressure. These are the times required for different fruits (all at medium—10 lb pressure):

Apples	5 minutes
Blackberries and apples combined	7 minutes
Blackcurrants	3–4 minutes
Damsons, plums and other stone fruit	5 minutes
Gooseberries	3 minutes
Marrow	1–2 minutes
Pears (cooking)	7 minutes
Quinces	5 minutes

7. Soft fruits, such as raspberries and strawberries, need very little preliminary softening and are therefore not usually cooked in a pressure cooker.

8. When two fruits (e.g. blackberries and apples) are combined, the cooking times may vary somewhat.

SWISS CHERRY JAM

As cherries are lacking in pectin, this jam will give only a light set.

2 kg (4 lb) cherries (e.g. Morello or May Duke),
*   washed and stoned (see note below)*
juice of 3 lemons
1.5 kg (3 lb) sugar
a knob of butter
75 ml (5 tbsp) kirsch (optional)

Crack a few of the cherry stones in a nutcracker and remove the kernels. Put the cherries, kernels and lemon juice in a pan and simmer very gently for about 45 minutes until really soft, stirring from time to time to prevent sticking.

Remove from the heat, add the sugar, stirring until dissolved, then add a knob of butter and boil rapidly for about 30 minutes. Test for a set and, when setting point is reached, take the pan off the heat and remove any scum with a slotted spoon. Stir in the kirsch, then pot and cover the jam in the usual way.

Makes about 2.5 kg (5 lb)

Note   Cherry stones are easy to remove with a cherry stoner, but if you haven't got one, use the cherries with their stones and remove them from the pan with a slotted spoon as they rise to the surface.

STRAWBERRY JAM

1.75 kg (3½ lb) strawberries, washed and hulled
45 ml (3 tbsp) lemon juice
1.5 kg (3 lb) sugar
a knob of butter

Place the strawberries in a preserving pan with the lemon juice and simmer gently, stirring occasionally, for 20–30 minutes until really soft.

Take the pan off the heat, add the sugar, stirring until dissolved, then add a knob of butter and boil rapidly for about 20 minutes. Test for a set and, when setting point is reached, take the pan off the heat and remove any scum with a slotted spoon. Allow the jam to cool for 15–20 minutes to prevent the fruit rising in the jars, then stir gently and pot and cover in the usual way.

Makes about 2.5 kg (5 lb)

ROSY TOMATO JAM

5 lemons, washed and halved
water
1 kg (2 lb) red tomatoes, skinned and quartered
1 kg (2 lb) sugar
a knob of butter

Squeeze the juice out of the lemons, reserving the pips. Remove the remaining flesh from the lemon halves and reserve. Strip the excess pith away from the lemon rind and cut the rind into thin strips. Place in a saucepan, add 150 ml (¼ pint) water and simmer, covered, for 20 minutes.

Remove the cores and seeds from the tomato quarters and tie in a piece of muslin with the lemon pips and flesh. Measure the lemon juice, make it up to 1.8 litres (3 pints) with water and pour into a preserving pan. Shred the tomato flesh and add to the pan with the softened lemon shreds, liquid and muslin bag. Simmer gently for about 40 minutes until tender. Remove the muslin bag and squeeze it well, allowing the juice to run back into the pan. Remove the pan from the heat, add the sugar, stirring until dissolved, then add a knob of butter and boil rapidly for 20 minutes. Test for a set and, when setting point is reached, take the pan off the heat and

remove any scum with a slotted spoon. Pot and cover the jam in the usual way.

Makes about 1.5 kg (3 lb)

WHOLE STRAWBERRY JAM
Illustrated in colour on page 25

1.25 kg (2½ lb) small strawberries, washed and
*   hulled*
45 ml (3 tbsp) lemon juice
1.5 kg (3 lb) sugar
a knob of butter
227-ml (8-fl oz) bottle of commercial pectin

Place the strawberries in a preserving pan with the lemon juice and sugar. Leave to stand for 1 hour, stirring occasionally. Heat slowly, stirring, until the sugar has dissolved, then add a small knob of butter to reduce foaming. Bring to the boil and boil rapidly for 4 minutes, stirring occasionally. Remove the pan from the heat and stir in the pectin. Cool for at least 20 minutes to prevent the fruit rising in the jars, then pot and cover in the usual way.

Makes about 2.5 kg (5 lb)

HONEY-PINEAPPLE JAM

1.5 kg (3 lb) ripe pineapple, peeled, cored and
*   chopped*
juice of 1 lemon
750 g (1½ lb) thick honey
half a 227-ml (8-fl oz) bottle of commercial
*   pectin*

Crush the pineapple thoroughly with a rolling pin or masher and place in a preserving pan with the lemon juice and honey. Mix well, bring to the boil and simmer for 20 minutes, stirring occasionally. Remove from the heat and stir in the pectin. Bring to the boil for 1 minute and remove any scum with a slotted spoon. Pot and cover in the usual way.

Makes about 1.25 kg (2½ lb)

UNCOOKED FREEZER JAM

This jam has a set similar to a conserve (see page 142). It will keep for up to six months in a freezer.

1.5 kg (3 lb) raspberries or strawberries, hulled
2 kg (4 lb) caster sugar
60 ml (4 tbsp) lemon juice
227-ml (8-fl oz) bottle of commercial pectin

Place the fruit in a large bowl and very lightly crush with a fork. Stir in the sugar and lemon juice and leave at room temperature, stirring occasionally, for about 1 hour until the sugar has dissolved. Gently stir in the pectin and continue stirring for a further 2 minutes. Pour the jam into small plastic containers, leaving a little space at the top to allow for expansion. Cover and leave at room temperature for a further 24 hours. Label and freeze. To serve, thaw at room temperature for about 1 hour.

Makes about 3.5 kg (7 lb)

ROSE PETAL JAM

This unusual jam has a strong, distinctive flavour. It should be eaten in small quantities and is delicious on biscuits served with tea, as it is in Russia, or as a sweetmeat. It is well worth making if you have an abundance of roses. Pick deep red, heavily-scented roses.

250 g (8 oz) rose petals
500 g (1 lb) sugar
1.2 litres (2 pints) water
juice of 2 lemons

Pick the roses when they are in full bloom, remove the petals and snip off the white bases. Cut the petals into small pieces, but not too finely. Place in a bowl and add 250 g (8 oz) sugar. Cover and leave overnight. This will extract the scent and darken the petals.

Pour the water and lemon juice into a saucepan and stir in the remaining sugar. Heat gently until the sugar has dissolved, but do not boil. Stir in the rose petals and simmer gently for 20 minutes. Bring to the boil and boil for about 5 minutes until thick. (This jam is not brought to setting point.) Pot and cover in the usual way.

Makes about 500 g (1 lb)

CARROT JAM

1 kg (2 lb) large carrots, trimmed and peeled
3 lemons, washed
1.2 litres (2 pints) water
1 kg (2 lb) sugar
25 g (1 oz) blanched almonds
15 ml (1 tbsp) brandy

Slice or chop the carrots. Grate the rind from the lemons and squeeze out the juice, reserving the pips. Roughly chop the lemon pith and tie tightly in a piece of muslin with the pips. Put the carrots, grated lemon rind and juice, muslin bag and water into a preserving pan and bring to the boil. Boil for about 1 hour until the carrots are tender.

Remove the muslin bag. Drain the carrots and press them through a sieve or liquidise in a blender. Return the pulp to a clean pan with the sugar. Heat gently, stirring, until the sugar has dissolved. Bring to the boil and boil rapidly for about 10 minutes. Test for a set and, when setting point is reached, take the pan off the heat and remove any scum with a slotted spoon. Split the almonds and stir them into the jam with the brandy. Pot and cover in the usual way.

Makes about 2 kg (4 lb)

Note If liked, angelica or preserved ginger may be used instead of the almonds.

MELON AND GINGER JAM

2 kg (4 lb) honeydew melon (prepared weight),
    seeded, skinned and diced
2 kg (4 lb) sugar
25 g (1 oz) root ginger
thinly pared rind and juice of 3 lemons
a knob of butter

Place the prepared melon in a bowl, sprinkle
with about 500 g (1 lb) of the sugar and leave
to stand overnight. Crush or 'bruise' the
ginger with a rolling pin or weight to release
the flavour from the fibres and tie it in a piece
of muslin with the lemon rind. Place in a
preserving pan with the melon and lemon
juice. Simmer gently for 30 minutes, then
remove the pan from the heat and add the rest
of the sugar. Stir until the sugar has dissolved,
add a knob of butter and boil gently for about
30 minutes until the melon looks transparent.
Test for a set and, when setting point is

reached, take the pan off the heat, remove the
muslin bag and any scum with a slotted
spoon. Pot and cover the jam as usual.

Makes about 2.5 kg (5 lb)

PRUNE JAM

6 whole cloves
1 blade of mace
5 cm (2 inches) cinnamon stick
1 kg (2 lb) prunes, washed and soaked overnight
1.2 litres (2 pints) water
juice of 2 lemons
1 kg (2 lb) sugar
a knob of butter

Tie the cloves, mace and cinnamon in a piece
of muslin. Drain the prunes and place them in
a preserving pan with the water, lemon juice
and muslin bag. Cover and simmer gently for
about 1 hour until the prunes are very soft.
Using a slotted spoon, remove the stones as
they rise to the surface.

Remove the muslin bag, then take the pan
off the heat and add the sugar, stirring until
dissolved. Add a knob of butter, then bring to
the boil and boil rapidly for 10 minutes. Test
for a set and, when setting point is reached,
take the pan off the heat and remove any
scum with a slotted spoon. Pot and cover the
jam in the usual way.

Makes about 3 kg (6 lb)

APPLE GINGER JAM

2 kg (4 lb) cooking apples
900 ml (1½ pints) water
250 g (8 oz) preserved ginger, drained and
    chopped
45 ml (3 tbsp) ginger syrup from the jar
grated rind and juice of 3 lemons
1.5 kg (3 lb) sugar

Peel, core and slice the apples and tie the cores
and peel in a piece of muslin. Put the apples
and muslin bag in a preserving pan with the
water and simmer gently until the fruit is
really soft and pulpy. Remove the muslin bag
and mash the apples or press them through a
nylon sieve.

Return the apple purée to the pan and add the ginger, ginger syrup, the rind and juice of the lemons and the sugar. Bring to the boil, stirring constantly, and boil rapidly for 10 minutes. Test for a set and, when setting point is reached, take the pan off the heat and remove any scum with a slotted spoon. Leave the jam to stand for 15 minutes before potting and covering in the usual way.

Makes 2.75–3.5 kg (5½–7 lb)

Note Windfall apples may be used in this recipe. The amount of ginger used can be varied according to taste.

PEACH JAM

This delicious preserve has only a light set.

2 kg (4 lb) peaches
1 lemon
450 ml (¾ pint) water
1.5 kg (3 lb) sugar
a knob of butter
227-ml (8-fl oz) bottle of commercial pectin

Skin, stone and chop the peaches, reserving the stones. Halve the lemon and squeeze out the juice. Cut up the peel and tie in a piece of muslin with the peach stones. Put the peaches, lemon juice and muslin bag into a preserving pan with the water. Bring to the boil, then simmer for about 30 minutes until the peaches are tender. Remove the muslin bag, squeezing well in a sieve with the back of a wooden spoon.

Remove the pan from the heat, add the sugar and stir until dissolved. Add a knob of butter, then bring to the boil and boil rapidly for 5–10 minutes. Remove the pan from the heat, add the pectin, return to the heat and boil for a further minute. Remove any scum with a slotted spoon and allow to cool slightly before potting and covering the jam in the usual way.

Makes about 3 kg (6 lb)

MULBERRY AND APPLE JAM

1.5 kg (3 lb) mulberries, washed
600 ml (1 pint) water
500 g (1 lb) cooking apples (prepared weight), peeled, cored and sliced
1.75 kg (3½ lb) sugar
a knob of butter

Place the mulberries in a preserving pan with half the water and simmer gently for about 20 minutes until they are soft and pulpy. Place the apples in a saucepan with the remaining water and simmer gently for about 20 minutes until they are soft and pulpy. Add the apples to the mulberries and stir in the sugar. Continue stirring until the sugar has dissolved, then add a knob of butter and boil the jam for about 10 minutes. Test for a set and, when setting point is reached, take the pan off the heat and remove any scum with a slotted spoon. Pot and cover the jam as usual.

Makes about 2.5 kg (5 lb)

APRICOT JAM

2 kg (4 lb) apricots, washed, halved and stoned
450 ml (¾ pint) water
juice of 1 lemon
2 kg (4 lb) sugar
a knob of butter

Crack a few of the apricot stones with a weight, nutcracker or hammer, take out the kernels and blanch in boiling water for 1 minute. Place the apricots, water, lemon juice and kernels in a preserving pan and simmer for about 15 minutes until they are soft and the contents of the pan are well reduced. Take the pan off the heat, add the sugar, stirring until dissolved, then add a knob of butter and boil the jam rapidly for about 15 minutes. Test for a set and, when setting point is reached, take the pan off the heat and remove any scum with a slotted spoon. Pot and cover the jam in the usual way.

Makes about 3.25 kg (6½ lb)

DRIED APRICOT JAM
Illustrated in colour on page 28

500 g (1 lb) dried apricots
1.8 litres (3 pints) water
juice of 1 lemon
1.5 kg (3 lb) sugar
50 g (2 oz) blanched almonds, split
a knob of butter

Put the apricots in a bowl, cover with the water and leave to soak overnight.

Place the apricots in a preserving pan with the soaking water and lemon juice. Simmer for about 30 minutes until soft, stirring from time to time. Remove the pan from the heat and add the sugar and blanched almonds. Stir until the sugar has dissolved, then add a knob of butter and boil rapidly for 20–25 minutes, stirring frequently to prevent sticking. Test for a set and, when setting point is reached, take the pan off the heat and remove any scum with a slotted spoon. Pot and cover the jam in the usual way.

Makes about 2.5 kg (5 lb)

QUICK APRICOT JAM

three 425-g (15-oz) cans apricot halves
30 ml (2 tbsp) lemon juice
500 g (1 lb) sugar

Drain the apricots, reserving the syrup. Put the apricots into an electric blender with 300 ml (½ pint) of the syrup, the lemon juice and the sugar. (If you are using a small blender, process the mixture in small amounts.) Blend until smooth, then pour into a saucepan and boil gently until thick. Pot and cover the jam in the usual way.

Makes about 1.5 kg (3 lb)

RASPBERRY JAM

2 kg (4 lb) raspberries, washed
2 kg (4 lb) sugar
a knob of butter

Place the fruit in a preserving pan and simmer very gently in its own juice for about 20 minutes, stirring carefully from time to time, until the fruit is really soft. Remove the pan from the heat and add the sugar, stirring until dissolved, then add a knob of butter and boil rapidly for about 30 minutes. Test for a set and, when setting point is reached, take the pan off the heat and remove any scum with a slotted spoon. Pot and cover the jam in the usual way.

Makes about 3.25 kg (6½ lb)

VARIATION
Loganberry jam
Illustrated in colour on page 27
Follow the above recipe, using loganberries instead of raspberries.

PLUM AND APPLE JAM

1 kg (2 lb) plums, washed, halved and stoned
1 kg (2 lb) apples, peeled, cored and sliced
900 ml (1½ pints) water
1.5 kg (3 lb) sugar
a knob of butter

Put the plums, apples and water in a preserving pan and boil for about 1 hour until the fruit is tender and the contents of the pan have been reduced by half. Remove the pan from the heat and add the sugar, stirring until dissolved, then add a knob of butter and boil rapidly for 10–15 minutes. Test for a set and, when setting point is reached, take the pan off the heat, remove any scum with a slotted spoon, then pot and cover in the usual way.

Makes about 2.5 kg (5 lb)

QUINCE AND MARROW JAM

Combining quinces with marrow is an economical way of using this delicious fruit, which is usually only available for a very short period each year.

1 kg (2 lb) quinces (prepared weight), peeled, cored and sliced
1 kg (2 lb) marrow (prepared weight), peeled, seeded and diced
900 ml (1½ pints) water
60 ml (4 tbsp) lemon juice
3 kg (6 lb) sugar
a knob of butter

Place the quinces and marrow in a preserving pan with the water and lemon juice. Simmer gently for about 45 minutes until tender and pulpy. Remove the pan from the heat and add the sugar, stirring until dissolved. Add a knob of butter and bring to the boil. Boil rapidly for 10 minutes. Test for a set and, when setting point is reached, take the pan off the heat and remove any scum with a slotted spoon. Pot and cover the jam in the usual way.

Makes about 5 kg (10 lb)

CHERRY AND APPLE JAM

1 kg (2 lb) sour cooking apples, washed
900 ml (1½ pints) water
2 kg (4 lb) Morello or May Duke cherries, washed
juice of 1 lemon
1.75 kg (3½ lb) sugar
a knob of butter

Slice the apples without peeling or coring, put them into a large saucepan with the water and simmer for 30–40 minutes until they are well pulped. Spoon them into a jelly bag (see page 34) and leave to strain for several hours.

Put the apple extract, which should weigh about 300 g (10 oz), into a preserving pan with the cherries and lemon juice and simmer gently for about 30 minutes until a large part of the moisture from the cherries has evaporated. Remove from the heat and stir in the sugar, then add a knob of butter, bring to the boil and boil for 10 minutes. Test for a set and, when setting point is reached, take the pan off the heat and remove any scum with a slotted spoon. Pot and cover the jam in the usual way.

Makes about 3 kg (6 lb)

Quince

CRANBERRY JAM

1 kg (2 lb) cranberries, washed
200 ml (7 fl oz) water
1 kg (2 lb) sugar
a knob of butter

Put the fruit and water in a preserving pan. Bring to the boil. Simmer for 30–40 minutes until the fruit is soft and the skins tender. Remove from the heat, add the sugar and stir carefully until dissolved. Add a knob of butter, bring the jam to the boil and boil rapidly for about 15 minutes. Test for a set and, when setting point is reached, remove the pan from the heat and remove any scum with a slotted spoon. Pot and cover the jam as usual.

Makes about 1.5 kg (3 lb)

GOOSEBERRY AND APPLE JAM

750 g (1½ lb) gooseberries (preferably red), topped, tailed and washed
1 kg (2 lb) cooking apples, peeled, cored and chopped
300 ml (½ pint) water
1.75 kg (3½ lb) sugar
a knob of butter

Put the fruit into a preserving pan, add the water, bring to the boil and simmer gently for about 30 minutes until the fruit is soft and pulpy.

Remove the pan from the heat, add the sugar, stirring until it has dissolved. Add a knob of butter, bring to the boil, stirring all the time, and continue to boil for 15 minutes. Test for a set and, when setting point is reached, take the pan off the heat and remove any scum with a slotted spoon. Pot and cover the jam in the usual way.

Makes about 2.5 kg (5 lb)

PEACH AND RASPBERRY JAM

1 kg (2 lb) fresh peaches (prepared weight), skinned, stoned and chopped
1 kg (2 lb) raspberries, washed
150 ml (¼ pint) water
1.5 kg (3 lb) sugar
a knob of butter

Crack the peach stones with a nutcracker or hammer, take out the kernels and tie them in a piece of muslin. Put the fruit and water into a preserving pan with the muslin bag and simmer gently for about 30 minutes until the fruit is tender. Remove the muslin bag, squeezing well.

Remove the pan from the heat, add the sugar and stir until dissolved. Add a knob of butter and boil for about 15 minutes, stirring occasionally. Test for a set and, when setting point is reached, take the pan off the heat and remove any scum with a slotted spoon. Pot and cover the jam in the usual way.

Makes about 2.5 kg (5 lb)

FRESH FIG JAM

500 g (1 lb) fresh figs, washed and sliced
250 g (8 oz) cooking apples, peeled, cored and sliced
grated rind of 1 lemon
juice of 3 lemons
500 g (1 lb) sugar
a knob of butter

Place the fruit in a preserving pan with the lemon rind and juice. Simmer gently for about 30 minutes until the fruit is quite tender. Remove the pan from the heat, add the sugar, stirring until dissolved. Add a knob of butter, bring to the boil and boil rapidly for 10 minutes. Test for a set and, when setting point is reached, take the pan off the heat and remove any scum with a slotted spoon. Pot and cover the jam in the usual way.

Makes about 1 kg (2 lb)

PLUM JAM

3 kg (6 lb) plums, washed
900 ml (1½ pints) water
3 kg (6 lb) sugar
a knob of butter

Place the plums and water in a preserving pan and simmer gently for about 30 minutes until the fruit is really soft and the contents of the pan are well reduced. Remove the pan from the heat, add the sugar, stirring until dissolved, then add a knob of butter and boil rapidly for 10–15 minutes. Test for a set and, when setting point is reached, take the pan off the heat. Using a slotted spoon, remove the stones and any scum from the surface of the jam. Pot and cover the jam in the usual way.

Makes about 5 kg (10 lb)

PINEAPPLE JAM

*1.5 kg (3 lb) pineapple (prepared weight), peeled,
    cored and finely chopped
450 ml ($\frac{3}{4}$ pint) water
juice of 1 lemon
1.25 kg ($2\frac{1}{2}$ lb) sugar
a knob of butter*

Put the pineapple in a preserving pan with the water and lemon juice and simmer gently for 45 minutes–1 hour until the pineapple is tender and the water has almost all evaporated. Remove the pan from the heat, add the sugar, stirring until dissolved. Add a knob of butter, bring to the boil and boil for about 10 minutes. Test for a set and, when setting point is reached, take the pan off the heat and remove any scum with a slotted spoon. Pot and cover the jam as usual.

Makes about 2 kg (4 lb)

CHERRY AND GOOSEBERRY JAM

*1.5 kg (3 lb) Morello or May Duke cherries,
    washed and stoned
750 g (1$\frac{1}{2}$ lb) red gooseberries, topped, tailed and
    washed
200 ml (7 fl oz) water
2.5 ml ($\frac{1}{2}$ level tsp) citric or tartaric acid
2 kg (4 lb) sugar
a knob of butter*

Place the cherries and gooseberries in a preserving pan and heat gently until the juice flows, then add the water and acid. Simmer for about 20 minutes until the fruit is tender. Remove the pan from the heat, add the sugar and stir until dissolved. Add a knob of butter, bring to the boil and boil rapidly for 10–15 minutes. Test for a set and, when setting point is reached, take the pan off the heat and

remove any scum with a slotted spoon. Pot and cover the jam in the usual way.

Makes about 3 kg (6 lb)

BLACKBERRY AND APPLE JAM
Illustrated in colour on page 96

*2 kg (4 lb) blackberries, washed
300 ml ($\frac{1}{2}$ pint) water
750 g (1$\frac{1}{2}$ lb) sour cooking apples (prepared
    weight), peeled, cored and sliced
3 kg (6 lb) sugar
a knob of butter*

Place the blackberries in a large saucepan with 150 ml ($\frac{1}{4}$ pint) of the water and simmer gently until soft. Put the apples in a preserving pan with the remaining 150 ml ($\frac{1}{4}$ pint) water and simmer gently until soft. Pulp with a wooden spoon or a potato masher.

Add the blackberries and sugar to the apple pulp, stirring until the sugar has dissolved, then add a knob of butter, bring to the boil and boil rapidly, stirring frequently, for about 10 minutes. Test for a set and, when setting point is reached, take the pan off the heat and remove any scum with a slotted spoon. Pot and cover the jam in the usual way.

Makes about 5 kg (10 lb)

LOGANBERRY AND CHERRY JAM

1.5 kg (3 lb) Morello cherries, washed
1.5 kg (3 lb) loganberries, washed
200 ml (7 fl oz) water
juice of 2 lemons
3 kg (6 lb) sugar
a knob of butter

Stone the cherries, reserving some of the stones. Place the fruit in a preserving pan with the water and lemon juice. Using a hammer, crack the reserved cherry stones and take out the kernels. Tie them in a piece of muslin and add to the pan. Bring to the boil and simmer for about 30 minutes until the fruit is tender. Remove the muslin bag, squeezing well and allowing the juice to run back into the pan.

Remove the pan from the heat, add the sugar, stir until dissolved, then add a knob of butter, bring to the boil and boil rapidly for 15–25 minutes. Test for a set and, when setting point is reached, remove the pan from the heat and skim off any scum with a slotted spoon. Pot and cover the jam as usual.

Makes about 5 kg (10 lb)

RASPBERRY AND GOOSEBERRY JAM

1.5 kg (3 lb) gooseberries, topped, tailed and
    washed
600 ml (1 pint) water
1.5 kg (3 lb) raspberries, washed
3 kg (6 lb) sugar
a knob of butter

Put the gooseberries in a pan with the water and heat very gently, mashing the fruit as it softens with a wooden spoon. Continue to cook for about 20 minutes until well reduced. Add the raspberries and cook until they are soft.

Remove the pan from the heat and add the sugar, stir until dissolved, then add a knob of butter, bring to the boil and boil rapidly for about 15 minutes. Test for a set and, when setting point is reached, take the pan off the heat and remove any scum with a slotted spoon. Pot and cover the jam as usual.

Makes about 5 kg (10 lb)

CHERRY AND REDCURRANT JAM

1 kg (2 lb) black cherries, washed and stoned
500 g (1 lb) redcurrants, washed and strung
150 ml ($\frac{1}{4}$ pint) water
1.5 kg (3 lb) sugar
a knob of butter

Place the fruit in a preserving pan with the water. Simmer gently for about 30 minutes until the fruit is very soft. Remove from the heat, add the sugar, stirring until dissolved, then add a knob of butter and boil rapidly for about 15 minutes. Test for a set and, when setting point is reached, take the pan off the heat and remove any scum with a slotted spoon. Pot and cover the jam as usual.

Makes about 2.25 kg (4$\frac{1}{2}$ lb)

BLACKCURRANT JAM

2 kg (4 lb) blackcurrants, washed and strung
1.8 litres (3 pints) water
3 kg (6 lb) sugar
a knob of butter

Place the fruit in a preserving pan with the water. Simmer gently for about 45 minutes until the fruit is soft and the contents of the pan are well reduced, stirring from time to time to prevent sticking. (As the skins of currants tend to be rather tough, it is important to cook the fruit really well before adding the sugar.)

Remove the pan from the heat, add the sugar to the fruit pulp, stir until dissolved, then add a knob of butter and boil rapidly for about 10 minutes. Test for a set and, when setting point is reached, take the pan off the heat and remove any scum with a slotted spoon. Pot and cover the jam as usual.

Makes about 5 kg (10 lb)

Whole strawberry jam (page 16)

Above: *Loganberries*

Opposite: *Loganberry jam (page 20)*

BLACKBERRY JAM

3 kg (6 lb) blackberries (not over-ripe), washed
juice of 2 lemons or 5 ml (1 level tsp) citric or
*   tartaric acid*
150 ml ($\frac{1}{4}$ pint) water
3 kg (6 lb) sugar
a knob of butter

Place the blackberries in a preserving pan with the lemon juice (or acid) and water. Simmer very gently for about 30 minutes until the blackberries are very soft and the contents of the pan are well reduced.

Remove from the heat, add the sugar, stir until dissolved, then add a knob of butter, bring to the boil and boil rapidly for about 10 minutes, stirring frequently. Test for a set and, when setting point is reached, take the pan off the heat and remove any scum with a slotted spoon. Pot and cover the jam as usual.

Makes about 5 kg (10 lb)

DAMSON JAM

2.5 kg (5 lb) damsons, washed
900 ml (1$\frac{1}{2}$ pints) water
3 kg (6 lb) sugar
a knob of butter

Place the damsons in a preserving pan with the water and simmer gently for about 30 minutes until the fruit is really soft and pulpy. Remove from the heat, add the sugar and stir until dissolved. Add a knob of butter, bring to the boil and boil rapidly for about 10 minutes. Using a slotted spoon, lift out the stones as they rise to the surface. Test for a set and, when setting point is reached, take the pan off the heat and remove any scum with a slotted spoon. Pot and cover the jam as usual.

Makes about 5 kg (10 lb)

GOOSEBERRY JAM

3 kg (6 lb) gooseberries (slightly under-ripe),
*   topped, tailed and washed*
1.2 litres (2 pints) water
3 kg (6 lb) sugar
a knob of butter

Place the gooseberries in a preserving pan with the water. Simmer gently for about 30 minutes until the fruit is really soft and reduced, mashing it to a pulp with a wooden spoon and stirring from time to time to prevent sticking.

Remove from the heat, add the sugar to the fruit pulp and stir until dissolved. Add a knob of butter, bring to the boil and boil rapidly for about 10 minutes. Test for a set and, when setting point is reached, take the pan off the heat and remove any scum with a slotted spoon. Pot and cover the jam in the usual way.

Makes about 5 kg (10 lb)

VARIATIONS
Ripe gooseberry jam
Substitute fully ripe gooseberries in the above recipe. This will produce a jam with a light set that is a pretty shade of pink.

Elderflower-flavoured gooseberry jam
A delicious and unusual flavour can be given to gooseberry jam by adding 6–8 elderflower heads to each 1 kg (2 lb) of fruit. Cut off the stems close to the flower and tie the flowers in a piece of muslin. Add the muslin bag to the jam when it comes to the boil, removing it before the jam is potted.

Dried apricot jam (page 20)

29

RASPBERRY AND REDCURRANT JAM

750 g (1½ lb) redcurrants, washed and strung
750 g (1½ lb) raspberries, washed
600 ml (1 pint) water
1.5 kg (3 lb) sugar
a knob of butter

Put the fruit in a preserving pan with the water. Simmer gently for about 20 minutes until the fruit is really soft. Remove from the heat, add the sugar and stir until dissolved. Add a knob of butter, bring the jam to the boil and boil rapidly for about 10 minutes. Test for a set and, when setting point is reached, take the pan off the heat and remove any scum with a slotted spoon. Pot and cover the jam in the usual way.

Makes about 2.5 kg (5 lb)

Note This jam tends to contain rather a lot of pips, but the amount can be reduced by cooking the two fruits separately, each in 300 ml (½ pint) water, and sieving the redcurrants before adding them to the raspberries. The yield will then be slightly less.

LOGANBERRY AND RHUBARB JAM

If preferred, raspberries can be used instead of loganberries.

1.5 kg (3 lb) rhubarb, washed and chopped
300 ml (½ pint) water
1.5 kg (3 lb) loganberries, washed
3 kg (6 lb) sugar
a knob of butter

Put the rhubarb in a preserving pan with the water and cook for about 15 minutes until the fruit is soft and broken up. Add the loganberries and continue to cook for about 30 minutes until they are tender and the contents of the pan are well reduced. Remove the pan from the heat, add the sugar and stir until dissolved. Add a knob of butter, bring the jam to the boil and boil rapidly for about 10 minutes. Test for a set and, when setting point is reached, take the pan off the heat and remove any scum with a slotted spoon. Pot and cover the jam in the usual way.

Makes about 5 kg (10 lb)

CRANBERRY AND APPLE JAM

700 g (1½ lb) cranberries, washed
700 g (1½ lb) cooking apples, peeled, cored and sliced
300 ml (½ pint) water
1.5 kg (3 lb) sugar
a knob of butter

Place the cranberries, apples and water in a preserving pan and simmer gently for about 30 minutes or until the fruit is tender. Remove the pan from the heat, add the sugar and stir until dissolved. Add a knob of butter, bring the jam to the boil and boil rapidly for about 10 minutes. Test for a set and, when setting point is reached, take the pan off the heat and remove any scum with a slotted spoon. Pot and cover in the usual way.

Makes about 2.5 kg (5 lb)

CHERRY AND PINEAPPLE JAM

*500 g (1 lb) fresh pineapple, skinned and finely
    chopped (prepared weight)*
1 kg (2 lb) Morello cherries, washed and stoned
juice of 1 lemon
1 kg (2 lb) sugar
*half a 227-ml (8-fl oz) bottle of commercial
    pectin*

Place the pineapple, cherries and lemon juice
in a preserving pan. Simmer gently for about
45 minutes until the fruit is tender. Remove
the pan from the heat, add the sugar, stirring
until dissolved, then add a knob of butter. Add
the pectin and boil rapidly for about 3
minutes. Take the pan off the heat and
remove any scum with a slotted spoon. Pot
and cover the jam in the usual way.

Makes about 2.5 kg (5 lb)

GREENGAGE JAM
Illustrated in colour on page 96

3 kg (6 lb) greengages, washed
600 ml (1 pint) water
3 kg (6 lb) sugar
a knob of butter

Put the greengages and water in a preserving
pan and simmer gently for about 30 minutes
until the fruit is really soft. Remove from the
heat, add the sugar and stir until dissolved.
Add a knob of butter, bring the jam to the boil
and boil rapidly for about 15 minutes. Using a
slotted spoon, lift out the stones as they rise to
the surface. Test for a set and, when setting
point is reached, take the pan off the heat and
remove any scum with a slotted spoon. Pot
and cover the jam in the usual way.

Makes about 5 kg (10 lb)

LIGHT SET RASPBERRY JAM
This jam has only a light set, but has a very
good colour and fresh fruit flavour.

1.25 kg (2$\frac{1}{2}$ lb) raspberries, washed
1.5 kg (3 lb) sugar

Put the raspberries in a preserving pan and
simmer very gently for about 10 minutes
until the juice flows, then bring to the boil and
boil gently for a further 10 minutes. Warm
the sugar in a heatproof bowl in the oven and
stir it into the fruit until it has dissolved. Bring
the jam back to the boil and boil for 2
minutes. Take the pan off the heat and
remove any scum with a slotted spoon. Pot
and cover the jam in the usual way.

Makes about 2.5 kg (5 lb)

SOMERSET APPLE JAM

1½ kg (3 lb) cooking apples, washed
100 g (4 oz) blackberries (see Note below)
300 ml (½ pint) water
300 ml (½ pint) cider
5 whole cloves
juice of 3 lemons
1.25 kg (2½ lb) sugar
a knob of butter

Slice the apples but do not peel or core them. Place them in a preserving pan with the blackberries, water, cider, cloves and lemon juice. Simmer gently for 25–30 minutes until the fruit is cooked to a pulp. Remove the cloves, then press the fruit through a sieve. Return the fruit pulp to the pan and stir in the sugar until dissolved. Add a knob of butter, bring to the boil and boil, stirring occasionally, for about 10 minutes. Test for a set and, when setting point is reached, take the pan off the heat and remove any scum with a slotted spoon. Pot and cover the jam as usual.

Makes about 2.5 kg (5 lb)

Note The blackberries are included in this recipe mostly to improve the colour of the jam. Other berries, such as raspberries or cranberries can be used instead.

BILBERRY JAM

This jam has a delicious flavour but is rather expensive to make unless you can pick the bilberries yourself.

1.25 kg (2½ lb) bilberries, washed
150 ml (¼ pint) water
45 ml (3 tbsp) lemon juice
1.5 kg (3 lb) sugar
a knob of butter
227-ml (8-fl oz) bottle of commercial pectin

Place the bilberries in a preserving pan with the water and lemon juice. Simmer gently for 10–15 minutes until the fruit is soft and just beginning to pulp. Remove the pan from the heat, add the sugar, stir until dissolved, then add a knob of butter, bring to the boil and boil rapidly for 3 minutes. Remove the pan from the heat, add the pectin, return to the heat and boil for a further minute. Allow to cool slightly before potting and covering the jam in the usual way.

Makes about 2.75 kg (5½ lb)

RHUBARB GINGER JAM

1.25 kg (2½ lb) rhubarb (prepared weight),
    chopped
1.25 kg (2½ lb) sugar
juice of 2 lemons
25 g (1 oz) root ginger
100 g (4 oz) preserved or crystallised ginger,
    chopped

Place the rhubarb in a large bowl in alternate layers with the sugar and lemon juice, cover and leave overnight.

Next day, bruise the root ginger slightly with a weight or rolling pin, and tie it in a piece of muslin. Put the rhubarb mixture into a preserving pan with the muslin bag, bring to the boil and boil rapidly for 15 minutes. Remove the muslin bag, add the preserved or crystallised ginger and boil for a further 5 minutes, or until the rhubarb is clear. Test for a set and, when setting point is reached, take the pan off the heat and remove any scum with a slotted spoon. Pot and cover the jam in the usual way.

Makes about 2.25 kg (4½ lb)

QUINCE JAM

1 kg (2 lb) quinces (prepared weight), peeled,
  cored and sliced
1 litre (1¾ pints) water
1.5 kg (3 lb) sugar
a knob of butter

Place the quinces in a preserving pan with the water and simmer very gently until the fruit is really soft and pulpy. Remove from the heat, add the sugar and stir until dissolved. Add a knob of butter, bring the jam to the boil and boil rapidly for 15–20 minutes. Test for a set and, when setting point is reached, remove the pan from the heat and remove any scum with a slotted spoon. Pot and cover the jam in the usual way.

Makes about 2.5 kg (5 lb)

Note If the quinces are really ripe, add the juice of 1 lemon with the sugar.

PEAR JAM

1.5 kg (3 lb) cooking or firm eating pears
grated rind and juice of 2 lemons
150 ml (¼ pint) water
1.25 kg (2½ lb) sugar
a knob of butter
half a 227-ml (8-fl oz) bottle of commercial
  pectin

Peel, core and chop the pears, reserving the peel and cores. Put the peel and cores in a saucepan with the lemon rind and water and boil for 10 minutes. Strain and pour the liquid into a preserving pan with the pear flesh and lemon juice. Simmer gently for 25–30 minutes until the pears are tender. Remove the pan from the heat, add the sugar and stir until it has dissolved. Add a knob of butter, bring to the boil and boil for 5–10 minutes. Remove the pan from the heat, add the pectin, return to the heat and boil for a further minute. Remove any scum with a slotted spoon and allow to cool slightly before potting and covering in the usual way.

Makes 1–1.25 kg (2–2½ lb)

Jellies

Jellies take longer to make than jams but are worth the extra trouble.

The equipment and method used for making jellies is similar to that used for jams (see page 10) but there are a few special, additional points.

The Fruit

Only fruits giving a good set (i.e. with a high pectin content—see page 11) are really suitable for jelly-making. Fruits with poor setting qualities can be combined with others with a higher pectin content.

Preparing the fruit Fruit for jelly-making needs very little preparation, though any damaged fruits should not be used. It is not necessary to peel or core fruit; just wash and roughly chop it. Any skin, core, stones or pips will be extracted when the pulp is strained.

Jelly-making

Cooking the fruit The first stage in jelly-making is to cook the fruit in water. The amount of water needed depends on how juicy the fruit is. Hard fruits should be covered with water. The cooking must be very slow and thorough to extract as much juice as possible, so only simmer the fruit gently until very tender. This takes from 30 minutes–1 hour, depending on the softness of the fruit. To save time, particularly when using hard fruits, this stage of jelly-making can be done in a pressure cooker (see opposite).

Straining off the juice After cooking, the fruit pulp is transferred to a jelly bag and left to drip until all the juice has been strained off. If you haven't got a jelly bag, improvise with a large piece of muslin or a double thickness of fine cloth (e.g. a clean tea-towel or cotton sheet). Whatever you use should first be scalded in boiling water. Suspend the bag or cloth between the legs of an upturned chair or stool with a large bowl placed underneath to catch the dripping juice. Leave until the dripping has stopped (overnight if necessary) and don't be tempted to squeeze or poke the bag or the finished jelly will be cloudy.

Double extraction If a fruit that is very high in pectin is being used, a double extraction can be made to increase the final yield. After the first straining, the pulp should be cooked again in a little water and then strained again. The two juices are then combined.

Adding the sugar The next stage in jelly-making is to add the sugar to the juice. If necessary, the pectin test (see page 11) can be carried out beforehand. If the result is poor, put the juice in a pan, boil, then test again.

Measure the strained juice (known as the extract), put it in a preserving pan and add the sugar. 600 ml (1 pint) extract rich in pectin will set with 500 g (1 lb) sugar, and 600 ml (1 pint) juice with a medium pectin content will set with 375 g (12 oz) sugar. Granulated sugar is suitable, though lump sugar or preserving crystals will cause less scum to be formed and will result in a clearer jelly. Stir the sugar into the juice, return the pan to the heat and bring to the boil, stirring until the sugar has dissolved. Continue boiling until setting point is reached, stirring occasionally. Test for setting point in the same way as for jam (see page 12). When setting point is reached (usually after boiling the jelly for about 10 minutes), remove any scum with a slotted spoon before quickly potting and covering as for jam (see page 12).

Yield

It is not practicable to state the exact yield in jelly recipes because the ripeness of the fruit and the time allowed for dripping both affect the quantity of juice obtained.

Pressure Cooking Jellies

The fruit used for making jellies can also be softened in the pressure cooker and this method is particularly useful for hard fruits.
1. Prepare the fruit.
2. Place the fruit in the pressure cooker (without the trivet) and allow only half the amount of water stated in the recipe.
3. Cook at medium (10 lb) pressure, then reduce the pressure at room temperature.
4. Mash the fruit well and pour it into a jelly bag or muslin cloth attached to the legs of an upturned stool. Finish as in the recipe.

Opposite are examples of the cooking times required for some fruits when cooked in a pressure cooker.

Apples	7 minutes	Gooseberries	3 minutes
Blackberries and apples combined	9 minutes	Pears (cooking)	9 minutes
Blackcurrants	4 minutes	Quinces	7 minutes
Damsons, plums and other stone fruit	5 minutes	Citrus fruits	25 minutes

APPLE JELLY
(see page 36)

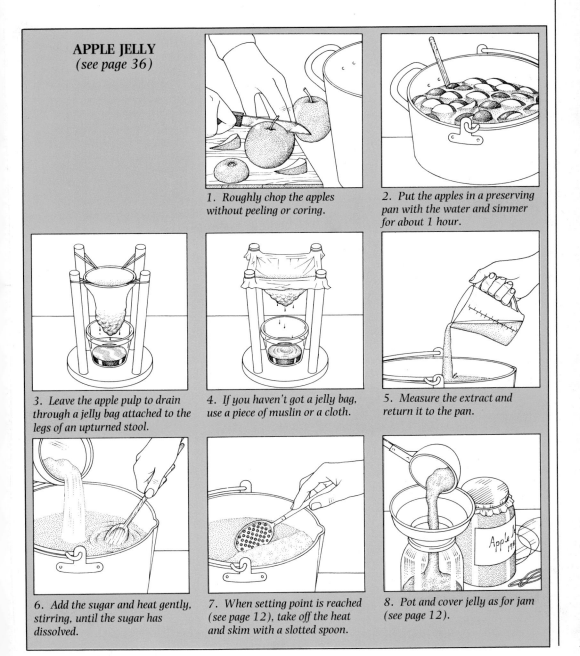

1. Roughly chop the apples without peeling or coring.

2. Put the apples in a preserving pan with the water and simmer for about 1 hour.

3. Leave the apple pulp to drain through a jelly bag attached to the legs of an upturned stool.

4. If you haven't got a jelly bag, use a piece of muslin or a cloth.

5. Measure the extract and return it to the pan.

6. Add the sugar and heat gently, stirring, until the sugar has dissolved.

7. When setting point is reached (see page 12), take off the heat and skim with a slotted spoon.

8. Pot and cover jelly as for jam (see page 12).

APPLE JELLY

2.75 kg (5½ lb) cooking apples, washed
juice of 2 lemons
water
sugar

Remove any bruised or damaged portions from the apples and cut them into thick chunks without peeling or coring. Put the apples in a preserving pan with the lemon juice and sufficient water to cover. Simmer gently for about 1 hour until the apples are really soft and the liquid is well reduced (by about one third). Stir from time to time to prevent sticking. Spoon the apple pulp into a jelly bag or cloth attached to the legs of an upturned stool, and leave to strain into a large bowl for at least 12 hours.

Discard the pulp remaining in the jelly bag. Measure the extract and return it to the pan with 500 g (1 lb) sugar for each 600 ml (1 pint) extract. Heat gently, stirring until the sugar has dissolved, then boil rapidly for about 10 minutes. Test for a set and, when setting point is reached, take the pan off the heat and remove any scum with a slotted spoon. Pot and cover the jelly as usual.

Note Windfalls or cooking apples are the best to use for this jelly. Dessert apples should not be used for jelly-making. As the colour of Apple jelly is sometimes unattractive, a few blackberries, raspberries, redcurrants, cranberries or loganberries can be added with the apples to give the preserve a better colour.

MINT JELLY
Illustrated in colour on page 96

2.5 kg (5 lb) cooking apples, washed
1.2 litres (2 pints) water
a few sprigs of fresh mint
1.2 litres (2 pints) distilled vinegar
sugar
90–120 ml (6–8 level tbsp) chopped fresh mint
a few drops of green food colouring

Remove any bruised or damaged portions from the apples and roughly chop them into thick chunks without peeling or coring. Place them in a large saucepan with the water and mint sprigs. Bring to the boil, then simmer

gently for about 45 minutes until soft and pulpy. Stir from time to time to prevent sticking. Add the vinegar and boil for a further 5 minutes.

Spoon the apple pulp into a jelly bag or cloth attached to the legs of an upturned stool, and leave to strain into a large bowl for at least 12 hours.

Discard the pulp remaining in the jelly bag. Measure the extract and put it in a preserving pan with 500 g (1 lb) sugar for each 600 ml (1 pint) extract. Heat gently, stirring, until the sugar has dissolved, then boil rapidly for about 10 minutes. Test for a set and, when setting point is reached, take the pan off the heat and remove any scum with a slotted spoon. Stir in the chopped mint and add a few drops of green food colouring. Allow to cool slightly, then stir well to distribute the mint and pot and cover the jelly in the usual way.

VARIATION
Herb jellies
Other fresh herbs, such as rosemary, parsley, sage and thyme, can be used equally as well as mint. Serve these herb jellies with roast meats—rosemary jelly (illustrated in colour on page 38) with lamb; parsley jelly with gammon; sage jelly with pork; and thyme jelly with poultry.

Gooseberry and elderflower jelly (page 40)

BRAMBLE JELLY

2 kg (4 lb) slightly under-ripe blackberries, washed
juice of 2 lemons or 7.5 ml (1½ level tsp) citric or tartaric acid
450 ml (¾ pint) water
sugar

Put the blackberries, lemon juice (or acid) and water into a preserving pan and simmer gently for about 1 hour until the fruit is really soft and pulpy. Stir from time to time to prevent sticking. Spoon the blackberry pulp into a jelly bag or cloth attached to the legs of an upturned stool and leave to strain into a large bowl for at least 12 hours.

Discard the pulp remaining in the jelly bag. Measure the extract and return it to the pan with 500 g (1 lb) sugar for each 600 ml (1 pint) extract. Stir until the sugar has dissolved, then boil rapidly for about 10 minutes. Test for a set and, when setting point is reached, take the pan off the heat and remove any scum with a slotted spoon. Pot and cover the jelly in the usual way.

Rosemary jelly (page 36)

CRAB-APPLE JELLY

Serve with roast beef. A few cloves or some bruised root ginger may be added while the apples are cooking to give extra flavour.

2.75 kg (5½ lb) crab-apples, washed
1.8 litres (3 pints) water
sugar

Cut the crab-apples into quarters without peeling or coring and put them in a preserving pan with the water. Bring to the boil and simmer gently for about 1½ hours until the fruit is soft and pulpy, adding a little more water if necessary. Stir from time to time to prevent sticking. Spoon the fruit pulp into a jelly bag or cloth attached to the legs of an upturned stool, and leave to strain into a large bowl for at least 12 hours.

Discard the pulp remaining in the jelly bag. Measure the extract and return it to the pan with 500 g (1 lb) sugar for each 600 ml (1 pint) extract. Heat gently, stirring, until the sugar has dissolved, then boil rapidly for about 10 minutes. Test for a set and, when setting point is reached, take the pan off the heat and remove any scum with a slotted spoon. Pot and cover the jelly as usual.

GOOSEBERRY JELLY

This preserve is pink in colour, not green as you might expect. Serve with veal, poultry or pork.

2 kg (4 lb) gooseberries, washed
water
sugar

Put the gooseberries in a preserving pan with sufficient water to cover. Bring to the boil, then simmer gently for 45 minutes–1 hour until the fruit is really soft and pulpy. Stir from time to time to prevent sticking. Spoon the fruit pulp into a jelly bag or cloth attached to the legs of an upturned stool, and leave to strain into a large bowl for at least 12 hours.

Discard the pulp remaining in the jelly bag. Measure the extract and return it to the pan with 500 g (1 lb) sugar for each 600 ml (1 pint) extract. Heat gently, stirring, until the sugar has dissolved, then boil rapidly for about 15 minutes. Test for a set and, when setting point is reached, take the pan off the heat and remove any scum with a slotted spoon. Pot and cover the jelly as usual.

VARIATIONS
Gooseberry mint jelly
Cook the gooseberries with a few sprigs of mint and add finely chopped fresh mint to the jelly before potting.

Gooseberry and elderflower jelly
Illustrated in colour on page 37
Tie two large elderflower heads in a piece of muslin. When the jelly has reached setting point, remove from the heat, add the muslin bag and stir around in the hot jelly for about 3 minutes. This will produce a good flavour that is not over-dominant. Remove the muslin bag and pot and cover the jelly in the usual way.

HONEY APPLE JELLY

1.25 kg (2½ lb) thin honey
300 ml (½ pint) pure apple juice
227-ml (8-fl oz) bottle of commercial pectin

Put the honey and apple juice in a large saucepan and bring rapidly to the boil. Add the pectin, stirring constantly, and bring back to the boil. Continue boiling rapidly for 5 minutes, then take the pan off the heat. Remove any scum with a slotted spoon. Pot and cover the jelly in the usual way.

Makes about 1.5 kg (3 lb)

BLACKBERRY AND APPLE JELLY

1 kg (2 lb) cooking apples, washed
2 kg (4 lb) blackberries, washed
1.2 litres (2 pints) water
sugar

Remove any bruised or damaged portions from the apples and cut them into thick chunks without peeling or coring. Place the apples and blackberries in a preserving pan with the water and simmer gently for about 1 hour until the fruit is really soft and pulpy. Stir from time to time to prevent sticking. Spoon the fruit pulp into a jelly bag or cloth attached to the legs of an upturned stool, and leave to strain into a large bowl for at least 12 hours.

Discard the pulp remaining in the jelly bag. Measure the extract and return it to the pan with 500 g (1 lb) sugar for each 600 ml (1 pint) extract. Heat gently, stirring, until the sugar has dissolved, then boil rapidly for about 10 minutes. Test for a set and, when setting point is reached, take the pan off the heat and remove any scum with a slotted spoon. Pot and cover the jelly as usual.

PORT AND CURRANT JELLY

1.5 kg (3 lb) red or blackcurrants, washed
600 ml (1 pint) water
sugar
45 ml (3 tbsp) port

There is no need to remove the currants from their stalks. Place the currants in a preserving pan with the water and simmer gently for about 30 minutes until the fruit is really soft and pulpy. Stir from time to time to prevent sticking. Spoon the fruit pulp into a jelly bag or cloth attached to the legs of an upturned stool, and leave to strain into a large bowl for at least 12 hours.

Discard the pulp remaining in the jelly bag. Measure the extract and return it to the pan with 500 g (1 lb) sugar for each 600 ml (1 pint) extract. Heat gently, stirring, until the sugar has dissolved, then boil rapidly for about 15 minutes. Test for a set and, when setting point is reached, remove the pan from the heat. Stir in the port, remove any scum with a slotted spoon and pot and cover the jelly in the usual way.

JAPONICA JELLY

750 g (1½ lb) japonicas, washed and roughly
  chopped
30 ml (2 tbsp) lemon juice
1.8 litres (3 pints) water
sugar

Place the fruit in a preserving pan with the lemon juice and water and simmer gently for 45 minutes–1 hour until the fruit is very soft and the contents of the pan are reduced by about one third. Stir from time to time to prevent sticking. Spoon the fruit pulp into a jelly bag or cloth attached to the legs of an upturned stool, and leave to strain into a large bowl for at least 12 hours.

Discard the pulp remaining in the jelly bag. Measure the extract and return it to the pan with 500 g (1 lb) sugar for each 600 ml (1 pint) extract. Heat gently, stirring, until the sugar has dissolved, then boil rapidly for about 10 minutes. Test for a set and, when setting point is reached, take the pan off the heat and remove any scum with a slotted spoon. Pot and cover the jelly as usual.

DAMSON AND APPLE JELLY

3 kg (6 lb) cooking apples, washed
1.5 kg (3 lb) damsons, washed
2.4 litres (4 pints) water
sugar

Remove any bruised or damaged portions from the apples and roughly chop them into large chunks without peeling or coring. Place the apples and damsons in a preserving pan with the water and simmer gently for about 1 hour until the fruit is really soft and pulpy. Stir from time to time to prevent sticking. Spoon the fruit pulp into a jelly bag or cloth attached to the legs of an upturned stool, and leave to strain into a large bowl for at least 12 hours.

Discard the pulp remaining in the jelly bag. Measure the extract and return it to the pan with 500 g (1 lb) sugar for each 600 ml (1 pint) extract. Heat gently, stirring, until the sugar has dissolved, then boil rapidly for about 10 minutes. Test for a set and, when setting point is reached, take the pan off the heat and remove any scum with a slotted spoon. Pot and cover the jelly as usual.

QUINCE JELLY

This jelly makes a good accompaniment to serve with game.

2 kg (4 lb) quinces, washed and roughly chopped
3.6 litres (6 pints) water
grated rind and juice of 3 lemons
sugar

Place the fruit in a preserving pan with 2.4 litres (4 pints) of the water and the lemon rind and juice. Simmer, covered, for 1 hour until the fruit is tender. Stir from time to time to prevent sticking. Spoon the fruit pulp into a jelly bag or cloth attached to the legs of an upturned stool, and leave to strain into a large bowl for at least 12 hours.

Return the pulp in the jelly bag to the pan and add the remaining water. Bring to the boil, simmer gently for 30 minutes, then strain again through a jelly bag or cloth for at least 12 hours.

Discard the pulp remaining in the jelly bag. Combine the two lots of extract and measure. Return to the pan with 500 g (1 lb) sugar for each 600 ml (1 pint) extract. Heat gently, stirring, until the sugar has dissolved, then boil rapidly for about 10 minutes. Test for a set and, when setting point is reached, take the pan off the heat and remove any scum with a slotted spoon. Pot and cover the jelly in the usual way.

ROWAN-BERRY JELLY

Rowan-berries are the fruit of the mountain ash tree. They produce rather a bitter jelly, but it is delicious with rich meats, such as game or venison.

1.5 kg (3 lb) firm, ripe rowan-berries, washed
600 ml (1 pint) water
juice of 1 lemon
sugar

Place the berries in a preserving pan with the water and lemon juice. Bring to the boil, then simmer gently for 45 minutes–1 hour until the fruit is very soft and pulpy. Stir from time to time to prevent sticking. Spoon the fruit pulp into a jelly bag or cloth attached to the legs of an upturned stool, and leave to strain into a large bowl for at least 12 hours.

Discard the pulp remaining in the jelly bag. Measure the extract and return to the pan with 500 g (1 lb) sugar for each 600 ml (1 pint) extract. Heat gently, stirring, until the sugar has dissolved, then bring to the boil and boil rapidly for about 10 minutes. Test for a set and, when setting point is reached, take the pan off the heat and remove any scum with a slotted spoon. Pot and cover the jelly in the usual way.

ROSE HIP JELLY

1 kg (2 lb) cooking apples, washed
500 g (1 lb) ripe rose hips, washed
water
sugar

Remove any bruised or damaged portions from the apples, then roughly chop them without coring or peeling. Place in a preserving pan with the rose hips and add just enough water to cover. Bring to the boil, then simmer gently for about 45 minutes until the fruit is soft and pulpy. Stir from time to time to prevent sticking. Break the fruit down with a wooden spoon, then spoon the pulp into a jelly bag or cloth attached to the legs of an upturned stool. Leave to strain into a large bowl for at least 12 hours.

Discard the pulp remaining in the jelly bag. Measure the extract and return to the pan with 500 g (1 lb) sugar for each 600 ml (1 pint) extract. Stir until the sugar has dissolved. Bring to the boil and boil rapidly for about 15 minutes. Test for a set and, when setting point is reached, take the pan off the heat and remove any scum with a slotted spoon. Pot and cover the jelly as usual.

BITTER LIME JELLY WITH PERNOD

4 limes, washed and sliced
3.6 litres (6 pints) water
sugar
15 ml (1 tbsp) Pernod

Place the limes in a preserving pan with the water and simmer gently for 1 hour until the fruit is soft. Spoon the fruit into a jelly bag or cloth attached to the legs of an upturned stool, and leave to strain into a large bowl for at least 12 hours.

Discard the pulp remaining in the jelly bag. Measure the extract and return it to the pan with 500 g (1 lb) sugar for each 600 ml (1 pint) extract. Heat gently, stirring, until the sugar has dissolved, then boil rapidly for 10–15 minutes. Test for a set and, when setting point is reached, remove the pan from the heat and stir in the Pernod. Remove any scum with a slotted spoon, and pot and cover the jelly in the usual way.

Note If a less acid jelly is preferred, add 2.5 ml ($\frac{1}{4}$ level tsp) bicarbonate of soda to the water when cooking the limes.

CRANBERRY AND APPLE JELLY

This jelly is delicious served as an accompaniment to roast turkey.

1.5 kg (3 lb) cooking apples, washed
1 kg (2 lb) cranberries, washed
water
sugar

Remove any bruised or damaged portions from the apples, then roughly chop them without peeling or coring. Place the apples and cranberries in a preserving pan with sufficient water to cover and simmer gently for 45 minutes–1 hour until the fruit is really soft and pulpy. Stir from time to time to prevent sticking. Spoon the pulp into a jelly bag or cloth attached to the legs of an upturned stool, and leave to strain into a large bowl for at least 12 hours.

Discard the pulp remaining in the jelly bag. Measure the extract and return it to the pan with 500 g (1 lb) sugar for each 600 ml (1 pint) extract. Bring to the boil, stirring, until the sugar has dissolved, then boil rapidly for about 10 minutes. Test for a set and, when setting point is reached, take the pan off the heat and remove any scum with a slotted spoon. Pot and cover the jelly as usual.

SLOE JELLY

2 kg (4 lb) sloes, washed
water
sugar

Prick the sloes all over, using a darning needle. Place the sloes in a preserving pan, add a little water—hardly enough to cover—and bring to the boil and simmer very gently for 1½–2 hours until the fruit is very soft and pulpy. Stir from time to time to prevent sticking. Spoon the fruit pulp into a jelly bag or cloth attached to the legs of an upturned stool, and leave to strain into a large bowl for at least 12 hours.

Discard the pulp remaining in the jelly bag. Measure the extract and return it to the pan with 500 g (1 lb) sugar for each 600 ml (1 pint) extract. Heat gently, stirring, until the sugar has dissolved, then boil rapidly for about 10 minutes. Test for a set and, when setting point is reached, take the pan off the heat and remove any scum with a slotted spoon. Pot and cover the jelly as usual.

REDCURRANT JELLY

1.5 kg (3 lb) redcurrants, washed
600 ml (1 pint) water
sugar

There is no need to remove the currants from their stalks. Place them in a preserving pan with the water and simmer gently for about 30 minutes until the fruit is soft and pulpy. Stir from time to time to prevent sticking. Spoon the fruit pulp into a jelly bag or cloth attached to the legs of an upturned stool, and leave to strain for at least 12 hours.

Discard the pulp remaining in the jelly bag. Measure the extract and return it to the pan with 500 g (1 lb) sugar for each 600 ml (1 pint) extract. Heat gently, stirring, until the sugar has dissolved, then boil rapidly for about 15 minutes. Test for a set and, when setting point is reached, take the pan off the heat and remove any scum with a slotted spoon. Pot and cover the jelly as usual.

VARIATION
Redcurrant mint jelly
Add a few sprigs of fresh mint when cooking the fruit and some finely chopped fresh mint before potting the jelly.

FOUR-FRUIT JELLY

500 g (1 lb) redcurrants, washed
500 g (1 lb) raspberries, washed
500 g (1 lb) Morello or May Duke cherries,
*   washed*
500 g (1 lb) strawberries, washed
60 ml (4 tbsp) lemon juice
600 ml (1 pint) water
sugar

It is not necessary to string the redcurrants. Place all the fruit in a preserving pan with the lemon juice and water. Simmer gently for about 1 hour until the fruit is really soft and pulpy. Stir from time to time to prevent sticking. Spoon the fruit pulp into a jelly bag or cloth attached to the legs of an upturned stool, and leave to strain into a large bowl for at least 12 hours.

Discard the pulp remaining in the jelly bag. Measure the extract and return it to the pan with 500 g (1 lb) sugar for each 600 ml (1 pint) extract. Heat gently, stirring, until the sugar has dissolved, then boil rapidly for about 10 minutes. Test for a set and, when setting point is reached, take the pan off the heat and remove any scum with a slotted spoon. Pot and cover the jelly as usual.

GRAPE JELLY

Serve as an accompaniment to roast poultry, veal or game.

500 g (1 lb) black grapes, washed
500 g (1 lb) cooking apples, washed
juice of 1 lemon
300 ml (½ pint) water
sugar

Place the grapes in a preserving pan and lightly crush them with a potato masher. Remove any bruised or damaged portions from the apples, roughly chop them without peeling or coring and add them to the pan. Add the lemon juice and water. Simmer gently for about 30 minutes until the fruit is very soft and pulpy. Stir from time to time to prevent sticking. Spoon the fruit pulp into a jelly bag or cloth attached to the legs of an upturned stool, and leave to strain into a large bowl for at least 12 hours.

Discard the pulp remaining in the jelly bag. Measure the extract and return it to the pan with 500 g (1 lb) sugar for each 600 ml (1 pint) extract. Heat gently, stirring, until the sugar has dissolved, then boil rapidly for about 10 minutes. Test for a set and, when setting point is reached, take the pan off the heat and remove any scum with a slotted spoon. Pot and cover the jelly as usual.

GUAVA JELLY

Serve as an accompaniment to poultry.

1 kg (2 lb) guavas, washed and sliced
900 ml (1½ pints) water
sugar
juice of 2 lemons

Place the fruit and water in a preserving pan, bring to the boil and simmer gently for 30 minutes until the fruit is really soft and pulpy. Stir from time to time to prevent sticking. Spoon the fruit pulp into a jelly bag or cloth attached to the legs of an upturned stool, and leave to strain into a large bowl for at least 12 hours.

Discard the pulp remaining in the jelly bag. Measure the extract and return it to the pan with 500 g (1 lb) sugar for each 600 ml (1 pint) extract and the lemon juice. Heat gently, stirring, until the sugar has dissolved, then boil rapidly for about 15 minutes. Test for a set and, when setting point is reached, take the pan off the heat and remove any scum with a slotted spoon. Pot and cover the jelly in the usual way.

ORANGE AND THYME JELLY

2 kg (4 lb) oranges, washed
500 g (1 lb) lemons, washed
3 litres (5 pints) water
120 ml (8 level tbsp) chopped fresh thyme
sugar

Slice the oranges and lemons then cut the slices into quarters. Place in a preserving pan with the water and 60 ml (4 level tbsp) chopped thyme. Bring to the boil, then simmer gently for about $1\frac{1}{4}$ hours until the fruit is soft. Stir from time to time to prevent sticking. Spoon the fruit pulp into a jelly bag or cloth attached to the legs of an upturned stool, and leave to strain into a large bowl for at least 12 hours.

Discard the pulp remaining in the jelly bag. Measure the extract and return it to the pan with 500 g (1 lb) sugar for each 600 ml (1 pint) extract. Heat gently, stirring until the sugar has dissolved, then boil rapidly for about 15 minutes. Test for a set and, when setting point is reached, take the pan off the heat and remove any scum with a slotted spoon. Stir in the remaining chopped thyme. Allow the jelly to cool slightly, then stir well to distribute the thyme. Pot and cover as usual.

CURRANT AND APPLE JELLY

This jelly is excellent with poultry or roast beef.

1 kg (2 lb) red or blackcurrants, washed
1 kg (2 lb) cooking apples, washed
1.5 litres ($2\frac{1}{2}$ pints) water
sugar

There is no need to remove the stalks from the currants. Remove any bruised or damaged portions from the apples and slice them without peeling or coring. Place the fruit in a preserving pan and add the water. Simmer very gently for about 1 hour until the fruit is thoroughly cooked and pulpy. Stir from time to time to prevent sticking. Spoon the fruit pulp into a jelly bag or cloth attached to the legs of an upturned stool, and leave to strain into a large bowl for at least 12 hours.

Discard the pulp remaining in the jelly bag. Measure the extract and return it to the pan with 500 g (1 lb) sugar for each 600 ml (1 pint) extract. Heat gently, stirring, until the sugar has dissolved, then boil rapidly for 8–10 minutes. Test for a set and, when setting point is reached, take the pan off the heat and remove any scum with a slotted spoon. Pot and cover the jelly in the usual way.

47

ELDERBERRY JELLY

Serve as an accompaniment to pork.

1 kg (2 lb) cooking apples, washed
1 kg (2 lb) elderberries, washed
water
sugar

Remove any bruised or damaged portions from the apples and roughly chop them without peeling or coring. Place them in a saucepan with just enough water to cover and simmer gently for about 1 hour until the fruit is very soft and pulpy. Put the elder-berries in another saucepan with just enough water to cover and simmer gently for about 1 hour until the fruit is very soft and tender. Combine the two lots of fruit. Spoon the fruit pulp into a jelly bag or cloth attached to the legs of an upturned stool, and leave to strain into a large bowl for at least 12 hours.

Discard the pulp remaining in the jelly bag. Measure the extract and return it to the pan with 375 g (12 oz) sugar for each 600 ml (1 pint) extract. Heat gently, stirring, until the sugar has dissolved, then boil rapidly for about 10 minutes. Test for a set and, when setting point is reached, take the pan off the heat and remove any scum with a slotted spoon. Pot and cover the jelly as usual.

VARIATION
Bilberry jelly
If preferred, follow the above recipe, using bilberries instead of elderberries.

RASPBERRY JELLY

2 kg (4 lb) raspberries, washed
sugar

Put the raspberries in a preserving pan and heat very gently until the juices flow, then simmer for about 1 hour until they are quite soft and pulpy. Stir from time to time to prevent sticking. Spoon the pulp into a jelly bag or cloth attached to the legs of an upturned stool, and leave to strain into a large bowl for at least 12 hours.

Discard the pulp remaining in the jelly bag. Measure the extract and return it to the pan with 500 g (1 lb) sugar for each 600 ml (1 pint) extract. Heat gently, stirring, to dissolve the sugar, then bring to the boil and boil rapidly for about 10 minutes. Test for a set and, when setting point is reached, take the pan off the heat and remove any scum with a slotted spoon. Pot and cover the jelly in the usual way.

VARIATION
Loganberry jelly
If preferred, follow the above recipe, using loganberries instead of raspberries.

MULBERRY AND APPLE JELLY

1.25 kg (2½ lb) sour cooking apples, washed
1.5 kg (3 lb) mulberries, washed
1.8 litres (3 pints) water
juice of 2 lemons or 7.5 ml (1½ level tsp) citric
  acid
sugar

Remove any bruised or damaged portions from the apples and roughly chop them without peeling or coring. Place the apples and mulberries in a preserving pan with the water and lemon juice or acid. Simmer gently for about 1 hour, mashing from time to time, until the fruit is very soft and the contents of the pan have reduced considerably. Spoon the fruit pulp into a jelly bag or cloth attached to the legs of an upturned stool, and leave to strain into a large bowl for at least 12 hours.

Discard the pulp remaining in the jelly bag. Measure the extract and return it to the pan with 500 g (1 lb) sugar for each 600 ml (1 pint) extract. Heat gently, stirring, until the sugar has dissolved, then boil rapidly for about 10 minutes. Test for a set and, when setting point is reached, remove the pan from the heat. Remove any scum with a slotted spoon. Pot and cover the jelly as usual.

BLACKCURRANT JELLY

2 kg (4 lb) blackcurrants, washed
about 1.5 litres (2½ pints) water
sugar

There is no need to remove the fruit from the stalks. Put into a preserving pan with the water and simmer gently for about 1 hour until the fruit is really soft and pulpy. Stir from time to time to prevent sticking. Spoon the fruit pulp into a jelly bag or cloth attached to the legs of an upturned stool, and leave to strain into a large bowl for at least 12 hours.

Discard the pulp in the jelly bag. Measure the extract and return it to the pan with 500 g (1 lb) sugar for each 600 ml (1 pint) extract. Heat gently, stirring, until the sugar has dissolved, then boil rapidly for about 15 minutes. Test for a set and, when setting point is reached, take the pan off the heat and remove any scum with a slotted spoon. Pot and cover the jelly in the usual way.

QUICK MINT JELLY

300 ml (½ pint) distilled vinegar
500 g (1 lb) sugar
50 g (2 oz) fresh mint
227-ml (8-fl oz) bottle of commercial pectin
2–3 drops of green food colouring

Place the vinegar and sugar in a large saucepan with half the mint sprigs. Heat gently, stirring, until the sugar has dissolved. Strain through a sieve to remove the mint, return the vinegar syrup to the pan and bring to the boil. Boil for 1 minute, then stir in the pectin. Bring to the boil and boil for 2 minutes. Chop the remaining mint and stir into the pan with the food colouring. Allow to cool slightly, then stir to distribute the mint. Pot and cover the jelly in the usual way.

Marmalades

Marmalade is a preserve that is nearly always made from citrus fruits and is most commonly seen on the breakfast table. At one time marmalade was made from a variety of fruits, but nowadays other fruits are only used in recipes which combine them with citrus fruits. The method used for making marmalade is very similar to that used for jam (see page 10) but with a few special points to remember.

The Fruit
Seville or bitter oranges make the best marmalades with a pleasing flavour and appearance. Sweet oranges give marmalade a rather cloudy appearance and the pith does not turn as translucent as that of Seville oranges. Sweet oranges are usually only used in combination with other citrus fruits.

The best time to make marmalade is in January and February when Seville oranges are available. Fortunately, it is possible to freeze Seville oranges (see notes on freezing on page 173, and a method for making marmalade from frozen oranges on page 52).
Preparing the fruit The peel of citrus fruits is tougher than that of most fruits used for jam-making and must therefore be evenly shredded, either by hand or in the slicer attachment of a food mixer, or in a food processor. You can choose the thickness of peel that you prefer. Do not use a coarse mincer to cut up the peel as it produces a paste-like marmalade. If you are making a very large quantity of marmalade, however, it may be a good idea to mince half the peel and cut the remainder by hand.

There are several methods of preparing and softening the fruit, each resulting in a different type of marmalade, such as coarse-cut, thin-cut and fine-shred jelly marmalade. The method you choose for peeling and preparing the fruit depends on the recipe you are using and precise instructions are given.

It is sometimes suggested that the peel should be cut up and soaked in water over-night to help soften it. However, soaking is not essential and the long, first cooking stage is usually sufficient. Sometimes it may be more convenient to prepare the fruit one day and make the marmalade the next day, in which case the peel should be left in water overnight to prevent it drying out.

Cooking Marmalade
First cooking Cooking times required for marmalades are usually much longer than for jams—at least 1 hour and very often 2–3

Navel

Seville

Kumquat

Valencia

Jaffa

Tangerine

hours. Consequently, larger quantities of water are needed to allow for evaporation. The purpose of the first cooking stage is to extract the pectin, reduce the contents of the pan by about half and to really soften the peel. Failure to do this is one of the most common reasons why a marmalade will not set. You can shorten the cooking time by using a pressure cooker (see page 52).

If you wish to double the recipe quantities, it may be necessary to adjust the cooking time and to use an extra large pan.

SEVILLE ORANGE MARMALADE
(see page 52)

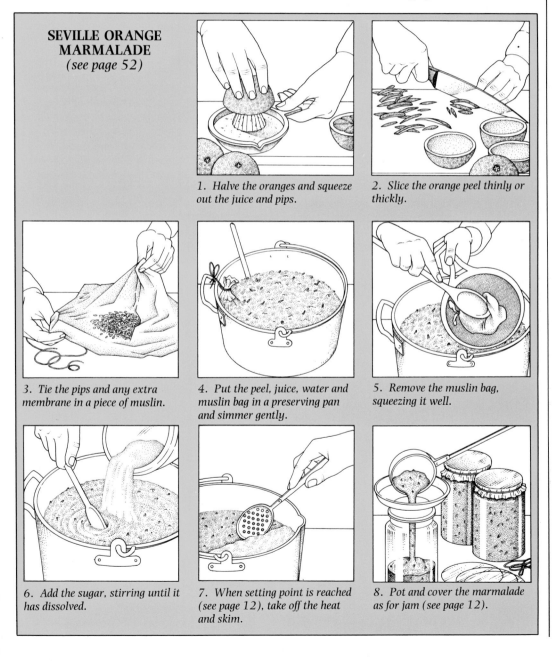

1. Halve the oranges and squeeze out the juice and pips.

2. Slice the orange peel thinly or thickly.

3. Tie the pips and any extra membrane in a piece of muslin.

4. Put the peel, juice, water and muslin bag in a preserving pan and simmer gently.

5. Remove the muslin bag, squeezing it well.

6. Add the sugar, stirring until it has dissolved.

7. When setting point is reached (see page 12), take off the heat and skim.

8. Pot and cover the marmalade as for jam (see page 12).

Extracting the pectin Much of the pectin in oranges is contained in the pips and membranes, and it is important that it is all extracted. Put all the pips, and any membrane that has come away from the peel during squeezing, in a clean piece of muslin. If you haven't got any muslin, improvise by using an old, large, clean handkerchief. Tie the muslin or handkerchief in a bundle with a long piece of string, then tie the string to the handle of the pan so that the bundle hangs down into the marmalade and can easily be removed after cooking. Cook this with the fruit for the first cooking then take it out, squeezing it as much as possible, letting the pulpy juice run back into the pan. A good way to do this is to press the bag in a nylon sieve with the back of a wooden spoon. Discard the contents of the muslin bag.

Second cooking The sugar is added at the beginning of the second cooking stage and stirred in until it dissolves. The marmalade is then boiled rapidly for 15–20 minutes until setting point is reached. Prolonged boiling after the addition of sugar gives marmalade a dark colour. Test for a set in the same way as for jams (see page 12). As soon as setting point is reached, remove the pan from the heat and skim the marmalade with a slotted spoon to remove any scum.

Potting and Covering

Before potting, leave the marmalade to cool slightly for 10–15 minutes, then stir to distribute the peel. This will prevent the peel rising in the jars. Pot and cover as for jam (see page 12).

Pressure Cooking Marmalade

Follow the instructions given for jam on page 14, but add only a quarter of the amount of water required in the recipe when the fruit is cooked under pressure. The second quarter is added with the sugar. Cook citrus fruits for 20 minutes at medium (10 lb) pressure. (See recipe on page 61.)

SEVILLE ORANGE MARMALADE

Illustrated in colour on pages 55 and 56

1.5 kg (3 lb) Seville oranges, washed
juice of 2 lemons
3.6 litres (6 pints) water
3 kg (6 lb) sugar

Halve the oranges and squeeze out the juice and pips. Tie the pips, and any extra membrane that has come away during squeezing, in a piece of muslin. Slice the orange peel thinly or thickly, as preferred, and put it in a preserving pan with the fruit juices, water and muslin bag. Simmer gently for about 2 hours until the peel is really soft and the liquid reduced by about half. Remove the muslin bag, squeezing it well and allowing the juice to run back into the pan. Add the sugar, stirring until it has dissolved, then boil the mixture rapidly for about 15 minutes. Test for a set and, when setting point is reached, take the pan off the heat and remove any scum with a slotted spoon. Pot and cover the marmalade in the usual way.

Makes about 5 kg (10 lb)

VARIATIONS
Seville orange marmalade (whole fruit method)
As an alternative method, place the whole washed fruit in a saucepan with the water. Cover and simmer gently for about 2 hours until a fork pierces the peel easily. Remove the fruit from the pan and leave to cool a little, then cut it up, thinly or thickly, with a knife and fork. Save the pips and tie them in a piece of muslin. Put the muslin bag in the liquid in

the saucepan, add the lemon juice and boil for 5 minutes.

Weigh a preserving pan, put the fruit in it, add the liquid from the saucepan, discarding the muslin bag, and boil off the excess liquid until the contents weigh 2.25 kg ($4\frac{1}{2}$ lb). Add the sugar, stirring until it has dissolved, then bring to the boil and boil rapidly for about 15 minutes. Test for a set and, when setting point is reached, take the pan off the heat and remove any scum with a slotted spoon. Leave to stand for about 15 minutes then stir gently to distribute the peel. Pot and cover the marmalade in the usual way.

Whisky marmalade
Follow the recipe for Seville orange marmalade. When setting point is reached, take the pan off the heat, remove any scum with a slotted spoon, then stir in 150 ml ($\frac{1}{4}$ pint) whisky. Leave to stand for about 15 minutes, then stir to distribute the peel. Pot and cover the marmalade in the usual way.

Dark chunky marmalade (1)
Illustrated in colour on page 56
Follow the recipe for Seville orange marmalade. Cut the peel into thick slices. When the sugar is added, stir until it has dissolved, bring to the boil, then simmer gently for a further $1\frac{1}{2}$ hours until the colour of the marmalade has darkened. Test for a set and, when setting point is reached, take the pan off the heat and remove any scum with a slotted spoon. Pot and cover as usual.

Dark chunky marmalade (2)
Follow the recipe for Seville orange marmalade. Cut the peel into thick slices. Either replace the white sugar with the same quantity of demerara sugar, or stir in 30 ml (2 tbsp) black treacle with the white sugar.

THREE-FRUIT MARMALADE

4 ripe lemons, washed and halved
2 sweet oranges, washed and halved
2 grapefruits, washed
3.6 litres (6 pints) water
3 kg (6 lb) sugar

Altogether, the fruit should weigh a total of about 1.5 kg (3 lb). Squeeze the juice and pips out of the lemons and oranges. Peel the grapefruit and remove any pith and stringy parts from the flesh. Tie the pith, stringy parts and pips from all the fruits in a piece of muslin. Thinly cut the peel of all the fruits and chop the grapefruit flesh roughly. Put the peel, flesh, juice, water and muslin bag in a preserving pan. Simmer gently for $1-1\frac{1}{2}$ hours until the peel is really soft and the contents of the pan are reduced by half.

Remove the muslin bag from the pan, squeezing well and allowing the juice to run back into the pan. Add the sugar, stirring until dissolved, then boil rapidly for 15–20 minutes. Test for a set and, when setting point is reached, take the pan off the heat and remove any scum with a slotted spoon. Leave the marmalade to stand for 15 minutes, then stir to distribute the peel. Pot and cover the marmalade in the usual way.

Makes about 5 kg (10 lb)

SWEET ORANGE AND LEMON MARMALADE

2 sweet oranges, washed and thinly sliced
3 lemons, washed and thinly sliced
1.5 litres ($2\frac{1}{2}$ pints) water
1 kg (2 lb) sugar

Remove all the pips from the fruit and tie them in a piece of muslin. Put the fruit, water and muslin bag into a preserving pan and simmer gently for about $1\frac{1}{2}$ hours until the content of the pan is reduced by about half. Remove the muslin bag, squeezing it well and allowing the juice to run back into the pan. Add the sugar, stir until dissolved, then boil rapidly for about 10 minutes. Test for a set and, when setting point is reached, take the pan off the heat and remove any scum with a slotted spoon. Leave to stand for 15 minutes,

then stir gently to distribute the peel. Pot and cover the marmalade in the usual way.

Makes about 2 kg (4 lb)

ORANGE SHRED MARMALADE

1 kg (2 lb) Seville oranges, washed
juice of 2 lemons
2.7 litres ($4\frac{1}{2}$ pints) water
1.5 kg (3 lb) sugar

Peel off enough rind from the oranges, avoiding the pith, to weigh 100 g (4 oz). Cut the rind into thin strips. Cut up the rest of the fruit and simmer it in a covered preserving pan with the lemon juice and 1.5 litres ($2\frac{1}{2}$ pints) of the water for about 2 hours until the fruit is really soft.

Put the shredded rind in another pan with 600 ml (1 pint) of the water, cover and simmer gently until this also is really soft. Drain off the liquid from the shreds and add them to the fruit in the other pan. Pour the contents of the pan into a jelly bag or cloth attached to the legs of an upturned stool and leave to drip into a large bowl for 15 minutes.

Return the pulp remaining in the jelly bag to the pan with the remaining 600 ml (1 pint) water, simmer for a further 20 minutes, then pour into the jelly bag again and leave to drip for several hours.

Combine the two lots of extract and test for pectin (see page 11). If the liquid does not clot, reduce it slightly by rapid boiling, then test again. Add the sugar and stir until it has dissolved. Add the orange peel shreds from the jelly bag and boil rapidly for about 15 minutes. Test for a set and, when setting point is reached, take the pan off the heat and remove any scum with a slotted spoon. Leave the marmalade to stand for about 15 minutes, then stir to distribute the peel. Pot and cover in the usual way.

Makes about 2.5 kg (5 lb)

VARIATION
Lemon shred marmalade
Follow the recipe above but substitute lemons.

Seville orange marmalade (page 52)

GRAPEFRUIT MARMALADE

2 large grapefruit (about 1 kg, 2 lb), washed
4–5 lemons (about 500 g, 1 lb), washed
1.8 litres (3 pints) water
1.5 kg (3 lb) sugar

Pare the rinds from the grapefruit and lemons as thinly as possible, using a sharp knife or potato peeler, and cut it up finely. Remove the pith from the fruits and roughly cut up the flesh, removing and reserving any pips and saving the juice. Tie the pith and pips in a piece of muslin and put the peel, fruit, juice and water in a preserving pan with the muslin bag. Simmer gently for about $1\frac{1}{2}$ hours until the peel is really soft and the contents of the pan reduced by half.

Remove the muslin bag, squeezing it well and allowing the juice to run back into the pan. Add the sugar and stir until it has dissolved, then boil rapidly for 15–20 minutes. Test for a set and, when setting point is reached, take the pan off the heat and remove any scum with a slotted spoon. Leave to stand for about 15 minutes, then stir to distribute peel. Pot and cover as usual.

Makes about 2.25 kg ($4\frac{1}{2}$ lb)

LEMON MARMALADE
Illustrated in colour opposite

1.5 kg (3 lb) lemons, washed
3.6 litres (6 pints) water
3 kg (6 lb) sugar

For this recipe, weigh the empty preserving pan before you start.

Halve the lemons and squeeze out the juice and pips. Cut each 'cap' of peel in half and, with a sharp knife, remove the membrane and some of the pith. Tie the membrane, pith and pips in a piece of muslin. Slice the peel to the desired thickness and put it in the preserving pan with the juice, water and muslin bag.

Top (from left): *Diabetic marmalade (page 59),*
Lemon marmalade (above), Dark chunky
marmalade (page 53)
Bottom (from left): *Seville orange marmalade*
(page 52), Lemon marmalade (above), Seville
orange marmalade (page 52)

Bring to the boil, then simmer gently for about 2 hours until the peel is soft and the contents of the pan reduced by half.

Remove the muslin bag, squeezing out as much juice as possible. The contents of the pan should have reduced to 2.25 kg ($4\frac{1}{2}$ lb). Add the sugar, stir until dissolved, then bring to the boil and boil rapidly for about 15 minutes. Test for a set and, when setting point is reached, take the pan off the heat and remove any scum with a slotted spoon. Leave to stand for about 15 minutes, then stir to distribute the peel. Pot and cover the marmalade in the usual way.

Makes about 5 kg (10 lb)

VARIATION
Lime marmalade
As above, using limes instead of lemons.

WINDFALL MARMALADE

1 kg (2 lb) windfall apples
2 grapefruit, washed
4 lemons, washed
3 litres (5 pints) water
2.5 kg (5 lb) sugar

Peel, core and chop the apples, reserving the cores and peel. Pare the rinds from the grapefruit and lemons as thinly as possible, using a sharp knife or potato peeler, and shred the rind finely. Remove the pith from the fruits and roughly chop the flesh, removing and reserving any pips. Tie the citrus pith, pips, apple peel and cores in a piece of muslin. Put all the fruit in a preserving pan with the shredded rind, water and muslin bag. Bring to the boil, then simmer gently for about $2\frac{1}{2}$ hours until the peel is soft and the contents of the pan reduced by half.

Remove the muslin bag, squeezing well and allowing the juice to run back into the pan. Add the sugar, stir until it has dissolved, then boil rapidly for 15–20 minutes. Test for a set and, when setting point is reached, take the pan off the heat and remove any scum with a slotted spoon. Leave to stand for 15 minutes, then stir to distribute the peel before potting and covering in the usual way.

Makes about 4.5 kg (9 lb)

GINGER MARMALADE

500 g (1 lb) Seville oranges, washed
3.15 litres (5¼ pints) water
1.5 kg (3 lb) cooking apples, peeled, cored and
  sliced
3.25 kg (6½ lb) sugar
250 g (8 oz) preserved ginger, diced
20 ml (4 level tsp) ground ginger

Peel the oranges and shred the peel finely. Roughly chop the oranges, removing and reserving any tough membrane, pith, pips and juice. Tie the membrane, pith and pips in a piece of muslin. Put the peel, chopped orange, juice, muslin bag and all but 150 ml (¼ pint) water into a preserving pan and simmer for about 1½ hours until the peel is soft and the contents of the pan reduced by half. Remove the muslin bag, squeezing well and allowing the juice to run back into the pan.

Put the apples in a saucepan with the remaining 150 ml (¼ pint) water and simmer gently until the fruit is really soft and pulped. Combine the apples with the oranges in the preserving pan, add the sugar and stir until it has dissolved. Add the preserved ginger and the ground ginger and boil rapidly for about 15 minutes. Test for a set and, when setting point is reached, take the pan off the heat and remove any scum with a slotted spoon. Leave for about 15 minutes, then stir to distribute the peel and ginger. Pot and cover the marmalade in the usual way.

Makes about 5 kg (10 lb)

TANGERINE JELLY MARMALADE

As tangerines have a poor pectin content, they are unsuitable for marmalade making unless combined with another citrus fruit. Grapefruit is ideal as it is fairly rich in pectin and its flavour is sufficiently delicate not to mask the flavour of the tangerines.

1 kg (2 lb) tangerines, washed
1 large grapefruit, washed
1 lemon, washed
5 ml (1 level tsp) citric acid
3 litres (5 pints) water
1.5 kg (3 lb) sugar

All together, the fruit should weigh about 1.37 kg (2¾ lb). Peel the tangerines and cut the peel into fine shreds. Tie the shreds in a piece of muslin. Peel the grapefruit and lemon and cut the peel up finely. Roughly chop the flesh of all the fruit, reserving the juice, and put flesh, juice and peel in a preserving pan with the muslin bag. Add the citric acid and water and simmer for about 2 hours until the fruit is soft. Remove the muslin bag after 30 minutes, squeezing well and allowing the juice to run back into the pan. Untie the muslin bag and place the tangerine peel in a sieve, wash under cold water, drain and reserve. Spoon the pulped fruit into a jelly bag or cloth attached to the legs of an upturned stool and leave to drip for about 2 hours.

Pour the extract into a clean pan and add the sugar. Heat gently and stir until the sugar has dissolved. Bring to the boil, stir in the reserved peel and boil rapidly. Test for a set and, when setting point is reached, take the pan off the heat and quickly remove any scum with a slotted spoon. Leave to stand for 15 minutes, then stir to distribute the shreds. Pot and cover the marmalade in the usual way.

Makes about 2.5 kg (5 lb)

DIABETIC MARMALADE
Illustrated in colour on page 56

3 large oranges, washed
3 lemons, washed
1.2 litres (2 pints) water
1 kg (2 lb) Sorbitol powder
227-ml (8-fl oz) bottle of commercial pectin

Pare the rinds from the oranges and lemons as thinly as possible, using a sharp knife or a potato peeler, and shred the rind very finely. Halve the oranges and lemons and squeeze out the juice and pips. Tie the pips and pith in a piece of muslin. Put the fruit juices, shredded rind, muslin bag and water into a preserving pan, bring to the boil, then simmer gently for $1-1\frac{1}{2}$ hours until the peel is tender and the contents of the pan reduced by half.

Remove the muslin bag, squeezing out as much juice as possible. Add the Sorbitol powder and stir until it has dissolved, then bring to the boil and boil rapidly for 5 minutes. Remove from the heat and stir in the pectin. Boil for a further minute, then take the pan off the heat and remove any scum with a slotted spoon. Leave to cool for 15 minutes, then stir to distribute the peel. Pot and cover the marmalade in the usual way.

Makes about 2 kg (4 lb)

Note Small jars are recommended as the marmalade will not keep for long.

GREEN TOMATO MARMALADE

5 lemons, washed
water
1 kg (2 lb) green tomatoes
1.75 kg ($3\frac{1}{2}$ lb) sugar

Halve the lemons and squeeze out the juice. Remove the remaining flesh and reserve with the pips. Strip away the excess pith and cut the rind into thin strips. Place the rind in a saucepan, add 450 ml ($\frac{3}{4}$ pint) water and simmer, covered, for 20 minutes until soft.

Meanwhile, cut the tomatoes into quarters, remove the seeds and tie in a piece of muslin with the lemon pips and remaining lemon flesh. Shred the tomato flesh and place it in a preserving pan. Measure the lemon juice, make it up to 1.8 litres (3 pints) with water and add it to the pan with the muslin bag and the softened lemon shreds and liquid. Simmer all together for about 40 minutes until the tomato is tender.

Remove the muslin bag, squeezing well and allowing the juice to run back into the pan. Add the sugar, stir until it has dissolved, then boil rapidly for about 15 minutes. Test for a set and, when setting point is reached, take the pan off the heat and remove any scum with a slotted spoon. Leave to stand for about 15 minutes, then stir to distribute the peel. Pot and cover the marmalade in the usual way.

Makes about 2.5 kg (5 lb)

GINGER THREE-FRUIT MARMALADE

4 Seville oranges, washed
2 sweet oranges, washed
2 lemons, washed
250 g (8 oz) preserved ginger
3.6 litres (6 pints) water
2.5 kg (5 lb) sugar

Pare the rinds from the fruit as thinly as possible, using a sharp knife or potato peeler, and cut the rind into thin shreds. Squeeze the juice out of the fruit, reserving the pips. Tie the remaining pith and the pips in a piece of muslin. Cut the ginger into small strips. Place the shredded rind, the juice, ginger and muslin bag in a preserving pan and add the water. Simmer for 1½–2 hours until tender.

Remove the muslin bag, squeezing well to remove as much juice as possible. Add the sugar and stir until it has dissolved, then boil rapidly for 10–15 minutes. Test for a set and, when setting point is reached, take the pan off the heat and remove any scum with a slotted spoon. Leave to stand for about 15 minutes, then stir. Pot and cover in the usual way.

Makes about 4 kg (8 lb)

CROCK-POT MARMALADE

1 kg (2 lb) Seville oranges, washed
juice of 2 small lemons
1.2 litres (2 pints) water
2 kg (4 lb) sugar

Halve the oranges and squeeze out the juice, reserving any pips and pulp. Tie the pips and pulp in a piece of muslin. Slice the orange peel thinly and place in an electric casserole with the fruit juices, water and muslin bag. Place the lid in position and cook on high for 3–4 hours, or low for 6–8 hours, until the peel is tender.

Remove the muslin bag, squeezing it well and allowing the juice to run back into the pot. Pour the contents of the electric casserole into a large saucepan. Add the sugar and cook over a gentle heat, stirring, until the sugar has dissolved. Bring to the boil and boil rapidly for about 15 minutes. Test for a set and, when setting point is reached, take the pan off the heat and remove any scum with a slotted spoon. Leave to stand for 10 minutes, then stir well to distribute the peel. Pot and cover the marmalade in the usual way.

Makes about 3 kg (6 lb)

PRESSURE-COOKED MARMALADE

1.5 kg (3 lb) Seville oranges, washed
juice of 2 lemons
1.8 litres (3 pints) water
3 kg (6 lb) sugar

Halve the oranges and squeeze out the juice, reserving the pips and pulp. Tie the pips and pulp in a piece of muslin. Slice the orange peel thinly and place in a pressure cooker with the fruit juices, 900 ml (1½ pints) water and the muslin bag. Bring to medium (10 lb) pressure and cook for 20 minutes until the peel is soft. Leave the pan to cool at room temperature until the pressure is reduced.

Remove the muslin bag, squeezing it well and allowing the juice to run back into the cooker. Add the remaining water and the sugar and stir until the sugar has dissolved. Boil rapidly for 15 minutes. Test for a set and, when setting point is reached, take the pan off the heat and remove any scum with a slotted spoon. Leave the marmalade to stand for 15 minutes, then stir gently to distribute the peel. Pot and cover the marmalade as usual.

Makes about 5 kg (10 lb)

Note For further notes on pressure cooking marmalades, see page 52.

OXFORD MARMALADE
Illustrated in colour on page 96

This recipe is for a rather bitter dark chunky marmalade known as 'Oxford' marmalade.

1.5 kg (3 lb) Seville oranges
3.6 litres (6 pints) water
3 kg (6 lb) sugar

Peel the oranges and cut the peel into strips and the fruit into small pieces, reserving the pips. Put the pips into a small bowl. Put the strips of peel and chopped flesh into a large bowl. Bring the water to the boil and pour 600 ml (1 pint) over the pips and the remainder over the orange peel and flesh. Cover and leave for several hours or overnight.

The next day, the pips will be covered with a soft transparent jelly which must be washed off them into the orange peel and flesh. To do this, lift the pips out of the water with a slotted spoon and put them in a nylon sieve. Pour the water the pips were soaking in over the pips into the large bowl. Repeat the process, using water from the large bowl. Discard the pips.

Boil the peel, flesh and water until the peel is very soft—the longer this mixture boils the darker the marmalade will be. When the peel is quite soft, remove the pan from the heat and add the sugar, stirring until it has dissolved. Boil very gently until the marmalade is as dark as you like it, then boil rapidly for about 15 minutes. Test for a set and, when setting point is reached, take the pan off the heat and remove any scum with a slotted spoon. Leave to stand for 15 minutes, then stir to distribute the peel. Pot and cover the marmalade in the usual way.

Makes about 5 kg (10 lb)

Butters, Cheeses and Curds

Fruit butters, cheeses and curds are all traditional country preserves which are usually only made when there is a glut of fruit, as a large quantity of fruit produces only a comparatively small amount of finished preserve.

Butters and Cheeses

Fruit butters are soft and butter-like and can be used like jam. They do not keep very well so should only be made in small quantities and used up fairly quickly.

Cheeses are very thick preserves that are often served as an accompaniment to meat, poultry and game. The preserve is so thick that it can be potted in small moulds or jars and turned out whole when required. Cheeses store much better than butters and, in fact, improve on keeping.

The fruits most commonly used for making fruit butters and cheeses are apples, apricots, blackberries, gooseberries, damsons, medlars and quinces.

It is not practicable to state an exact yield in recipes for butters and cheeses.

Preparation and cooking Fruit for butter or cheese making only needs picking over and washing, although larger fruits should be roughly chopped. Put the prepared fruit in a preserving pan or large saucepan with just enough water to cover, and simmer until really soft. Press the fruit pulp through a nylon sieve, using a wooden spoon so that the fruit does not discolour. Measure the pulp and allow the following amounts of sugar: For *butters*, allow 225–375 g (8–12 oz) sugar to each 600 ml (1 pint) pulp. For *cheeses*, allow 375–500 g (12 oz–1 lb) sugar to each 600 ml (1 pint) pulp.

Return the pulp to the pan, add the sugar

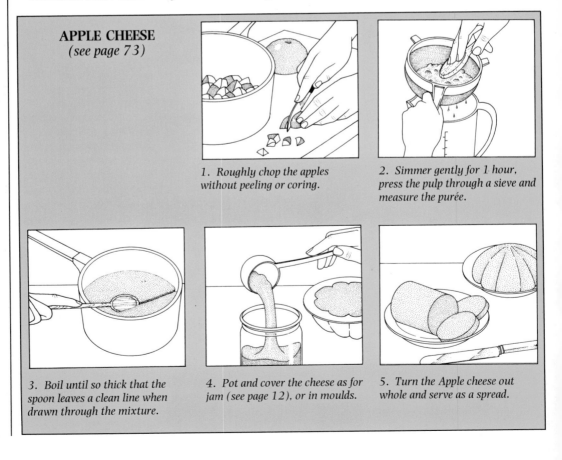

APPLE CHEESE
(see page 73)

1. *Roughly chop the apples without peeling or coring.*

2. *Simmer gently for 1 hour, press the pulp through a sieve and measure the purée.*

3. *Boil until so thick that the spoon leaves a clean line when drawn through the mixture.*

4. *Pot and cover the cheese as for jam (see page 12), or in moulds.*

5. *Turn the Apple cheese out whole and serve as a spread.*

and stir until dissolved. Boil gently until the required consistency is reached. Stir continuously to prevent the preserve sticking to the bottom of the pan as it cooks and thickens. Butters should be cooked until they are like thick cream. The finishing point is determined by consistency rather than by set or temperature—the cooled butter should be thick and almost set so that it may be spread like jam. Cheeses should be cooked until they are so thick that a spoon drawn across the bottom of the pan leaves a clean line through the preserve.

Potting For butters, prepare jars or small pots and cover as for jam (see page 12), or use caps and rings as for bottling (see page 120).

For cheeses, brush the inside of some small, prepared pots or jars (preferably straight-sided) or moulds with olive oil. This enables the preserve to be turned out. Pour in the cheese, cover as for jam (see page 12) and store for 3–4 months before using.

Curds

Made with eggs and butter as well as sugar and fruit, curds are not a true 'preserve' and should only be made in small quantities and eaten quickly. They will keep for up to a month in a cupboard or for up to 3 months in the refrigerator.

Cooking Cook curds very gently in the top of a double saucepan or in a bowl standing over a pan of simmering water, stirring all the time. The mixture should not be allowed to boil or it will curdle, and it should be cooked until it is thick enough to coat the back of a wooden spoon.

Potting and covering Strain the cooked curd through a fine sieve, to remove any lumps of egg white, before pouring into small jars. Fill the jars right to the top as the curd will thicken and shrink as it cools. Cover immediately as for jam (see page 12).

LEMON CURD
Illustrated in colour opposite and on page 67

grated rind and juice of 4 medium lemons
4 eggs
100 g (4 oz) butter
375 g (12 oz) caster sugar

Place all the ingredients in the top of a double saucepan or in a bowl standing over a pan of simmering water. Stir until the sugar has dissolved and continue heating gently for about 20 minutes until the curd thickens. Strain into jars and cover in the usual way.

Makes about 750 g (1½ lb)

Note Home-made lemon curd should be made in small quantities as it only keeps for about 1 month. Store in a cool place.

VARIATION
The fresh lemon juice can be replaced with 180 ml (12 tbsp) artificial lemon juice. To give extra tang, the grated rind of a fresh lemon can be added, if liked.

ORANGE CURD

grated rind and juice of 2 large oranges
juice of ½ a lemon
225 g (8 oz) caster sugar
100 g (4 oz) butter
3 egg yolks, beaten

Place all the ingredients in the top of a double saucepan or in a bowl standing over a pan of simmering water. Heat gently, stirring, for about 20 minutes until the sugar has dissolved and the mixture has thickened. Strain, pot and cover the curd in the usual way.

Makes about 500 g (1 lb)

GOOSEBERRY CURD

1.5 kg (3 lb) green gooseberries, topped, tailed and washed
450 ml (¾ pint) water
750 g (1½ lb) caster sugar
100 g (4 oz) butter
4 eggs, lightly beaten

Put the gooseberries and water in a saucepan and simmer gently for 20 minutes until tender. Using a wooden spoon, press the gooseberry pulp through a nylon sieve into the top of a double saucepan or a bowl standing over a pan of simmering water. Add the sugar, butter and eggs. Heat gently, stirring, for about 20 minutes until the sugar has dissolved and the mixture thickens. Strain.

Pot in small jars, cover in the usual way and store in a cool place. Use within 1 month.

Makes about 2 kg (4 lb)

THREE-FRUIT CURD

1 medium juicy grapefruit
1 medium juicy orange
2 thin-skinned lemons
50 g (2 oz) butter, softened
4 eggs
150 g (5 oz) caster sugar

Finely grate the rinds of the grapefruit, orange and one lemon into a bowl over a pan of simmering water or the top of a double saucepan. Halve the fruits and squeeze out the juice. Add 75 ml (5 tbsp) grapefruit juice, 45 ml (3 tbsp) orange juice and 60 ml (4 tbsp) lemon juice to the grated rinds with the butter, eggs and sugar. Whisk lightly to break up the eggs. Heat gently, stirring all the time, until the curd thickens sufficiently to coat the back of the spoon. Strain into small pots, taking care to fill them to the top. Cover as usual. Store in the refrigerator and use within 2 weeks.

Makes about 600 g (1¼ lb)

Lemon curd (above)

Above: *Apples, pears, plums and hazelnuts*

Opposite: Clockwise from top

Lemon curd cake filling (page 64),
Crunchy harvest butter (page 71),
Apricot and orange butter (page 70)

RASPBERRY CURD

375 g (12 oz) raspberries, washed
225 g (8 oz) cooking apples, peeled, cored and
*   chopped*
grated rind and juice of 1 orange
4 eggs, beaten
100 g (4 oz) butter
375 g (12 oz) sugar

Place the raspberries, apples, and orange rind and juice in a saucepan. Bring to the boil, then simmer for 20 minutes until the fruit is soft. Using a wooden spoon, press the fruit pulp through a nylon sieve into a bowl over a pan of simmering water or into a double saucepan. Add the eggs, butter and sugar. Heat gently, stirring, until the sugar has dissolved and continue heating gently, stirring frequently, for 35–40 minutes until the curd thickens. Strain the curd into small pots and cover in the usual way.

Makes about 750 g (1½ lb)

TANGERINE CURD

3 tangerines, washed
150 g (5 oz) caster sugar
100 g (4 oz) butter
3 egg yolks

Finely grate the rinds of 2 of the tangerines. Squeeze the juice from all the fruit and strain into the top of a double saucepan or a bowl standing over a pan of simmering water. Add the rind, sugar, butter and egg yolks. Heat gently, stirring, for about 20 minutes until the mixture thickens. Strain, pot and cover the curd in the usual way.

Makes about 500 g (1 lb)

Gooseberry cheese (page 72)

HONEY LEMON CURD

grated rind and juice of 4 lemons
5 eggs, beaten
100 g (4 oz) butter
225 g (8 oz) thick honey
50 g (2 oz) caster sugar

Put all the ingredients in the top of a double saucepan or in a deep bowl standing over a pan of simmering water. Heat gently, stirring frequently, for 10–20 minutes until the sugar has dissolved and the curd has thickened enough to coat the back of a wooden spoon.

Strain the curd into small pots and cover in the usual way. Stored in a cool place, preferably the refrigerator, this curd will keep for about 1 month.

Makes about 1 kg (2 lb)

Note You will need about 175 ml (6 fl oz) lemon juice, so squeeze another lemon if necessary.

APRICOT AND ORANGE BUTTER
Illustrated in colour on page 67

1.5 kg (3 lb) fresh apricots, skinned and stoned
grated rind and juice of 2 oranges
about 450 ml ($\frac{3}{4}$ pint) water
sugar

Place the apricots, orange rind and juice in a pan and add just enough water to cover. Simmer gently for about 45 minutes until the fruit is soft and pulpy. Using a wooden spoon, press the fruit pulp through a nylon sieve. Measure the purée and return it to the pan with 375 g (12 oz) sugar for each 600 ml (1 pint) purée. Heat gently, stirring, until the sugar has dissolved, then bring to the boil and boil for 30–40 minutes, stirring frequently, until the mixture is thick and like jam in consistency. Pot and cover in the usual way.

Makes about 1.5 kg (3 lb)

PLUM BUTTER

1.5 kg (3 lb) plums, skinned and stoned
grated rind and juice of 1 lemon
about 450 ml ($\frac{3}{4}$ pint) water
sugar

Place the plums, lemon rind and juice in a pan and add just enough water to cover. Simmer gently for 15–20 minutes until the fruit is soft and pulpy. Using a wooden spoon, press the fruit pulp through a nylon sieve and measure the purée. Return the purée to the pan and add 375 g (12 oz) sugar for each 600 ml (1 pint) purée. Heat gently, stirring, until the sugar has dissolved, then bring to the boil and boil for 20–25 minutes, stirring frequently, until the mixture thickens and is like jam in consistency. Pot and cover the butter in the usual way.

Makes about 1.25 kg (2$\frac{1}{2}$ lb)

BLACK BUTTER
Nièr beurre is a traditional preserve from the Channel Islands. It is thick, dark and spicy.

2.4 litres (4 pints) cider
1 kg (2 lb) cooking apples, peeled, cored and
* sliced*
2 kg (4 lb) eating apples, peeled, cored and sliced
grated rind and juice of 2 thin-skinned lemons
sugar
5 ml (1 level tsp) ground cinnamon
5 ml (1 level tsp) ground nutmeg

Pour the cider into a large, heavy-based saucepan and boil rapidly until reduced by half. Combine the apple slices and add half to the cider. Continue cooking and, when the apples are soft, add the remaining apples with the lemon rind and juice. Cook until well reduced and pulpy. Measure the pulp and add 375 g (12 oz) sugar for each 600 ml (1 pint) pulp. Return the pulp and sugar to the pan, add the spices and continue cooking, stirring frequently, until no free liquid remains. Keep the heat low towards the end of the cooking time as the preserve tends to spit. Pot and cover the butter as usual.

Makes about 4.25 kg (8$\frac{1}{2}$ lb)

CRUNCHY HARVEST BUTTER
Illustrated in colour on page 67

1.5 kg (3 lb) cooking apples, windfalls or crab-
apples, washed and chopped
about 1 litre (1¾ pints) water
sugar
25 g (1 oz) walnuts, finely chopped
45 ml (3 level tbsp) crunchy natural wheatgerm

Place the apples in a saucepan, cover with water and simmer gently for 1 hour until really soft and pulpy. Using a wooden spoon, press the apple pulp through a nylon sieve and measure the purée. Return the purée to the pan and add 375 g (12 oz) sugar for each 600 ml (1 pint) purée. Heat gently, stirring, until the sugar has dissolved, then bring to the boil and boil for 30–45 minutes, stirring frequently, until the mixture is thick and like jam in consistency. Stir in the walnuts and wheatgerm and pot and cover the butter in the usual way.

Makes about 1.5 kg (3 lb)

BLACKBERRY CHEESE

1 kg (2 lb) blackberries, washed
500 g (1 lb) cooking apples, peeled, cored and
diced
600 ml (1 pint) water
sugar

Place the blackberries, apples and water in a large saucepan or preserving pan. Bring to the boil and simmer gently for about 30 minutes until the blackberries are just tender. Using a wooden spoon, press the fruit pulp through a nylon sieve and measure the purée. Return the purée to the pan and add 375 g (12 oz) sugar for each 600 ml (1 pint) purée. Heat gently, stirring, until the sugar has dissolved, then bring to the boil and boil for about 30 minutes until the mixture is so thick that the wooden spoon leaves a clean line through the mixture when drawn across the bottom of the pan.

Pot and cover the Blackberry cheese in the usual way or, if preferred, prepare and fill a bowl or several small moulds (see page 63) from which the cheese can be turned out and served whole. Leave to set and cover as usual. Serve in wedges with bread and butter or with soft or crumbly cheese.

Makes about 1 kg (2 lb)

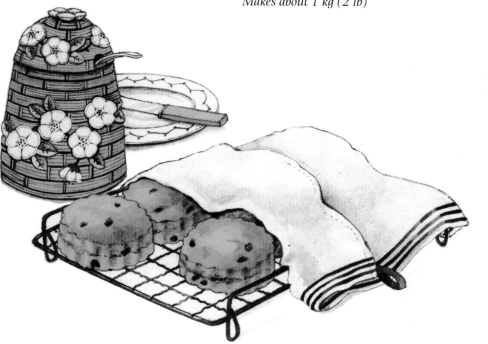

DAMSON CHEESE

1.5 kg (3 lb) damsons, washed
150–300 ml ($\frac{1}{4}$–$\frac{1}{2}$ pint) water
sugar

Place the fruit and water in a pan, cover and simmer gently for 15–20 minutes until the fruit is really soft. Scoop out the stones with a slotted spoon as they come to the surface. Using a wooden spoon, press the fruit pulp through a nylon sieve and measure the purée.

Return the purée to the pan and add 375 g (12 oz) sugar for each 600 ml (1 pint) purée. Heat gently, stirring, until the sugar has dissolved, then bring to the boil and boil gently, stirring frequently, for 30–40 minutes until so thick that the wooden spoon leaves a clean line through the mixture when drawn across the bottom of the pan.

Pot and cover the cheese in the usual way or, if preferred, prepare and fill a bowl or several small moulds (see page 63) from which the cheese can be turned out and served whole. Leave to set and cover as usual.

Makes about 1.5 kg (3 lb)

VARIATIONS
Gooseberry cheese
Illustrated in colour on page 68
Make as above, using 1.5 kg (3 lb) gooseberries and 150 ml ($\frac{1}{4}$ pint) water.

Damson and blackberry cheese
Make as above, using 500 g (1 lb) damsons and 1 kg (2 lb) blackberries.

QUINCE CHEESE

1.5 kg (3 lb) quinces, washed
water
sugar

Chop the quinces without peeling or coring, put them in a large saucepan and add just enough water to cover. Simmer gently for about 30 minutes until the fruit is really soft.

Using a wooden spoon, press the fruit pulp through a nylon sieve and measure the purée. Return the purée to the pan and add 500 g (1 lb) sugar for each 600 ml (1 pint) purée. Heat gently, stirring, until the sugar has dissolved, then bring to the boil and boil gently, stirring frequently, for 30–40 minutes until so thick that the wooden spoon leaves a clean line through the mixture when drawn across the bottom of the pan.

Pot and cover the cheese in the usual way or, if preferred, prepare and fill a bowl or several small moulds (see page 63) from which the cheese can be turned out and served whole. Leave to set and cover as usual.

Makes about 1.5 kg (3 lb)

APPLE CHEESE

1.5 kg (3 lb) cooking apples, windfalls or crab-apples, washed
about 1.2 litres (2 pints) water
2.5 ml ($\frac{1}{2}$ level tsp) ground cinnamon
1.25–2.5 ml ($\frac{1}{4}$–$\frac{1}{2}$ level tsp) ground cloves
sugar

Chop the apples without peeling or coring and put them in a large saucepan. Add just enough water to cover and simmer gently for about 1 hour until the apples are really soft and pulpy.

Using a wooden spoon, press the apple pulp through a nylon sieve and measure the purée. Return the purée to the pan and add the spices and 500 g (1 lb) sugar for each 600 ml (1 pint) purée. Heat gently, stirring, until the sugar has dissolved, then bring to the boil and boil gently, stirring frequently, for 30–45 minutes until so thick that the wooden spoon leaves a clean line through the mixture when drawn across the bottom of the pan.

Pot and cover the cheese in the usual way or, if preferred, prepare and fill a bowl or several small moulds (see page 63) from which the Apple cheese can be turned out and served whole. Serve as a spread, decorated with split almonds.

Makes about 1.5 kg (3 lb)

MEDLAR CHEESE

1 kg (2 lb) medlars, washed
2 lemons
300 ml ($\frac{1}{2}$ pint) water
sugar
5 ml (1 level tsp) mixed spice

Cut each medlar into four. Halve the lemons, squeeze out the juice and cut up the peel. Tie the peel in a piece of muslin with any pips. Put the fruit, lemon juice and muslin bag into a saucepan, add the water and simmer gently until the medlars are tender. Remove the muslin bag and, using a wooden spoon, press the fruit pulp through a nylon sieve. Measure the purée. Return the purée to the pan and add 375 g (12 oz) sugar for each 600 ml (1 pint) purée. Stir in the spice. Heat gently, stirring, until the sugar has dissolved, then bring to the boil and boil rapidly for about 5 minutes until the mixture is so thick that the spoon leaves a clean line through the mixture when drawn across the bottom of the pan.

Pot and cover the cheese in the usual way or, if preferred, prepare and fill a bowl or several small moulds (see page 63).

Makes about 1 kg (2 lb)

CRANBERRY CHEESE
Serves as an accompaniment to roast turkey.

750 g (1$\frac{1}{2}$ lb) cranberries, washed
900 ml (1$\frac{1}{2}$ pints) water
750 g (1$\frac{1}{2}$ lb) sugar

Place the cranberries in a saucepan with the water and simmer gently for about 1 hour until the fruit is tender. Using a wooden spoon, press the fruit pulp through a nylon sieve. Return the purée to a clean pan, add the sugar and heat gently, stirring. until the sugar has dissolved. Bring to the boil and boil rapidly for about 30 minutes until the mixture is so thick that the spoon leaves a clean line through the mixture when drawn across the bottom of the pan.

Pot and cover the cheese in the usual way or, if preferred, prepare and fill a bowl or several small moulds (see page 63).

Makes about 1 kg (2 lb)

Pickles

Pickles make delicious and attractive accompaniments to cold meats. They can be either sweet or sharp, or an interesting blend of both, and are made by preserving raw or lightly cooked vegetables or fruit in clear, spiced vinegar. Only crisp, fresh fruits and vegetables should be pickled.

Equipment for Pickling
Choose enamel-lined, aluminium or stainless steel pans. Avoid brass, copper or iron, as they tend to impart an unpleasant metallic flavour to the preserve. Use only nylon sieves.
Pickle jars Large, wide-necked bottles are recommended for pickling, though smaller jam jars can be used. Jars with screw-tops with plastic-coated linings such as those used for coffee jars and commercially prepared pickles are ideal. The number of jars needed for a specific quantity of pickles varies so much, depending on the size of the vegetables or fruit and how tightly they are packed, that it is not practicable to state exact numbers. Before filling with a hot pickle, jars should be pre-heated in the oven.

The Vinegar
Vinegar acts as the preserving agent in pickles and is a very important factor. It should be of the best quality, with an acetic acid content of at least 5 per cent. 'Barrelled' vinegars usually have only a 4–5 per cent acetic acid content and are not so good. The colour of vinegar is no indication of its strength; further distilling has the effect of rendering vinegar colourless. This 'white' vinegar gives a better appearance to light-coloured pickles, such as onions and cauliflower, but malt vinegar gives a rather better flavour. Wine vinegar is just as good as malt for pickling but is usually rather expensive. Vinegar to be used for pickling is normally given extra flavour by being infused with herbs and spices (see page 115).

Brining
When making sharp pickles, the vegetables are usually brined beforehand. This removes surplus water which would otherwise dilute the vinegar and render it too weak to act as a preservative to the vegetables. Ordinary table salt is quite suitable for brining.

Fruits for pickling do not require brining as they are usually lightly cooked before pickling and the surplus moisture evaporates during the cooking. Sweet pickles are mostly made of fruit as they contain more sugar.
Dry brining For cucumber, marrow, tomatoes and red cabbage. Prepare the vegetables according to the recipe and layer them in a bowl with salt, allowing 15 ml (1 level tbsp) salt to each 500 g (1 lb) vegetables. Cover and leave overnight.
Wet brining For cauliflower, walnuts and onions. Prepare the vegetables according to

the recipe and place in a large bowl. Cover with a brine solution, allowing 50 g (2 oz) salt dissolved in 600 ml (1 pint) water to each 500 g (1 lb) vegetables. Put a plate over the surface to ensure that the vegetables are kept under the liquid, cover and leave overnight.

Finishing

After brining, vegetables for pickling should be well rinsed in cold water, drained and then packed into jars to within 2.5 cm (1 inch) of the top. Pour spiced vinegar over, taking care to cover the vegetables well and to add at least 1 cm ($\frac{1}{2}$ inch) extra to allow for any evaporation which may take place. Leave a little space at the top of the jar to prevent the vinegar coming into contact with the cover. Cover securely with one of the following:
1. Metal or Bakelite caps, with a vinegar-proof lining.

2. Greaseproof paper and then a round of muslin dipped in melted paraffin wax or fat.
3. Preserving skin (sold in rolls) or vinegar-proof paper.
4. Large corks (previously boiled), covered with a piece of greaseproof paper tied down with string.

If the jars are not adequately covered, the vinegar will evaporate, the preserve shrink and the top dry out.

When pickling crisp, sharp vegetables, e.g. cabbage or onion, the vinegar is poured over cold. For softer pickles, such as plums or walnuts, hot vinegar is used.

Storing

Store pickles in a cool, dry, dark place and leave to mature for 2–3 months before eating. The exception is red cabbage, which loses its crispness after 2–3 weeks.

PICKLED RED CABBAGE
(Dry brining method)

PICKLED ONIONS
(Wet brining method)

(see page 81)

1. Layer red cabbage in a bowl, sprinkling each layer with salt, and leave overnight.

2. Drain the cabbage, rinse thoroughly, drain again and pack into jars.

1. Put skinned onions in a bowl, cover with brine and leave for 24–36 hours.

2. Drain and rinse the onions well and pack into jars.

3. Pour spiced vinegar into the jars and cover at once with airtight, vinegar-proof tops.

'BREAD AND BUTTER' PICKLE
Illustrated in colour on page 96

This cucumber pickle is best served with bread and butter—hence its name.

3 large ridge or smooth-skinned cucumbers, washed
4 large onions, skinned and sliced
45 ml (3 level tbsp) salt
450 ml ($\frac{3}{4}$ pint) distilled vinegar
150 g (5 oz) granulated sugar
5 ml (1 level tsp) celery seeds
5 ml (1 level tsp) mustard seeds

Slice the cucumbers, then layer the cucumber and onion slices in a large bowl, sprinkling each layer with salt. Leave for 1 hour, then drain and rinse well.

Put the vinegar, sugar, celery and mustard seeds in a pan and heat gently, stirring, until the sugar has dissolved, then bring to the boil and cook for 3 minutes. Pack the vegetable slices into pre-heated jars and add enough hot vinegar mixture to cover. Cover immediately with airtight, vinegar-proof tops.

Note This pickle must be stored in a dark place or the cucumber will lose its colour.

PICKLE STICKS
Illustrated in colour on page 95

3 large, firm cucumbers
salt
600 ml (1 pint) water
1 large carrot, trimmed and peeled
4 celery sticks, trimmed and washed
2 red peppers, washed and seeded
100 g (4 oz) French beans, trimmed and washed
450 ml ($\frac{3}{4}$ pint) wine vinegar
500 g (1 lb) granulated sugar
30 ml (2 level tbsp) mustard seeds
5 ml (1 level tsp) turmeric

Cut the cucumbers into sticks about 5 cm (2 inches) long and 0.5 cm ($\frac{1}{4}$ inch) wide and place in a large bowl. Stir 30 ml (2 level tbsp) salt into the water, pour over the cucumber and leave overnight.

The next day, drain and rinse the cucumber well. Cut the carrot, celery and peppers into sticks the same size as the cucumber and cook with the beans in boiling salted water for 2 minutes, then drain. Place all the vegetables, including the cucumber, in a large pan with the remaining ingredients and 10 ml (2 level tsp) salt. Bring to the boil, stirring, then pack into pre-heated jars and cover immediately with airtight and vinegar-proof tops.

PICKLED MUSHROOMS
Illustrated in colour on page 95

900 ml (1$\frac{1}{2}$ pints) malt vinegar
4 blades of mace
5 ml (1 level tsp) freshly ground pepper
10 ml (2 level tsp) salt
2 shallots, skinned and chopped
a few sprigs of marjoram
1 kg (2 lb) small button mushrooms, trimmed and wiped

Pour the vinegar into a large pan and add the mace, seasoning, shallots and marjoram. Bring to the boil and add the mushrooms. Simmer gently for about 10 minutes until the mushrooms are tender and have shrunk slightly. Spoon the mushrooms into pre-heated jars, pour over the hot vinegar and cover immediately with airtight and vinegar-proof tops.

Pickled red cabbage (page 81)

PICKLED BEETROOT

beetroot
salt
water
spiced vinegar (see page 115)

Weigh the beetroots and wash them carefully, taking care not to damage the skins. Wrap the beets in foil and bake in the oven at 180°C (350°F) mark 4 for 2–3 hours, depending on size, until tender, Alternatively, mix up a brine solution, allowing 50 g (2 oz) salt dissolved in 600 ml (1 pint) water for each 500 g (1 lb) beets. Put the beets in a large saucepan, cover with the brine solution and simmer gently for 1½–2 hours, depending on the size of the beets, until tender.

Leave the beets to cool, then skin and thinly slice them. Pack the slices into jars and cover with cold spiced vinegar. If beets were baked, add 10 ml (2 level tsp) salt for each 600 ml (1 pint) vinegar. Cover the jars immediately with airtight, vinegar-proof tops.

For longer keeping, dice the beetroot, pack loosely, cover with boiling vinegar and seal.

PICKLED CARROTS
Illustrated in colour on page 95

1.25 kg (2½ lb) young carrots, of uniform size, trimmed and scraped
water
600 ml (1 pint) distilled vinegar
250 g (8 oz) granulated sugar
25 g (1 oz) pickling spice

Place the carrots in a large saucepan and cover with cold water. Bring to the boil, simmer gently for 10 minutes until only half cooked, then drain. Pour the vinegar into another pan with 300 ml (½ pint) water and the sugar. Tie the pickling spices in a piece of muslin and add to the vinegar mixture. Bring to the boil and boil for 5 minutes, then remove the muslin bag. Add the carrots and boil for 10–15 minutes or until almost tender. Pack the carrots into pre-heated jars, cover them with the boiling vinegar and cover the jars at once with airtight, vinegar-proof tops.

Spiced pickled peaches, Cerises au vinaigre (page 84)

LEMON PICKLE
This is an unusual pickle to serve with curry.

500 g (1 lb) lemons, washed
45 ml (3 level tbsp) salt
5 ml (1 level tsp) turmeric
7.5 ml (1½ level tsp) chilli powder
10 ml (2 level tsp) garam masala (see below)

Cut the fruit into small pieces, remove any pips and catch any juice in a bowl. Mix the fruit pieces and juice with the salt, turmeric, chilli powder and garam masala. Put into a large screw-topped jar and keep in a warm cupboard or, when possible, in the hot sun for a week, giving it a good shake each day. The pickle is ready when the skins are tender. Store well covered.

Note Garam masala is a flavouring made by mixing 5 ml (1 level tsp) ground cloves, 5 ml (1 level tsp) ground cinnamon, 5 ml (1 level tsp) freshly ground black pepper, 5 ml (1 level tsp) ground cumin seeds and 5 ml (1 level tsp) ground cardamom seeds.

VARIATIONS
Sweet lemon pickle
Add 75 g (3 oz) demerara sugar to the ingredients above to give a sweet pickle. A few chillies may be added to make it hotter.

Lime pickle
Make lime pickle by using the same number of limes in the recipe above instead of lemons.

PICKLED MARROW
Illustrated in colour on page 95

750 g (1½ lb) marrow (prepared weight), seeded
  and diced
25 g (1 oz) salt
300 ml (½ pint) sweet spiced vinegar (see page
  115)
175 g (6 oz) granulated sugar
4-cm (1½-inch) piece of root ginger, bruised

Place the marrow in a bowl, sprinkle with salt
and leave for about 12 hours.

Drain and rinse the marrow well and place
in a saucepan with the vinegar, sugar and
ginger. Heat gently, stirring, until the sugar
has dissolved, then bring to the boil and
simmer gently for about 10 minutes until the
marrow is just tender but not broken up.
Remove the ginger. Pack the marrow into
pre-heated jars and cover with vinegar. Cover
at once with airtight, vinegar-proof tops.

ITALIAN-STYLE
PICKLED CAULIFLOWER
Illustrated in colour on page 95

1 kg (2 lb) cauliflower, washed
1.8 litres (3 pints) malt vinegar
30 ml (2 level tbsp) dried marjoram
salt and freshly ground pepper
½ a red pepper, seeded and chopped
60 ml (4 tbsp) olive oil

Divide the cauliflower into small florets and
cook in boiling salted water for 5 minutes.
Drain well and put in a bowl. Pour the
vinegar into a pan, bring to the boil and pour
over the florets. Leave for 24 hours.

Lift the florets out of the vinegar and drain
well. Put them in layers in jars, sprinkling the
marjoram, seasoning and chopped red pepper
between the layers. Pour in the vinegar to
cover the cauliflower, then add the oil. Cover
at once with airtight, vinegar-proof tops.

APPLE AND ONION PICKLE

375 g (12 oz) sour cooking apples, washed,
  cored and finely chopped
375 g (12 oz) onions, skinned and finely
  chopped
50 g (2 oz) sultanas
9 peppercorns
9 whole cloves
40 g (1½ oz) chillies
450 ml (¾ pint) distilled vinegar
7.5 ml (1½ level tsp) salt

Pack the apples, onions and sultanas in pre-
heated jars. Tie the spices in a piece of muslin.
Pour the vinegar into a saucepan, add the salt
and muslin bag and leave to soak for 30
minutes. Bring to the boil and simmer gently
for 10 minutes. Pour the boiling vinegar over
the apples and onions and cover immediately
with airtight and vinegar-proof tops. This
pickle is ready for use the next day.

PICKLED NASTURTIUM SEEDS
Pickled nasturtium seeds may be used as an
interesting substitute for capers in sauces.

nasturtium seeds
salt
water
spiced vinegar (see page 115)

Pick the seeds on a dry day and wash and dry
them well (checking carefully for insects).
Weigh the seeds and put them in a large bowl.
Mix up a brine solution, allowing 50 g (2 oz)
salt dissolved in 600 ml (1 pint) water for
each 500 g (1 lb) seeds. Pour the brine over
the seeds to cover and leave to soak for 12–24
hours.

Drain and rinse the nasturtium seeds well
and pack them into small jars, leaving room
for 1 cm (½ inch) vinegar above the seeds.
Cover with cold spiced vinegar and seal the
jars with airtight, vinegar-proof tops.

GREEN TOMATO AND ONION PICKLE

2 kg (4 lb) green tomatoes, sliced
750 g (1½ lb) large onions, skinned and sliced
75 ml (5 level tbsp) salt
2.4 litres (4 pints) malt vinegar
150 ml (¼ pint) black treacle or syrup
15 ml (1 level tbsp) mustard powder
10 ml (2 level tsp) curry powder
1.25 ml (¼ level tsp) cayenne pepper
5 ml (1 level tsp) mixed spice

Layer the tomato and onion slices in a bowl, sprinkling each layer liberally with salt, and leave for 24 hours.

Drain and rinse the tomatoes and onions well. Put the vinegar, treacle or syrup and spices into a saucepan and bring to the boil. Add the vegetables and cook very gently for 5 minutes. Pour into pre-heated jars and cover at once with airtight, vinegar-proof tops.

PICKLED ONIONS
Illustrated in colour on page 96

2 kg (4 lb) pickling onions
500 g (1 lb) salt
4.5 litres (8 pints) water
1.2 litres (2 pints) spiced vinegar (see page 115)

Place the onions, without skinning, in a large bowl. Dissolve half the salt in half the water, pour the brine over the onions and leave for 12 hours. Skin the onions, then cover with fresh brine, made with the remaining salt and water, and leave for a further 24–36 hours.

Drain and rinse the onions well and pack them into jars. Pour the spiced vinegar over the onions and cover the jars immediately with airtight and vinegar-proof tops. Leave for 3 months before use.

PICKLED RED CABBAGE
Illustrated in colour on page 77

about 1.5 kg (3 lb) firm, red cabbage, finely
* shredded*
2 large onions, skinned and sliced
60 ml (4 level tbsp) salt
2.4 litres (4 pints) spiced vinegar (see page 115)
15 ml (1 level tbsp) soft brown sugar

Layer the cabbage and onion in a large bowl, sprinkling each layer with salt, then cover and leave overnight.

The next day, drain the cabbage and onion thoroughly, rinse off the surplus salt and drain again. Pack into jars. Pour the vinegar into a pan and heat gently. Add the sugar and stir until dissolved. Leave to cool, then pour over the cabbage and onion and cover immediately with airtight and vinegar-proof tops.

Use within 2–3 weeks as the cabbage tends to lose its crispness.

PICKLED GHERKINS

500 g (1 lb) gherkins
50 g (2 oz) salt
600 ml (1 pint) water
600 ml (1 pint) light malt vinegar
5 ml (1 level tsp) whole allspice
5 ml (1 level tsp) black peppercorns
2 whole cloves
1 blade of mace

Put the gherkins in a large bowl. Dissolve the salt in the water and pour the brine solution over the gherkins. Leave to soak for 3 days.

Rinse, drain and dry the gherkins well, then pack them carefully in a jar. Pour the vinegar into a saucepan, add the spices and boil for 10 minutes. Pour over the gherkins, cover tightly and leave in a warm place for 24 hours.

Strain the vinegar out of the jars into a saucepan, boil it up and pour it over the gherkins again. Cover tightly and leave for another 24 hours. Repeat this process until the gherkins are a good green. Finally, pack the gherkins in jars, cover with vinegar, adding more if required, and cover with airtight and vinegar-proof tops.

PICKLED WALNUTS

500 g (1 lb) green walnuts
100 g (4 oz) salt
1.2 litres (2 pints) water
sweet spiced vinegar (see page 115)

Wipe the walnuts, prick well and put them in a bowl, rejecting any that feel hard when pricked. Dissolve half the salt in half the water, pour this brine over the walnuts and leave to soak for 7 days. Drain off and discard the brine, cover the walnuts with fresh brine and leave to soak for another 14 days.

Drain, rinse and dry the walnuts well, then spread them out and leave them exposed to the air until they blacken, then pack them into jars. Pour the spiced vinegar into a saucepan, bring to the boil, then pour over the walnuts. Leave to cool and, when cold, cover the jars with airtight and vinegar-proof tops. Store in a cool place for 5–6 weeks before use.

VARIATION
Pickled walnuts and onions
An interesting variation is obtained by pickling walnuts and onions together. Each should be prepared according to the directions given above and in the Pickled onions recipe on page 81. Place equal quantities of each in jars, arranged in alternate layers, and pour cold spiced vinegar over them.

PICKLED EGGS
Illustrated in colour on page 96

600 ml (1 pint) white wine or cider vinegar
6 garlic cloves, skinned
25 g (1 oz) pickling spice
small piece of orange rind
1 blade of mace
6 fresh, hard-boiled eggs, shelled

Put all the ingredients, except the eggs, in a heavy-based saucepan and bring to the boil. Cover tightly and simmer gently for 10 minutes. Leave to cool, then strain some of the spiced vinegar into a large wide-mouthed jar. Put in the eggs and top up the jar with more spiced vinegar. Cover with airtight and vinegar-proof tops and leave for at least 6 weeks before using. Add more eggs as convenient.

PICCALILLI
Illustrated in colour on page 95

3 kg (6 lb) mixed marrow, cucumber, beans,
*   small onions and cauliflower (prepared*
*   weight—see method)*
375 g (12 oz) salt
275 g (9 oz) granulated sugar
15 ml (1 level tbsp) mustard powder
7.5 ml (1½ level tsp) ground ginger
2 garlic cloves, skinned and crushed
1.5 litres (2½ pints) distilled vinegar
50 g (2 oz) plain flour
30 ml (2 level tbsp) turmeric

Seed the marrow and finely dice the marrow and cucumber. Top, tail and slice the beans, skin and halve the onions and break the cauliflower into small florets. Layer the vegetables in a large bowl, sprinkling each layer with salt. Add 3.6 litres (6 pints) water, cover and leave for 24 hours.

The next day, remove the vegetables and rinse and drain them well. Blend the sugar, mustard, ginger and garlic with 1 litre (2 pints) of the vinegar in a large pan. Add the vegetables, bring to the boil and simmer for 20 minutes until the vegetables are cooked but still crisp. Blend the flour and turmeric with the remaining vinegar and stir into the cooked vegetables. Bring to the boil and cook for 2 minutes. Spoon into pre-heated jars and cover immediately with airtight and vinegar-proof tops.

MIXED PICKLE
Illustrated in colour on page 95

*1.25 kg (2½ lb) mixed cauliflower, cucumber,
small onions, peppers and French beans
(prepared weight—see method)*
150 g (5 oz) salt
1.5 litres (2½ pints) spiced vinegar (see page 115)

Break the cauliflower into florets, peel and
dice the cucumber, skin the onions, seed and
slice the peppers and top, tail and slice the
beans. Layer the vegetables in a large bowl,
sprinkling each layer with salt. Add 1.5 litres
(2½ pints) water and leave overnight.
 The next day, rinse the vegetables, drain
well and dry on absorbent kitchen paper.
Pack the vegetables into jars and cover with
spiced vinegar. Cover the jars immediately
with airtight and vinegar-proof tops.

SWEET GREEN TOMATO PICKLE

300 ml (½ pint) malt vinegar
1 kg (2 lb) granulated sugar
5 ml (1 level tsp) ground cinnamon
150 ml (¼ pint) water
1.5 kg (3 lb) small green tomatoes, skinned

Place the vinegar, sugar, cinnamon and
water in a large saucepan. Heat gently, stirring,
until the sugar has dissolved, then bring
to the boil. Add the tomatoes and continue
cooking for 5 minutes. Pour into a bowl,
cover and leave for 1 week.
 Strain the vinegar into a large saucepan
and boil for 10 minutes. Add the tomatoes
and boil for a further 5 minutes. Pack into
pre-heated jars and cover immediately with
airtight and vinegar-proof tops.

GARDEN MINT PICKLE
This makes a delicious accompaniment for
cold lamb.

300 ml (½ pint) distilled vinegar
250 g (8 oz) granulated sugar
10 ml (2 level tsp) mustard powder
10 ml (2 level tsp) salt
1 cinnamon stick
5 ml (1 level tsp) peppercorns
1 blade of mace
750 g (1½ lb) cooking apples, peeled and sliced
250 g (8 oz) onions, skinned and sliced
25 g (1 oz) mint leaves, washed and chopped

Pour the vinegar into a saucepan and add the
sugar, seasoning and spices. Simmer very
gently for 30 minutes, then strain. Add the
apple and onion slices and continue cooking
gently for 10 minutes, then remove from the
heat and leave to cool.
 When cold, pack the apples and onions into
jars, sprinkling the chopped mint liberally
between the layers. Cover with the spiced
vinegar and seal the jars immediately with
airtight and vinegar-proof tops. Leave for a
month before use.

MIXED PICKLED BEANS
Illustrated in colour on page 95

*500 g (1 lb) mixed dried beans, soaked overnight
water*
1 small onion, skinned
1 bouquet garni
a few sprigs of fresh marjoram
1 litre (1¾ pints) distilled vinegar
30 ml (2 level tbsp) pickling spice
45 ml (3 level tbsp) granulated sugar

Drain the beans, place them in a large saucepan and cover with water. Add the onion and
bouquet garni and bring to the boil. Cover and
simmer for about 1½ hours until tender.
 Strain the beans, remove the onion and
bouquet garni and pack the beans into clean
jars. Add a few sprigs of marjoram to each jar.
Place the vinegar, pickling spice and sugar in
a saucepan and heat gently, stirring, until the
sugar has dissolved. Bring to the boil, cover
and simmer for 30 minutes. Strain the
vinegar and pour it over the beans in the jars.
Cover with vinegar-proof, airtight tops.

SPICED PICKLED PEACHES
Illustrated in colour on pages 78 and 95

about 30 whole cloves
1 kg (2 lb) freestone peaches, skinned, stoned and
  halved
500 g (1 lb) granulated sugar
300 ml ($\frac{1}{2}$ pint) white wine vinegar
thinly pared rind of $\frac{1}{2}$ a lemon
1 small cinnamon stick

Push two cloves into each peach half. Place the sugar, vinegar, lemon rind and cinnamon stick in a saucepan and heat gently, stirring, for about 5 minutes until the sugar has dissolved. Add the peach halves to the pan and simmer the fruit in the sweetened vinegar until soft.

Drain the fruit and pack into pre-heated jars. Continue boiling the vinegar until it is slightly reduced and beginning to thicken. Strain the vinegar syrup and pour sufficient over the fruit to cover. Cover the jars immediately with airtight and vinegar-proof tops and store for 2–3 months before use. Serve with cold ham or cold roast pork.

PICKLED APPLES

30 ml (2 level tbsp) whole cloves
18 cm (7 inches) cinnamon stick
30 ml (2 level tbsp) whole allspice
600 ml (1 pint) distilled vinegar
1 kg (2 lb) granulated sugar
2.5 ml ($\frac{1}{2}$ level tsp) salt
1 kg (2 lb) cooking apples, peeled, cored and
  quartered

Put all the ingredients, except the apples, into a large saucepan, heat gently, stirring, to dissolve the sugar, then bring to the boil. Add the apples and cook gently until they are soft but not mushy. Drain the apple segments, reserving the syrup, and pack them into pre-heated jars. Boil the syrup until it is beginning to thicken, then strain. Pour over the apples and seal the jars with airtight and vinegar-proof tops.

PICKLED ORANGE RINGS
Illustrated in colour on page 95

6 firm oranges, wiped
water
900 ml (1$\frac{1}{2}$ pints) distilled vinegar
750 g (1$\frac{1}{2}$ lb) granulated sugar
20 ml (4 level tsp) ground cloves
7.5 cm (3 inches) cinnamon stick
5 ml (1 level tsp) whole cloves

Slice the oranges into rounds 0.5 cm ($\frac{1}{4}$ inch) thick. Put the fruit into a large saucepan with just enough water to cover and simmer gently for 45 minutes until the rind is really soft.

Remove the oranges with a slotted spoon and add the vinegar, sugar, ground cloves and cinnamon to the juice in the pan. Bring to the boil and simmer gently for 10 minutes. Return the orange rings to the pan, a few at a time, and cook gently until the rind becomes transparent. Using a slotted spoon, lift the orange rings from the syrup and pack them into pre-heated jars. Continue to boil the syrup for about 15 minutes until it begins to thicken, then leave to cool and pour it over the orange rings. Add a few whole cloves to each jar and cover immediately with airtight and vinegar-proof tops. Serve as an accompaniment to roast duck, chicken, turkey or cold ham.

CERISES AU VINAIGRE
Illustrated in colour on pages 78 and 95

500 g (1 lb) granulated sugar
300 ml ($\frac{1}{2}$ pint) distilled vinegar
4 whole cloves
1 small cinnamon stick
1 kg (2 lb) cherries, washed

Put the sugar, vinegar and spices into a saucepan and heat gently, stirring, until the sugar has dissolved. Add the cherries and simmer gently for about 5 minutes until the fruit is cooked but not broken up. Lift the cherries out of the pan with a slotted spoon and pack them into pre-heated jars. Strain the sweetened vinegar to remove the spices, then return it to the pan and boil until it becomes syrupy. Pour over the cherries and cover the jars immediately with airtight and vinegar-proof tops. Serve with drinks.

PICKLED BANANAS

2 blades of mace
1 small cinnamon stick
6 whole cloves
300 ml ($\frac{1}{2}$ pint) distilled vinegar
375 g (12 oz) demerara sugar
12 under-ripe bananas

Tie the spices in a piece of muslin and put in a saucepan with the vinegar and sugar. Heat gently, stirring, until the sugar has dissolved, then boil for 15 minutes. Meanwhile, peel the bananas and cut them into slices about 0.5 cm ($\frac{1}{4}$ inch) thick. Add them to the vinegar and cook gently until almost tender. Carefully lift out the banana slices with a slotted spoon and pack into pre-heated jars. Strain the syrup to remove the spices and pour over the bananas. Cover immediately with airtight and vinegar-proof tops.

SPICED PEARS

1 kg (2 lb) firm eating pears, peeled, cored and
  quartered
450 ml ($\frac{3}{4}$ pint) cider vinegar
300 ml ($\frac{1}{2}$ pint) water
500 g (1 lb) granulated sugar
1 cinnamon stick
10 whole cloves
1 small piece of root ginger

Place the pears in a saucepan, cover with boiling water and cook gently for about 5 minutes until almost tender, then drain. Pour the vinegar into a pan and add the water, sugar, cinnamon, cloves and root ginger. Heat gently, stirring, until the sugar has dissolved, then boil for 5 minutes. Add the pears and continue cooking until the pears are transparent. Remove the pears with a slotted spoon and pack them into pre-heated jars. Strain the vinegar syrup to remove the spices and pour over the pears to cover. Cover the jars immediately with airtight and vinegar-proof tops. Spiced pears are delicious served as an accompaniment to cold turkey.

SPICED PRUNES

Serve spiced prunes with roast pork or turkey.

500 g (1 lb) prunes, washed
cold tea
450 ml ($\frac{3}{4}$ pint) distilled vinegar
250 g (8 oz) granulated sugar
7.5 ml (1$\frac{1}{2}$ level tsp) mixed spice

Put the prunes in a large bowl, cover with cold tea and leave to soak overnight. Pour the vinegar into a pan and add the sugar and spice. Heat gently, stirring, until the sugar has dissolved, then bring to the boil. Put the prunes in another pan with a little of the tea and simmer gently for 10–15 minutes until soft, then drain, reserving the juice. Add 300 ml ($\frac{1}{2}$ pint) of the prune juice to the vinegar. Pack the prunes into small jars and pour over the syrup. Cover immediately with airtight and vinegar-proof tops.

PICKLED DAMSONS

1.75 kg (3$\frac{1}{2}$ lb) firm ripe damsons, washed
1 kg (2 lb) granulated sugar
600 ml (1 pint) distilled vinegar
5 ml (1 level tsp) ground allspice
15 ml (1 level tbsp) ground ginger
5 ml (1 level tsp) ground mace
15 ml (1 level tbsp) ground cloves

Prick the fruit, put it into a large saucepan with the sugar and add the vinegar and spices. Heat gently, stirring, until the sugar has dissolved, then cook until the damsons are tender but not broken up. Drain well, reserving the liquid, and pack the damsons into jars. Return the syrup to the pan and boil for 15 minutes, then strain through muslin. Pour into the jars. Cover tightly and leave overnight.

The next day, pour off the syrup into a saucepan, re-boil and pour over the fruit again. Repeat on four successive days, then seal with airtight and vinegar-proof tops.

SIMPLE SWEET PICKLED FRUIT

1 kg (2 lb) hard pears, peeled, cored and
quartered; or hard plums, washed; or diced
melon flesh
water
1 kg (2 lb) granulated sugar
900 ml (1$\frac{1}{2}$ pints) distilled vinegar
2 whole cloves

Put the fruit in a large saucepan, cover with water and cook gently until soft, then drain well. Meanwhile, put the sugar, vinegar and cloves in another pan. Heat gently, stirring, until the sugar has dissolved, then boil for 30 minutes. Add the fruit to the vinegar syrup and boil for 15 minutes, then pour into pre-heated jars and cover immediately with air-tight and vinegar-proof tops. Store for 6 months before using.

PICKLED DATES

Illustrated in colour on page 95

1.5 litres (2½ pints) distilled vinegar
40 g (1½ oz) pickling spices
375 g (12 oz) soft brown sugar
1.5 kg (3 lb) dates, halved and stoned

Pour the vinegar into a saucepan and add the spices and sugar. Heat gently, stirring, until the sugar has dissolved, then boil for about 45 minutes until the liquid is reduced by half. Place the dates in pre-heated jars, pour the hot syrup over them and leave to cool. When cold, cover the jars with airtight and vinegar-proof tops. Store for 3 months before using.

SWEET-SOUR APRICOTS

375 ml (12 fl oz) wine vinegar
275 g (9 oz) granulated sugar
500 g (1 lb) apricots
1 small cinnamon stick

Pour the vinegar into a saucepan, add the sugar and heat gently, stirring, until the sugar has dissolved, then bring to the boil. Peel the apricots. (If the skins are difficult to remove, plunge the fruit into boiling water for a few seconds, then into cold water before peeling.) Put the apricots in a jar, packing as lightly as possible, add the cinnamon stick and slowly pour in the hot vinegar syrup. Cover immediately with an airtight and vinegar-proof top.

These pickled apricots are best left for a month before using. Serve with pork, ham or chicken.

PICKLED PLUMS

500 g (1 lb) granulated sugar
thinly pared rind of ½ a lemon
2 whole cloves
a small piece of root ginger
300 ml (½ pint) malt vinegar
1 kg (2 lb) plums

Place all the ingredients, except the plums, in a saucepan. Heat gently, stirring, until the sugar has dissolved, then bring to the boil. Leave until cold, then strain, return to the pan and bring to the boil again. Prick the plums, place them in a deep bowl, pour the spiced vinegar over, cover and leave for 5 days.

Strain off the vinegar into a saucepan, bring to the boil and pour over the fruit again. Cover and leave for another 5 days.

Strain off the vinegar into a saucepan and bring to the boil again. Pack the plums into jars, pour the boiling vinegar over and cover the jars immediately with airtight and vinegar-proof tops.

SPICED CRAB-APPLES

3 kg (6 lb) crab-apples, trimmed and washed
900 ml (1½ pints) water
2–3 strips of lemon peel
500 g (1 lb) granulated sugar
450 ml (¾ pint) wine vinegar
1 cinnamon stick
1–2 whole cloves
3 peppercorns

Put the crab-apples in a large saucepan with the water and strips of lemon peel and simmer gently until just tender. Remove the pan from the heat and drain, reserving the liquid. Place the sugar and vinegar in a pan and add 900 ml (1½ pints) of the liquid from the fruit. Tie the spices in a piece of muslin and add to the liquid. Heat gently, stirring, until the sugar has dissolved, then bring to the boil and boil for 1 minute. Add the crab-apples and simmer gently for 30–40 minutes until the syrup has reduced to a coating consistency. Remove the muslin bag after 30 minutes. Pack the fruit in small jars, pour over the syrup and cover with airtight and vinegar-proof tops.

PIQUANT GOOSEBERRIES
Illustrated in colour on page 95

1 kg (2 lb) gooseberries, topped, tailed and
*   washed*
150 ml (¼ pint) malt vinegar
1 kg (2 lb) granulated sugar

Place the gooseberries, vinegar and half the sugar in a saucepan. Heat gently, stirring, until the sugar has dissolved, then simmer for about 10 minutes until the gooseberries are tender. Using a slotted spoon, remove any scum, then lift out the gooseberries and pack them into pre-heated jars.

Add the remaining sugar to the vinegar, stir until it has dissolved, then bring to the boil and boil gently for about 20 minutes until syrupy. Remove any scum with a slotted spoon. Pour the syrup over the gooseberries and cover the jars immediately with airtight and vinegar-proof tops.

PICKLED MELON RIND

500 g (1 lb) melon rind, thinly pared
100 g (4 oz) salt
1.5 litres (2½ pints) water
600 ml (1 pint) distilled vinegar
500 g (1 lb) granulated sugar
1 small cinnamon stick
6–8 whole cloves
2–3 drops of green food colouring (optional)

Cut the melon rind into strips and place in a saucepan. Dissolve the salt in 1.2 litres (2 pints) water and pour into the saucepan with the melon rind. Bring to the boil and simmer gently for 30 minutes. Drain off the salt water, rinse, cover with fresh water, bring to the boil and cook for a further 10 minutes. Change the water again and continue boiling gently until the rind is tender. Remove from the heat, cover and leave to stand overnight.

Pour the vinegar into a saucepan with 300 ml (½ pint) water and the sugar. Add the spices and heat gently, stirring, to dissolve the sugar. Add the drained rind, bring to the boil and simmer gently for 1½ hours until the syrup is thick and the rind is clear. Remove the spices, add colouring if desired and spoon into jars. Cover with airtight and vinegar-proof tops. Serve with ham.

SWEET PICKLED LIMES

250 g (8 oz) salt
4.5 litres (7½ pints) water
18 limes, washed
900 ml (1½ pints) distilled vinegar
625 g (1 lb 5 oz) granulated sugar
4 cinnamon sticks
30 ml (2 level tbsp) whole allspice
15 ml (1 level tbsp) whole cloves

Dissolve the salt in 1.5 litres (2½ pints) of the water to make a brine. Pour over the limes and leave overnight. Drain, then place the limes in a large pan. Add the remaining water and simmer gently until the limes are tender. Drain and prick the limes with a darning needle. Place the vinegar, sugar, cinnamon, allspice and cloves in a pan. Bring to the boil and boil for 5 minutes. Add the limes and simmer for 20 minutes. Pack the limes into pre-heated jars, strain the vinegar syrup and pour over the limes. Cover the jars with airtight and vinegar-proof tops.

SPICED PICKLED MELON

150 ml (¼ pint) distilled vinegar
450 ml (¾ pint) water
1 small cinnamon stick
2.5 ml (½ level tsp) ground cloves
500 g (1 lb) granulated sugar
1 kg (2 lb) cubed melon flesh
250 g (8 oz) fresh cherries, stoned, or one 213-g
*   (7½-oz) can stoned cherries, drained*

Pour the vinegar and water into a saucepan and add the cinnamon, cloves and sugar. Heat gently, stirring, until the sugar has dissolved, then bring to the boil and add the melon and cherries. Simmer, covered, for about 40 minutes until the melon is transparent and tender. Remove the cinnamon stick, spoon the pickle into pre-heated jars and cover immediately with airtight and vinegar-proof tops.

Note   Reserve the melon rind and use it to make Pickled melon rind (opposite).

PICKLED JERUSALEM ARTICHOKES

Jerusalem artichokes
salt
water
spiced vinegar (see page 115)

Wash and scrape the artichokes. Dissolve 25 g (1 oz) salt in 600 ml (1 pint) water for every 500 g (1 lb) artichokes and cook the artichokes in this brine until tender but not too soft. Drain and leave until cold. Pack the artichokes into jars, fill up with cold spiced vinegar and cover in the usual way.

PICKLED LEMONS

These lemons are particularly good with veal.

12 lemons
salt
1.8 litres (3 pints) spiced vinegar (see page 115)

Wash the lemons thoroughly and peel very thinly. Put the lemons in a large, wide-necked jar, covering each layer thoroughly with salt. Leave for about 10 days until the lemons feel soft.

Wipe off most of the salt and place the lemons in a clean jar. Bring the spiced vinegar to boiling point and pour over the lemons immediately. Cover and store for 3 months before using.

PICKLED CAULIFLOWER

cauliflowers
salt
water
spiced vinegar (see page 115)

Choose young cauliflowers with tight heads and divide them into small florets, breaking rather than cutting them. Dissolve 50 g (2 oz) salt in 600 ml (1 pint) water for every 500 g (1 lb) cauliflower, pour over the florets and leave to stand overnight.

The next day, rinse and drain the cauliflower thoroughly. Pack into jars, pour over cold spiced vinegar and cover the jars in the usual way.

PICKLED CUCUMBERS

cucumbers
salt
spiced vinegar (see page 115)

Split the unpeeled cucumbers from end to end and cut into 5-cm (2-inch) pieces. Place in a large bowl, cover with salt and leave for 24 hours.

Drain off the liquid, rinse and drain the cucumber and pack into jars. Fill up with cold spiced vinegar, cover in the usual way and leave to mature for about 3 months.

PICKLED BLACKBERRIES

500 g (1 lb) granulated sugar
300 ml ($\frac{1}{2}$ pint) spiced vinegar (see page 115)
7 g ($\frac{1}{4}$ oz) whole cloves
7 g ($\frac{1}{4}$ oz) allspice
7 g ($\frac{1}{4}$ oz) cinnamon stick
1 kg (2 lb) blackberries, washed

Place the sugar and vinegar in a saucepan. Tie the spices in a piece of muslin, add to the pan and simmer gently for 3–4 minutes.

Remove the muslin bag, add the blackberries and cook the fruit in the vinegar for 5 minutes. Remove the blackberries from the pan with a slotted spoon and place them in pre-heated jars. Continue to boil the vinegar mixture until it forms a syrup, then pour over the fruit. Cover the jars with airtight and vinegar-proof tops. Store the blackberries for 2–3 weeks before using.

MOCK OLIVES

small green plums
salt
water
spiced vinegar (see page 115)

Use small plums, before the stones have properly formed—test by piercing with a needle. Wash the plums. Dissolve 50 g (2 oz) salt in 600 ml (1 pint) water for each 500 g (1 lb) plums and pour this brine over the plums. Leave for 3 days, then drain and dry on absorbent kitchen paper. Pack into clean jars, cover with cold spiced vinegar and seal in the usual way with airtight and vinegar-proof tops. Serve with drinks.

Chutneys and Relishes

Chutneys and relishes are made from mixtures of fruits and/or vegetables cooked with vinegar and spices which act as preservatives. The main difference between chutneys and relishes is in the finished texture. Chutneys are made from very finely chopped or sliced fruits and/or vegetables which are cooked very slowly to produce the characteristic smooth texture and mellow flavour. The finished texture of a relish is far more chunky since the ingredients used are cut larger and cooking time is shorter.

Preparation and Cooking

Chutneys The fruits and/or vegetables for a chutney should be finely chopped, sliced or minced. Bruised and poorly-shaped ingredients can very often be used as their appearance in the finished preserve is of no account. They are cooked to a pulp with vinegar, sugar, spices and salt. Chutneys should be simmered very slowly, uncovered to allow evaporation. The chutney is ready when no excess liquid remains and the mixture is the consistency of a thick sauce. The cooking time will vary between 1 and 4 hours, depending mostly on the depth of the contents of the pan.

Relishes The fruits and/or vegetables for a relish should be cut into chunks and cooked for a fairly short time so that the ingredients retain their shape. Some relishes do not need cooking at all.

Equipment

The equipment used for making chutneys and relishes is the same as for making pickles (see page 74).

GREEN TOMATO CHUTNEY
(see page 100)

1. Finely mince the apples and onions.

2. Thinly slice the tomatoes.

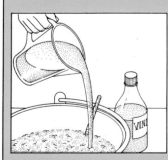

3. Put all the ingredients in a preserving pan and pour in the vinegar.

4. Cook gently until no excess liquid remains and spoon the chutney into pre-heated jars.

5. Cover with airtight, vinegar-proof tops.

Potting and Covering
Chutneys and relishes should be potted and covered in the same way as pickles (see pages 74 and 75). Pour the hot mixture into clean, dry, pre-heated jars and cover immediately with airtight, vinegar-proof tops.

Storing
Chutneys and relishes should be stored in a cool, dry, dark place and allowed to mature for 2–3 months before eating.

RED TOMATO CHUTNEY
Illustrated in colour on page 105

2 kg (4 lb) red tomatoes, skinned (see method)
30 ml (2 level tbsp) mustard seeds
15 ml (1 level tbsp) whole allspice
5 ml (1 level tsp) cayenne pepper
250 g (8 oz) demerara or granulated sugar
20 ml (4 level tsp) salt
450 ml ($\frac{3}{4}$ pint) distilled vinegar

Before skinning the tomatoes, immerse them in boiling water for 1–2 minutes and then plunge them into cold. The skins will then peel off easily.

Tie the mustard seeds and allspice in a piece of muslin and place in a large saucepan with the cayenne pepper and skinned tomatoes. Simmer gently for about 45 minutes, breaking down the tomatoes with a wooden spoon, until reduced to a pulp. Add the sugar, salt and vinegar. Continue simmering until no excess liquid remains and the mixture is thick. Spoon into pre-heated jars and cover at once with airtight, vinegar-proof tops.

Makes about 1 kg (2 lb)

APRICOT AND APPLE CHUTNEY

500 g (1 lb) dried apricots, soaked overnight
2 kg (4 lb) cooking apples, peeled, cored and chopped
500 g (1 lb) onions, skinned and sliced
375 g (12 oz) seedless raisins
500 g (1 lb) demerara sugar
600 ml (1 pint) distilled vinegar
15 ml (1 level tbsp) salt
15 ml (1 level tbsp) ground mixed spice

Drain the apricots and chop roughly. Place them, and all the remaining ingredients in a preserving pan and simmer gently for about 1 hour until the mixture thickens and no excess liquid remains. Pour the chutney into pre-heated jars and cover immediately with airtight and vinegar-proof tops.

Makes about 3.5 kg (7 lb)

PLUM CHUTNEY
Illustrated in colour on pages 106 and 107

This chutney is excellent served with sliced cold meats, such as pork or ham.

30 ml (2 level tbsp) pickling spice
1 kg (2 lb) plums, halved, stoned and chopped
250 g (8 oz) red tomatoes, skinned and chopped
900 ml (1½ pints) malt vinegar
500 g (1 lb) onions, skinned and chopped
500 g (1 lb) cooking apples, peeled, cored and
*   chopped*
500 g (1 lb) carrots, trimmed, peeled and diced
100 g (4 oz) sultanas
500 g (1 lb) demerara sugar
15 ml (1 level tbsp) salt

Tie the pickling spice in a piece of muslin. Place all the ingredients in a pan with the muslin bag. Bring to the boil and simmer for about 2½ hours, stirring occasionally, until thick. Remove the muslin bag. Spoon into pre-heated jars and cover immediately with air-tight and vinegar-proof tops.

Makes about 2.25 kg (4½ lb)

HOT INDIAN CHUTNEY
This hot, thick chutney makes a very good accompaniment to curry.

750 g (1½ lb) cooking apples, peeled, cored and
*   sliced*
500 g (1 lb) onions, skinned and finely chopped
750 g (1½ lb) soft brown sugar
1.5 litres (2½ pints) malt vinegar
500 g (1 lb) seedless raisins, chopped
4 garlic cloves, skinned and crushed
20 ml (4 level tsp) salt
30 ml (2 level tbsp) ground ginger
45 ml (3 level tbsp) mustard powder
30 ml (2 level tbsp) paprika
15 ml (1 level tbsp) ground coriander

Place all the ingredients in a large saucepan and bring to the boil. Simmer gently for about 3 hours, stirring occasionally, until no excess liquid remains and the chutney is thick and pulpy. Spoon into pre-heated jars and cover at once with airtight, vinegar-proof tops.

94 | *Makes about 2.25 kg (4½ lb)*

APPLE AND TOMATO CHUTNEY
This chutney makes an excellent accompaniment to cold meats.

1 kg (2 lb) cooking apples, peeled, cored and
*   sliced*
water
15 ml (1 level tbsp) mustard seeds
1 kg (2 lb) tomatoes, sliced
375 g (12 oz) onions, skinned and chopped
1 garlic clove, skinned and chopped
250 g (8 oz) sultanas
375 g (12 oz) demerara sugar
25 ml (5 level tsp) curry powder
5 ml (1 level tsp) cayenne pepper
20 ml (4 level tsp) salt
900 ml (1½ pints) malt vinegar

Put the apples in a large saucepan with a very small quantity of water. Cook gently, stirring occasionally, until tender. Tie the mustard seeds in a piece of muslin and add to the apples with the remaining ingredients. Bring to the boil, reduce the heat and simmer gently, stirring occasionally, for about 3 hours until the chutney is thick and no excess liquid remains. Remove the muslin bag, spoon the chutney into pre-heated jars and cover at once with airtight, vinegar-proof tops.

Makes about 2.5 kg (5 lb)

Top (from left): *Mixed pickle (page 83), Pickled marrow (page 80), Pickled orange rings, Cerises au vinaigre (page 84)*
Centre (from left): *Spiced pickled peaches (page 84), Pickled carrots (page 79), Piccalilli (page 82), Pickled mushrooms (page 76), Cerises au vinaigre (page 84)*
Bottom (from left): *Piquant gooseberries (page 88), Pickled dates (page 87), Pickle sticks (page 76), Mixed pickled beans (page 83), Italian-style pickled cauliflower (page 80)*

TOMATO RELISH
Illustrated in colour on page 108

1.5 kg (3 lb) tomatoes, skinned and sliced
500 g (1 lb) cucumber or marrow, peeled, seeded
*   and roughly chopped*
50 g (2 oz) salt
2 garlic cloves, skinned and finely chopped
1 large red pepper, washed, seeded and roughly
*   chopped*
450 ml ($\frac{3}{4}$ pint) malt vinegar
15 ml (1 level tbsp) mustard powder
2.5 ml ($\frac{1}{2}$ level tsp) ground allspice
2.5 ml ($\frac{1}{2}$ level tsp) mustard seeds

Layer the tomatoes and cucumber or marrow in a bowl, sprinkling each layer with salt. Cover and leave overnight.

Next day, drain and rinse well and place in a large saucepan. Add the garlic and pepper. Blend the vinegar with the dry ingredients, stir into the pan and bring slowly to the boil. Boil gently for about 1 hour, stirring occasionally, until the mixture is soft. Spoon the relish into pre-heated jars and cover immediately with airtight and vinegar-proof tops. Store for 3–4 months before use.

Makes about 1.5 kg (3 lb)

Top (from left): *Pickled eggs (page 82), 'Bread and butter' pickle (page 76)*
Bottom (from left): *Pickled onions (page 81), Blackberry and apple jam (page 23), Greengage jam (page 31), Oxford marmalade (page 61), Mint jelly (page 36)*

MIXED FRUIT CHUTNEY

500 g (1 lb) dried apricots, washed and chopped
500 g (1 lb) stoned dates, roughly chopped
750 g (1$\frac{1}{2}$ lb) cooking apples, peeled, cored and
*   chopped*
500 g (1 lb) bananas, peeled and sliced
250 g (8 oz) onions, skinned and finely chopped
500 g (1 lb) demerara sugar
grated rind and juice of 1 lemon
10 ml (2 level tsp) ground mixed spice
10 ml (2 level tsp) ground ginger
10 ml (2 level tsp) curry powder
10 ml (2 level tsp) salt
900 ml (1$\frac{1}{2}$ pints) distilled or cider vinegar

Place all the ingredients in a large preserving pan or saucepan. Heat gently, stirring, until the sugar has dissolved, then bring to the boil. Reduce the heat and simmer gently for about 1 hour, stirring occasionally, until no excess liquid remains and the mixture is thick and pulpy. Spoon into pre-heated jars and cover at once with airtight, vinegar-proof tops.

Makes about 3.5 kg (7 lb)

DATE AND ORANGE CHUTNEY

500 g (1 lb) oranges
500 g (1 lb) onions, skinned
750 g (1$\frac{1}{2}$ lb) dates, stoned
250 g (8 oz) sultanas
750 g (1$\frac{1}{2}$ lb) granulated sugar
100 g (4 oz) golden syrup
30 ml (2 level tbsp) salt
1.25 ml ($\frac{1}{4}$ level tsp) cayenne pepper
1.5 litres (2$\frac{1}{2}$ pints) malt vinegar

Finely grate the rind of the oranges. Peel off the pith and slice the oranges, discarding the pips. Mince together the oranges, onions, dates and sultanas. Place the sugar, syrup, salt, pepper and vinegar in a large saucepan. Heat gently, stirring, until the sugar has dissolved, then bring to the boil and add the minced fruits and half the orange rind. Simmer gently, stirring occasionally, for about 1 hour until no excess liquid remains and the mixture is thick. Stir in the remaining orange rind, spoon the chutney into pre-heated jars and cover immediately with airtight and vinegar-proof tops.

MUSTARD RELISH
Illustrated in colour on page 108

175 g (6 oz) cucumber, washed and finely
chopped
175 g (6 oz) onion, skinned and finely chopped
250 g (8 oz) cauliflower, washed and broken
into florets
100 g (4 oz) tomatoes, roughly chopped
1 medium green pepper, washed, seeded and
finely chopped
1 medium red pepper, washed, seeded and finely
chopped
250 g (8 oz) fresh gherkins, thickly sliced
25 g (1 oz) salt
1.2 litres (2 pints) water
15 ml (1 level tbsp) mustard seeds
275 g (9 oz) granulated sugar
25 g (1 oz) plain flour
2.5 ml ($\frac{1}{2}$ level tsp) mustard powder
2.5 ml ($\frac{1}{2}$ level tsp) turmeric
450 ml ($\frac{3}{4}$ pint) malt vinegar

Place all the vegetables in a large bowl.
Dissolve the salt in the water and pour over
the vegetables. Cover and leave to stand
overnight.

Drain and rinse the vegetables well. Blend
the mustard seeds, sugar, flour, mustard
powder and turmeric together in a large
saucepan, then gradually stir in the vinegar.
Bring to the boil, stirring. Add the drained
vegetables and simmer, uncovered, for 30
minutes. Stir gently from time to time to
prevent sticking. Spoon the relish into pre-
heated jars and cover immediately with airtight and vinegar-proof tops.

Makes about 1.5 kg (3 lb)

DAMSON CHUTNEY
Serve this chutney with ham.

1.75 kg (3$\frac{1}{2}$ lb) damsons, washed
2 medium onions, skinned and chopped
1 garlic clove, skinned and crushed
250 g (8 oz) seedless raisins, chopped
100 g (4 oz) stoned dates, chopped
750 g (1$\frac{1}{2}$ lb) soft brown sugar
1.5 litres (2$\frac{1}{2}$ pints) malt vinegar
15 g ($\frac{1}{2}$ oz) salt
25 g (1 oz) ground ginger
1.25 ml ($\frac{1}{4}$ level tsp) ground allspice

Mix all the ingredients together in a large
saucepan and simmer uncovered, stirring
occasionally, for 1$\frac{1}{2}$–2 hours until no excess
liquid remains and the mixture is thick. Scoop
out the damson stones with a slotted spoon.
Pour the chutney into pre-heated jars and
cover immediately with airtight and vinegar-
proof tops.

Makes about 2 kg (4 lb)

Note   If preferred, plums can be used in the
above recipe instead of damsons.

AUBERGINE PEPPER CHUTNEY

500 g (1 lb) aubergines, trimmed, washed and
chopped
1 medium red pepper, washed, seeded and
chopped
1 medium green pepper, washed, seeded and
chopped
1 medium onion, skinned and chopped
1 garlic clove, skinned and crushed
1 large cooking apple, peeled, cored and chopped
250 g (8 oz) demerara sugar
600 ml (1 pint) malt vinegar
5 ml (1 level tsp) salt

Place all the ingredients in a large saucepan.
Bring to the boil and simmer gently, stirring
occasionally, for 1$\frac{1}{2}$ hours until no excess
liquid remains and the mixture is thick. Spoon
into pre-heated jars and cover immediately
with airtight and vinegar-proof tops.

Makes about 1.5 kg (3 lb)

BANANA CHUTNEY

1 kg (2 lb) cooking apples, peeled, cored and
*   roughly chopped*
250 g (8 oz) seedless raisins
250 g (8 oz) stoned dates, chopped
2 kg (4 lb) bananas, peeled and sliced
250 g (8 oz) onions, skinned and chopped
10 ml (2 level tsp) salt
375 g (12 oz) demerara sugar
30 ml (2 level tbsp) ground ginger
2.5 ml (½ level tsp) cayenne pepper
600 ml (1 pint) distilled vinegar

Place the prepared fruit and onions in a
preserving pan and sprinkle with the salt,
sugar and spices. Pour in the vinegar and
bring gently to the boil. Simmer gently,
stirring occasionally, for about 1 hour until
no excess liquid remains and the mixture is
soft and pulpy. Spoon the chutney into pre-
heated jars and cover immediately with airtight and vinegar-proof tops. This chutney is
delicious served with curry.

Makes about 3.5 kg (7 lb)

SWEETCORN RELISH

6 corn cobs, trimmed and leaves and silk removed
½ a small white cabbage, trimmed and roughly
*   chopped*
2 medium onions, skinned and halved
1½ red peppers, washed, seeded and quartered
10 ml (2 level tsp) salt
30 ml (2 level tbsp) flour
2.5 ml (½ level tsp) turmeric
175 g (6 oz) granulated sugar
10 ml (2 level tsp) mustard powder
600 ml (1 pint) distilled vinegar

Cook the corn cobs in boiling salted water for
3 minutes, then drain. Using a sharp knife,
cut the corn from the cobs. Coarsely mince the
cabbage, onions and red peppers and combine
with the corn.
  Blend the salt, flour, turmeric, sugar and
mustard together in a saucepan, then
gradually stir in the vinegar. Heat gently,
stirring, until the sugar has dissolved, then
bring to the boil. Add the vegetables and
simmer for 25–30 minutes, stirring occasionally. Spoon the relish into pre-heated jars and
cover immediately with airtight and vinegar-
proof tops.

Makes about 2.5 kg (5 lb)

PEACH CHUTNEY

a small piece of root ginger, bruised
6 ripe peaches, stoned, skinned and sliced
100 g (4 oz) sultanas
2 large onions, skinned and finely chopped
15 ml (1 level tbsp) salt
375 g (12 oz) demerara sugar
300 ml (½ pint) malt vinegar
15 ml (1 level tbsp) mustard seeds
grated rind and juice of 1 lemon

Tie the root ginger in a piece of muslin. Place
all the ingredients in a large saucepan with
the muslin bag. Heat gently, stirring, until the
sugar has dissolved, then bring to the boil and
simmer for about 1¾ hours, stirring occasionally, until no excess liquid remains and the
mixture is thick. Remove the muslin bag.
Spoon the chutney into pre-heated jars and
cover immediately with airtight and vinegar-
proof tops. Store for 2–3 months before
serving with poultry, pork or lamb.

Makes about 1.25 kg (2½ lb)

VARIATION
Apricot chutney
Follow the above recipe, using apricots
instead of peaches.

GREEN TOMATO CHUTNEY

This is a lightly spiced, smooth-textured chutney.

500 g (1 lb) cooking apples, peeled, cored and
    minced
250 g (8 oz) onions, skinned and minced
1.5 kg (3 lb) green tomatoes, thinly sliced
250 g (8 oz) sultanas
250 g (8 oz) demerara sugar
10 ml (2 level tsp) salt
450 ml ($\frac{3}{4}$ pint) malt vinegar
4 small pieces of dried root ginger
2.5 ml ($\frac{1}{2}$ level tsp) cayenne pepper
5 ml (1 level tsp) mustard powder

Place all the ingredients in a large saucepan. Bring to the boil, reduce the heat and simmer gently for about 2 hours, stirring occasionally, until the ingredients are tender, reduced to a thick consistency, and no excess liquid remains. Remove the ginger, spoon the chutney into pre-heated jars and cover at once with airtight, vinegar-proof tops.

Makes about 1.5 kg (3 lb)

PEAR CHUTNEY

This chutney is delicious with cold pork.

1.5 kg (3 lb) pears, peeled, cored and sliced
500 g (1 lb) cooking apples, peeled, cored and
    chopped
250 g (8 oz) seedless raisins, chopped
250 g (8 oz) sultanas
500 g (1 lb) onions, skinned and chopped
1.2 litres (2 pints) malt vinegar
500 g (1 lb) demerara sugar
1.25 ml ($\frac{1}{4}$ level tsp) cayenne pepper
2.5 ml ($\frac{1}{2}$ level tsp) ground nutmeg
10 ml (2 level tsp) salt

Place all the fruits and vegetables in a large saucepan with the vinegar, sugar, spices and salt. Bring to the boil and simmer gently, stirring occasionally, for about 2$\frac{1}{2}$ hours until the mixture is thick and no excess liquid remains. Spoon the chutney into pre-heated jars and cover immediately with airtight and vinegar-proof tops. Store for 2–3 months before serving.

Makes about 2.5 kg (5 lb)

LEMON AND APPLE CHUTNEY

2 lemons, washed
water
300 ml ($\frac{1}{2}$ pint) cider vinegar
90 ml (6 tbsp) thin honey
250 g (8 oz) granulated sugar
2.5 ml ($\frac{1}{2}$ level tsp) ground ginger
250 g (8 oz) cooking apples, peeled, cored and
    sliced
1 medium onion, skinned and finely chopped
25 g (1 oz) sultanas

Halve the lemons lengthways and slice thinly, discarding any pips. Put the lemon slices in a saucepan with sufficient water to cover and simmer gently for 45 minutes until tender. Remove the lemon slices from the pan with a slotted spoon. Stir the vinegar, honey, sugar and ginger into the pan juices and heat gently, stirring continuously, until the sugar has dissolved.

Add the apples to the liquid with the onion, sultanas and cooked lemon. Bring to the boil and simmer gently, uncovered, for 20–25 minutes, stirring occasionally, until the onion is soft and no excess liquid remains. Spoon the chutney into pre-heated jars and cover at once with airtight, vinegar-proof tops.

Makes about 1 kg (2 lb)

BEETROOT CHUTNEY

1.5 kg (3 lb) raw beetroot, peeled and grated
1 kg (2 lb) cooking apples, peeled, cored and
    chopped
500 g (1 lb) onions, skinned and chopped
500 g (1 lb) seedless raisins
1.5 litres (2$\frac{1}{2}$ pints) malt vinegar
1.25 kg (2$\frac{1}{2}$ lb) granulated sugar
30 ml (2 level tbsp) ground ginger
juice of 1 lemon

Place all the ingredients in a preserving pan and bring to the boil. Simmer gently, uncovered, stirring occasionally, for about 2$\frac{1}{2}$ hours, until no excess liquid remains and the mixture is thick. Spoon the chutney into pre-heated jars and cover immediately with airtight and vinegar-proof tops.

Makes about 4 kg (8 lb)

SWEET MIXED CHUTNEY

1 kg (2 lb) marrow, peeled, seeded and finely
   chopped
1 cucumber, washed and finely chopped
750 g (1½ lb) tomatoes, skinned and finely
   chopped
1.2 litres (2 pints) malt vinegar
450 ml (¾ pint) distilled vinegar
500 g (1 lb) demerara sugar
30 ml (2 level tbsp) salt
30 ml (2 level tbsp) turmeric
5 ml (1 level tsp) ground cloves
7.5 ml (1½ level tsp) ground ginger

Place all the ingredients in a large saucepan.
Bring to the boil, stirring, and simmer gently,
uncovered, for about 3 hours, stirring
occasionally, until the mixture is fairly dark
and thick. Spoon the chutney into pre-heated
jars and cover immediately with airtight and
vinegar-proof tops. Store for 2–3 months
before eating.

Makes about 2 kg (4 lb)

Note Courgettes may be used instead of
marrow, and there is no need to peel them.

RHUBARB ORANGE CHUTNEY

1 kg (2 lb) rhubarb, trimmed, washed and
   chopped
grated rind and juice of 2 oranges
500 g (1 lb) onions, skinned and chopped
900 ml (1½ pints) malt vinegar
1 kg (2 lb) demerara sugar
500 g (1 lb) seedless raisins
5 ml (1 level tsp) whole allspice
15 ml (1 level tbsp) mustard seeds
15 ml (1 level tbsp) peppercorns

Place the rhubarb, orange rind and juice,
onions, vinegar, sugar and raisins in a large
saucepan. Tie the spices in a piece of muslin
and add to the ingredients in the pan. Bring to
the boil and simmer gently, uncovered, for
about 1½ hours, stirring occasionally, until
the mixture is thick and pulpy and no excess
liquid remains. Remove the muslin bag, spoon
the chutney into pre-heated jars and cover
immediately with airtight and vinegar-proof
tops. Store for 2–3 months before eating.

Makes about 4 kg (8 lb)

ALL-YEAR-ROUND CHUTNEY

This is a very useful chutney for, as its name implies, it can be made at any time of the year and needs no cooking.

500 g (1 lb) onions, skinned
500 g (1 lb) cooking apples, cored
500 g (1 lb) sultanas
500 g (1 lb) stoned dates
500 g (1 lb) soft brown sugar
5 ml (1 level tsp) ground ginger
5 ml (1 level tsp) ground allspice
15 ml (1 level tbsp) salt
2.5 ml ($\frac{1}{2}$ level tsp) pepper
600 ml (1 pint) malt vinegar

Mince the onions, apples, sultanas and dates and mix together in a large bowl. Stir in the sugar, spices and seasonings and pour over the vinegar. Stir well and leave for 24 hours, stirring from time to time, so that the flavours are well blended.

Spoon the chutney into pre-heated jars and cover immediately with airtight and vinegar-proof tops. Store for 2–3 months before eating.

Makes about 3.25 kg (6$\frac{1}{2}$ lb)

PUMPKIN CHUTNEY

1 kg (2 lb) pumpkin (prepared weight), peeled, cored and seeded
500 g (1 lb) tomatoes, skinned and roughly chopped
500 g (1 lb) onions, skinned and roughly chopped
1 garlic clove, skinned and crushed
50 g (2 oz) sultanas
750 g (1$\frac{1}{2}$ lb) soft brown sugar
600 ml (1 pint) white wine vinegar
5 ml (1 level tsp) ground allspice
15 ml (1 level tbsp) salt
5 ml (1 level tsp) freshly ground black pepper

Cut the pumpkin flesh into 1-cm ($\frac{1}{2}$-inch) cubes and place all the ingredients in a preserving pan. Bring to the boil and simmer gently for about 1 hour, stirring occasionally, especially towards the end of the cooking time, until no excess liquid remains and the mixture is thick. Spoon the chutney into pre-heated jars and cover immediately with airtight and vinegar-proof tops.

Makes about 2.5 kg (5 lb)

CUCUMBER AND CELERY RELISH
Illustrated in colour on page 108

3 cucumbers
2 large onions, skinned and chopped
4 large celery sticks, trimmed, washed and diced
1 green pepper, washed, seeded and diced
30 ml (2 level tbsp) salt
100 g (4 oz) granulated sugar
45 ml (3 level tbsp) mustard powder
75 ml (5 level tbsp) plain flour
5 ml (1 level tsp) turmeric
300 ml ($\frac{1}{2}$ pint) cider vinegar

Cut the cucumber into 0.5-cm ($\frac{1}{4}$-inch) cubes and place in a bowl. Add the onion, celery, green pepper and salt to the cucumber and stir. Leave to stand for 30 minutes, then drain. Mix the sugar, mustard, flour and turmeric with the cider vinegar. Add the chopped vegetables and cook over a medium heat for about 30 minutes, stirring to prevent burning. Spoon the relish into pre-heated jars and cover immediately with airtight and vinegar-proof tops. Store in a dark place or it will lose its colour.

Makes about 1.75 kg ($3\frac{1}{2}$ lb)

GREEN FIG CHUTNEY

1.5 kg (3 lb) fresh figs, washed and sliced
500 g (1 lb) onions, skinned and sliced
175 g (6 oz) dates, stoned and chopped
100 g (4 oz) preserved ginger, chopped
1.2 litres (2 pints) malt vinegar
375 g (12 oz) demerara sugar
175 g (6 oz) seedless raisins
2.5 ml ($\frac{1}{2}$ level tsp) cayenne pepper
5 ml (1 level tsp) salt

Place all the ingredients in a preserving pan. Bring to the boil and simmer gently for about 4 hours until no excess liquid remains and the mixture is thick. Spoon the chutney into pre-heated jars and cover immediately with air-tight and vinegar-proof tops.

Makes about 2 kg (4 lb)

AMERICAN CRANBERRY CHUTNEY

750 g ($1\frac{1}{2}$ lb) cranberries, washed
300 ml ($\frac{1}{2}$ pint) distilled vinegar
250 g (8 oz) sultanas
100 g (4 oz) seedless raisins
100 g (4 oz) granulated sugar
15 g ($\frac{1}{2}$ oz) salt
10 ml (2 level tsp) ground allspice
10 ml (2 level tsp) ground cinnamon

Place all the ingredients in a preserving pan and simmer gently for about 30 minutes until the fruit is tender and the mixture is of a thick consistency. Pour into pre-heated jars and cover immediately with airtight and vinegar-proof tops.

Makes about 1.5 kg (3 lb)

SWEET MANGO CHUTNEY
This chutney makes a delicious accompaniment to serve with roast beef and is particularly good with a curry.

2 kg (4 lb) yellow mangoes, peeled, stoned and
  sliced
250 g (8 oz) cooking apples, peeled, cored and
  chopped
250 g (8 oz) onions, skinned and chopped
100 g (4 oz) seedless raisins
600 ml (1 pint) distilled vinegar
375 g (12 oz) demerara sugar
15 ml (1 level tbsp) ground ginger
3 garlic cloves, skinned and crushed
5 ml (1 level tsp) grated nutmeg
2.5 ml ($\frac{1}{2}$ level tsp) salt

Place all the ingredients in a preserving pan. Bring to the boil and simmer gently, stirring occasionally, for about $1\frac{1}{2}$ hours until no excess liquid remains and the mixture is thick. Spoon the chutney into pre-heated jars and cover immediately with airtight and vinegar-proof tops. Store this chutney for 2–3 months before eating.

Makes about 2.25 kg ($4\frac{1}{2}$ lb)

PEAR AND LEMON CHUTNEY

2 kg (4 lb) pears, peeled, cored and chopped
500 g (1 lb) onions, skinned and chopped
375 g (12 oz) seedless raisins, chopped
50 g (2 oz) stem ginger, chopped
grated rind and juice of 2 lemons
250 g (8 oz) soft brown sugar
30 ml (2 level tbsp) salt
1.2 litres (2 pints) distilled vinegar
2 garlic cloves, skinned and crushed
6 chillies, crushed
4 whole cloves

Place the pears, onions, raisins, ginger, lemon rind and juice, sugar, salt and vinegar in a preserving pan. Tie the garlic, chillies and cloves in a piece of muslin and add to the pan. Bring to the boil, and simmer gently, uncovered, for about 2 hours, stirring occasionally, until the mixture is thick and no excess liquid remains. Remove the muslin bag, spoon the chutney into pre-heated jars and cover immediately with airtight and vinegar-proof tops. Store for 2–3 months before eating.

Makes about 2 kg (4 lb)

SPICED PEPPER CHUTNEY

3 red peppers, washed, seeded and finely chopped
3 green peppers, washed, seeded and finely
    chopped
500 g (1 lb) onions, skinned and sliced
500 g (1 lb) tomatoes, skinned and chopped
500 g (1 lb) apples, peeled, cored and chopped
250 g (8 oz) demerara sugar
5 ml (1 level tsp) ground allspice
450 ml ($\frac{3}{4}$ pint) malt vinegar
5 ml (1 level tsp) peppercorns
5 ml (1 level tsp) mustard seeds

Place the peppers in a preserving pan with the onions, tomatoes, apples, sugar, allspice and vinegar. Tie the peppercorns and mustard seeds in a piece of muslin and add to the pan. Bring to the boil and simmer over a medium heat for about 1$\frac{1}{2}$ hours until soft, pulpy and well reduced. Remove the muslin bag, spoon the chutney into pre-heated jars and cover at once with airtight, vinegar-proof tops.

Makes about 1.75 kg (3$\frac{1}{2}$ lb)

MARROW AND APPLE CHUTNEY

2 kg (4 lb) marrow, peeled and chopped
75 g (3 oz) salt
1 kg (2 lb) cooking apples, peeled, cored and
    finely chopped
500 g (1 lb) shallots or onions, skinned and
    chopped
500 g (1 lb) soft brown sugar
1.2 litres (2 pints) distilled vinegar
5 ml (1 level tsp) ground ginger
15 g ($\frac{1}{2}$ oz) pickling spice

Put the marrow pieces into a large bowl in layers with the salt and leave for 12 hours or overnight.

Next day, rinse the marrow pieces, drain off the water and put them into a preserving pan. Add the apples, shallots or onions, sugar, vinegar and spice. (If using whole spice, put them into a muslin bag.) Cook gently but steadily, uncovered, for about 2 hours, stirring from time to time, until the chutney becomes thick with no excess liquid. Remove the muslin bag, if used. Pour into pre-heated jars while still warm and cover immediately with airtight and vinegar-proof tops.

Makes about 3 kg (6 lb)

Red tomato chutney (page 93)
OVERLEAF: *Plum chutney (page 94)*

APPLE CHUTNEY

This is a light chutney, fruity but not spiced, which is good with pork and poultry.

1.5 kg (3 lb) cooking apples, peeled, cored and
   diced
1.5 kg (3 lb) onions, skinned and chopped
500 g (1 lb) sultanas or seedless raisins
grated rind and juice of 2 lemons
750 g (1½ lb) demerara sugar
600 ml (1 pint) malt vinegar

Put the apples, onions, sultanas or raisins, lemon rind and juice, sugar and vinegar in a preserving pan. Bring to the boil and simmer, uncovered, stirring occasionally, for about 3 hours until the mixture is of a thick consistency, with no excess liquid remaining. Spoon the chutney into pre-heated jars and cover immediately with airtight and vinegar-proof tops.

Makes about 3 kg (6 lb)

VARIATIONS
Blender apple chutney
An electric blender can be used to produce a smoother texture, if preferred. In this case, bring all the ingredients, except the sultanas or raisins, to the boil and simmer until really soft. Pour into the blender goblet, a little at a time, and blend until smooth. Return to the saucepan with the sultanas or raisins and cook for a further 15 minutes or until thick. Pot and cover in the usual way.

Gooseberry chutney
Follow the recipe above, replacing the apples with 1.5 kg (3 lb) gooseberries, topped, tailed and washed.

RHUBARB CHUTNEY

2.5 kg (5 lb) rhubarb, trimmed, washed and cut
   into small pieces
500 g (1 lb) onions, skinned and minced
1 kg (2 lb) granulated sugar
30 ml (2 level tbsp) ground ginger
50 g (2 oz) ground mixed spice or 15–30 ml
   (1–2 level tbsp) curry powder
10 ml (2 level tsp) salt
900 ml (1½ pints) vinegar

Place the rhubarb, onions, sugar, spices, salt and 300 ml (½ pint) of the vinegar in a pan and cook slowly until the rhubarb is tender. Add the remaining vinegar and simmer gently, stirring occasionally, until no excess liquid remains and the mixture is thick. Spoon the chutney into pre-heated jars and cover at once with airtight, vinegar-proof tops.

Makes about 3 kg (6 lb)

Clockwise from top: *Cucumber and celery relish (page 103), Tomato relish (page 97), Mustard relish (page 98)*

Sauces, Ketchups and Vinegars

Sauces, ketchups and vinegars are savoury, sometimes sweet, accompaniments to foods providing a complementary piquant flavour. They all contain vinegar, which is the preservative, and herbs and/or spices. A sauce contains a mixture of fruit and vegetables and a ketchup is the extract of a single fruit or vegetable, and is a little thinner than a sauce.

Sauces

Home-made bottled sauces are chutney-type mixtures of fruit, vegetables, vinegar, spices and sugar which are sieved after cooking. They usually have one predominating flavour. Use an open pan for cooking unless otherwise stated. Since most sauces have a low acid content, they are liable to ferment and must be sterilised after bottling. Allow sauces to mature for at least 1 month before using. Some of the thinner, more pungent sauces, such as Yorkshire relish, do not need sterilising and can be used immediately. These sauces can also be used as flavourings in other dishes.

Ketchups

Cooked with vinegar and other ingredients, a ketchup is the extract of a single fruit or vegetable. After cooking, the mixture is sieved. Like sauces, ketchups need sterilising if they have a low acid content. Home-made tomato ketchup is full of goodness and more economical than the bought kind.

Flavoured Vinegars

Vinegars are flavoured by infusing with fruit, herbs or spices. Fruit vinegars, used as cordials, are said to be good for sore throats. Fruit and herb vinegars make an interesting addition to salad dressings. Spiced vinegars are often used in pickles to give added flavour.

Bottling and Sterilising

Use bottles with metal or plastic screw caps, screw stoppers or corks. Heat the bottles in the oven at 140°C (275°F) mark 1 and boil the caps or corks in water for 10 minutes immediately before using. Screw-capped bottles should be filled to just under 2.5 cm (1 inch) from the top and corked bottles to within 3.5 cm (1½ inches) of the top. Seal with the cap or cork immediately after filling. If using corks, they must be tied down with wire or with a strong piece of cloth and string as soon as the bottles have been filled and corked. This will prevent the corks blowing out during the sterilising process.

Wrap the bottles in cloth or newspaper and

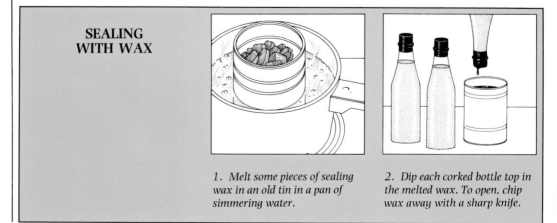

SEALING WITH WAX

1. Melt some pieces of sealing wax in an old tin in a pan of simmering water.

2. Dip each corked bottle top in the melted wax. To open, chip wax away with a sharp knife.

stand them upright in a deep pan with an upturned plate, a pad of newspaper or a folded cloth on the base. Fill up with warm water to reach the necks of the bottles. Heat to 76°C (170°F) or simmering point if no thermometer is available. Simmer, maintaining this temperature, for 30 minutes. Remove the bottles and tighten any screw caps used. Push in the corks and, when the bottles are partly cooled, coat the corks with melted paraffin wax to make them airtight. Store the bottles in a cool, dark place.

GREEN TOMATO SAUCE
(see page 112)

1. Wash and finely chop the tomatoes, onions and apples.

2. Put the empty bottles on a baking sheet and warm them in the oven before use.

3. Put the ingredients in a preserving pan and simmer for about 1 hour.

4. Press the pulp through a nylon sieve into another pan.

5. Boil caps or corks in water for about 10 minutes before use.

6. Pour the sauce into warmed bottles and cork, securing the corks with string.

7. Wrap each bottle in a cloth and stand them in a large pan. Fill with warm water.

8. Push the corks firmly into the bottles and seal with wax as shown opposite.

111

MINT SAUCE

Illustrated in colour on page 117

Mint sauce is traditionally served with lamb.

100 g (4 oz) fresh mint, washed, dried and finely
chopped
225 g (8 oz) granulated sugar
300 ml ($\frac{1}{2}$ pint) vinegar

Put the chopped mint into dry, wide-necked jars. Dissolve the sugar in the vinegar, stirring with a wooden spoon, and bring to the boil. Leave until cold. Pour over the mint and seal to make the jars airtight.

To serve, lift out sufficient mint with a wooden spoon, together with a little of the liquid. Put into a jug or sauce boat and add a little fresh vinegar.

Makes about 300 ml ($\frac{1}{2}$ pint)

GREEN TOMATO SAUCE

1.5 kg (3 lb) green tomatoes, washed and finely
chopped
500 g (1 lb) apples, washed and finely chopped
2 small onions or shallots, skinned and finely
chopped
225 g (8 oz) granulated sugar
5 ml (1 level tsp) ground pickling spice
2.5 ml ($\frac{1}{2}$ level tsp) freshly ground pepper
2.5 ml ($\frac{1}{2}$ level tsp) mustard powder
10 ml (2 level tsp) salt
300 ml ($\frac{1}{2}$ pint) vinegar
gravy browning to colour

Place all the ingredients in a large saucepan and simmer gently for 1 hour, stirring occasionally. Press through a nylon sieve and return to the pan. Bring to the boil and simmer for a few minutes. Pour the hot sauce into warm bottles, seal and sterilise.

Makes about 900 ml (1$\frac{1}{2}$ pints)

HORSERADISH SAUCE

Serve with roast beef or smoked fish.

225 g (8 oz) horseradish root, washed and
peeled
600 ml (1 pint) boiling water
5 ml (1 level tsp) salt
distilled vinegar

For the sauce
5 ml (1 level tsp) prepared mustard
5 ml (1 level tsp) caster sugar
salt and freshly ground pepper
60 ml (4 tbsp) double cream
10 ml (2 tsp) distilled vinegar

Grate or shred the horseradish and place immediately in boiling salted water for 1 minute to preserve the colour. (Grated horseradish is very pungent so keep it well away from your eyes.) Drain, then pack into warm jars. Cover at once with hot vinegar and seal with airtight and vinegar-proof tops.

To make the Horseradish sauce, add the sauce ingredients to 30–45 ml (2–3 level tbsp) of the grated horseradish and serve.

HOT WELLINGTON SAUCE

500 g (1 lb) red tomatoes, washed and chopped
1 onion, skinned and chopped
1 lemon, washed and chopped
1 kg (2 lb) apples, peeled, cored and chopped
1.2 litres (2 pints) malt vinegar
1.2 litres (2 pints) water
15 g ($\frac{1}{2}$ oz) whole mixed spice
25 g (1 oz) salt
225 g (8 oz) soft brown sugar
5 ml (1 tsp) soy sauce

Place the tomatoes, onion and fruit in a large saucepan and cover with the vinegar and water. Tie the spice in a piece of muslin and add to the pan with the salt and sugar. Bring to the boil, then simmer for about 3 hours until well reduced. Remove the muslin bag and press the mixture through a nylon sieve. Add the soy sauce and return to the pan. Simmer for 15 minutes, stirring occasionally, until the sauce thickens. Pour the hot sauce into warm bottles, seal and sterilise.

Makes about 900 ml (1$\frac{1}{2}$ pints)

ELDERBERRY SAUCE

This is a delicious accompaniment to fish dishes.

2 kg (4 lb) elderberries, washed and stripped
2 medium onions, skinned and chopped
20 ml (4 level tsp) salt
600 ml (1 pint) spiced vinegar (see page 115)
1.5 kg (3 lb) granulated sugar

Place all the ingredients in a saucepan and simmer gently until they are well broken down and the onions are tender. Press through a nylon sieve and return to the pan. Simmer until the sauce has thickened and no excess vinegar remains on top. Pour the hot sauce into warm bottles, seal and sterilise.

PLUM SAUCE

Serve with pork or ham.

2 kg (4 lb) plums, washed and stoned
225 g (8 oz) onions, skinned and sliced
100 g (4 oz) currants
600 ml (1 pint) spiced vinegar (see page 115)
225 g (8 oz) granulated sugar
25 g (1 oz) salt

Place the plums, onions and currants in a saucepan with 300 ml ($\frac{1}{2}$ pint) of the spiced vinegar and simmer for 30 minutes. Press through a nylon sieve and return to the pan with the remaining vinegar, the sugar and salt. Simmer for about 1 hour or until the sauce is thick and creamy. Pour the hot sauce into warm bottles, seal and sterilise.

Makes about 1.2 litres (2 pints)

TOMATO KETCHUP

A family favourite to serve with fish and chips, sausages and grills.

3 kg (6 lb) ripe tomatoes, sliced
225 g (8 oz) granulated sugar
300 ml ($\frac{1}{2}$ pint) distilled spiced vinegar (see
 page 115)
15 ml (1 tbsp) tarragon vinegar (optional)
pinch of cayenne pepper
5 ml (1 level tsp) paprika pepper
5 ml (1 level tsp) salt

Place the tomatoes in a pan and cook over a very low heat until they pulp; reduce by boiling until the pulp thickens, stirring frequently. Press through a nylon sieve and return to the pan, together with the other ingredients. Simmer until the mixture thickens. Pour the hot ketchup into warm bottles, seal and sterilise.

Makes about 1.2 litres (2 pints)

MUSHROOM KETCHUP

A delicious accompaniment to chicken and fish dishes.

1.5 kg (3 lb) mushrooms, washed and roughly
 broken
75 g (3 oz) salt
5 ml (1 tsp) peppercorns
5 ml (1 tsp) whole allspice
2.5 ml ($\frac{1}{2}$ level tsp) ground mace
2.5 ml ($\frac{1}{2}$ level tsp) ground ginger
1.25 ml ($\frac{1}{4}$ level tsp) ground cloves
600 ml (1 pint) distilled vinegar

Put the mushrooms in a bowl and sprinkle with the salt. Cover and leave overnight. Rinse away the excess salt, drain and mash with a wooden spoon. Place in a saucepan with the spices and vinegar, then cover and simmer for about 30 minutes or until the excess vinegar is absorbed. Press through a nylon sieve. Pour the ketchup into warm bottles, seal and sterilise.

Makes about 900 ml (1$\frac{1}{2}$ pints)

HERB VINEGARS
Illustrated in colour on page 118

Fill bottles with sprigs of leaves from freshly gathered herbs such as rosemary, tarragon, mint, thyme, marjoram, basil, dill, sage or parsley. Use either a mixture of herbs or one variety. Fill with a good quality red or white wine vinegar, then cover and leave in a cool, dry place for about 6 weeks. Strain through muslin. Taste and add more vinegar if the flavour is too strong. Pour into bottles and seal with airtight and vinegar-proof tops. Use when making salad dressings.

FRUIT VINEGARS
Illustrated in colour on page 118

These are usually made with raspberries, blackberries or blackcurrants and are used like a cordial. A fruit vinegar can also be used to replace wine vinegar in salad dressings.

Place the washed fruit in a bowl and break it up slightly with the back of a wooden spoon. For each 500 g (1 lb) fruit, pour in 600 ml (1 pint) malt vinegar. Cover with a cloth and leave to stand for 3–4 days, stirring occasionally. Strain through muslin and add 500 g (1 lb) sugar to each 600 ml (1 pint). Boil for 10 minutes then cool, strain again, pour into bottles and seal with airtight and vinegar-proof tops. Add a few whole pieces of fruit to each bottle, if liked.

SPICED VINEGAR
Illustrated in colour on page 118

1.2 litres (2 pints) vinegar
30 ml (2 tbsp) blade mace
15 ml (1 tbsp) whole allspice
15 ml (1 tbsp) whole cloves
18 cm (7 inches) cinnamon stick
6 peppercorns
1 small bay leaf

Place the vinegar, spices and bay leaf in a saucepan, bring to the boil and pour into a bowl or bottles. Cover to preserve the flavour and leave to marinate for 2 hours. Strain through muslin, pour into clean bottles and seal with airtight and vinegar-proof tops.

An even better result is obtained if the spices are left to stand in unheated vinegar for 1–2 months.

Note If the individual spices are not available, use 25–50 g (1–2 oz) pickling spice.

Different brands of pickling spice will vary considerably; for example, some contain whole chillies, giving a hotter flavour.

SWEET SPICED VINEGAR

1.8 litres (3 pints) vinegar
500 g (1 lb) granulated sugar
7.5 ml (1½ level tsp) salt
5 ml (1 tsp) whole mixed spice
5 ml (1 tsp) peppercorns
2.5 ml (½ tsp) whole cloves

Place the vinegar, sugar, salt and spices in a saucepan, bring to the boil and pour into a bowl. Cover with a plate to preserve the flavour and leave to marinate for 2 hours. Strain through muslin, pour into bottles and seal with airtight and vinegar-proof tops.

GARLIC VINEGAR

3 garlic cloves, skinned and sliced
600 ml (1 pint) distilled vinegar

Place the garlic in a warm bottle. Heat the vinegar in a saucepan and bring to the boil. Pour on to the garlic and leave to cool. Seal with a vinegar-proof top and leave in a cool place for about 6 weeks. Taste, and if sufficiently flavoured, strain through a nylon sieve. Re-bottle and seal with an airtight, vinegar-proof top. Use the vinegar in salad dressings.

PEAR SAUCE

8 large ripe dessert pears, peeled, cored and
    chopped
450 ml ($\frac{3}{4}$ pint) water
50 g (2 oz) caster sugar
5 ml (1 level tsp) pickling spice
1 cinnamon stick
5 ml (1 level tsp) whole cloves

Place the pears in a large pan with the water, sugar and spices. Bring to the boil and cook for about 10 minutes until tender and broken up. Press the mixture through a nylon sieve. Return the purée to a clean pan, bring to the boil and boil for 5 minutes, stirring occasionally, until the sauce thickens. Pour the hot sauce into warm bottles. Seal and sterilise.

Makes about 300 ml ($\frac{1}{2}$ pint)

HOT TOMATO AND APPLE SAUCE

500 g (1 lb) tomatoes, washed and chopped
500 g (1 lb) cooking apples, peeled, cored and
    chopped
2 medium onions, skinned and chopped
150 ml ($\frac{1}{4}$ pint) distilled vinegar
100 g (4 oz) granulated sugar
12 peppercorns
8 whole cloves
15 g ($\frac{1}{2}$ oz) root ginger
2 chillies
15 g ($\frac{1}{2}$ oz) salt

Place the tomatoes, apples and onions in a saucepan, cover and cook gently until soft, then add all the remaining ingredients. Simmer for about 30 minutes, uncovered, then press the mixture through a nylon sieve. Return to the pan and cook gently for about 15 minutes, stirring occasionally, until the sauce thickens. Pour the hot sauce into warm bottles, seal and sterilise.

Makes about 600 ml (1 pint)

Mint sauce (page 112)

PIQUANT RELISH

25 g (1 oz) garlic, skinned and chopped
25 g (1 oz) canned anchovies, drained
6–8 chillies
1.2 litres (2 pints) malt vinegar
300 ml ($\frac{1}{2}$ pint) soy sauce
15 g ($\frac{1}{2}$ oz) whole cloves
7 g ($\frac{1}{4}$ oz) allspice
grated rind and juice of 1 lemon

Pound the garlic, anchovies and chillies together and put in a pan with the vinegar and other ingredients. Bring to the boil and simmer for 30 minutes. Press through a nylon sieve and leave until cold. Bottle and seal.

Makes about 1.2 litres (2 pints)

YORKSHIRE RELISH

Although Yorkshire relish is not perhaps as well known as Worcestershire sauce, it was once very popular. These thin pungent sauces have their origins in India, and recipes were brought back to this country by British people who had enjoyed them while in India.

600 ml (1 pint) water
25 g (1 oz) black peppercorns
7 g ($\frac{1}{4}$ oz) cayenne pods or dried chilli
15 g ($\frac{1}{2}$ oz) whole cloves
100 g (4 oz) salt
225 g (8 oz) granulated sugar
30 ml (2 tbsp) gravy browning
1.2 litres (2 pints) vinegar

Put all the ingredients into a saucepan, bring to the boil and simmer for 5–10 minutes. Leave to cool, then press through a nylon sieve. Put the sauce into warm bottles and seal.

Makes about 1.8 litres (3 pints)

Top (from left): *Mint vinegar, Raspberry vinegar, Sage vinegar (page 114)*
Bottom (from left): *Thyme vinegar, Rosemary vinegar (page 114), Spiced vinegar (page 115)*

119

Bottling

Bottling is a process of preserving by sterilisation, which kills yeasts and moulds already present on the food and prevents others spreading into the bottling jars. This is done by heating the jars of fruit in the oven, in a water bath or in a pressure cooker and then sealing the jars while hot.

It is not possible to use bottling as a method of preserving meat, fish, poultry or vegetables in the home. In order to kill the bacteria which can lead to food poisoning, the food must be preserved in acid conditions—which is why most fruits can be bottled successfully—or heated to extremely high temperatures. Heat processing carried out at home, even when using a pressure cooker, is inadequate and cannot ensure that bottled vegetables are free from bacteria. Extra acid needs to be added when bottling tomatoes but almost any type of fruit can be bottled, providing the general rules for preparing and processing are followed. As with any other preserving process, the fruit must be fresh, sound, clean and properly ripe—neither too soft, nor too hard. Choose fruits of a similar shape, size and ripeness for any one bottle. Fruit should be prepared according to the chart on pages 128 and 129.

Bottling Jars

These are wide-necked jars with glass caps or metal discs, secured by screw-bands or clips. If the cap or disc has no integral rubber gasket, a thin rubber ring is inserted between it and the top of the bottle. Neither the rubber rings nor the metal discs with fitted seals should be used more than once. Jars can be obtained in different sizes ranging from 500 g (1 lb) upwards.

Before use, check all jars and fittings for any flaw and test to make sure they will be airtight. To do this, fill the jars with water, put the fittings in place, then turn them upside-down. Any leak will show in 10 minutes.

Jars must be absolutely clean, so wash them well and rinse in clean hot water. There is no need to dry them—the fruit slips into place more easily if the jar is wet.

Syrup for Bottling

Fruit may be preserved in either syrup or water, but syrup imparts a much better flavour and colour (see following recipe).

SUGAR SYRUP

225 g (8 oz) granulated sugar
600 ml (1 pint) water

Dissolve the sugar in half the water. Bring to the boil for 1 minute, then add the remaining water. (This method cuts the time required for the syrup to cool.) If the syrup is to be used while still boiling, keep a lid on the pan to prevent evaporation, which would alter the strength. Lemon and orange rind, liqueurs or whole spices can be added to the syrup if liked.

Golden syrup may be substituted for sugar. In this case, put the syrup and water into a pan, bring to the boil and simmer for 5 minutes before use. The flavour will, of course, be different.

Packing the Fruit

Put the fruit in the jars layer by layer, using a packing spoon or the handle of a wooden spoon to push down the fruit. When a jar is full, the fruit should be firmly and securely wedged in place, without bruising or squashing. The more closely the fruit is packed, the less likely it is to rise after the shrinkage which may occur during processing.

Normal pack Most fruit should be packed as above and the jars then filled up with syrup or water before or after processing.

Tight pack Fruit such as gooseberries and chopped rhubarb may be packed much more tightly, leaving space for only a very little syrup or water to be added. Fruit packed in this way is best used as a dessert without further cooking. If packed in the normal way, use gooseberries and rhubarb in pies or other made-up dishes which require further cooking.

Solid pack Apple slices and tomato halves may be packed so tightly into jars that they need no syrup or water added either before or after processing.

Processing

Bottles can be sterilised in the oven, in a water bath or in the pressure cooker. The method you choose will depend on the equipment you have and the time available.

Oven method The advantages of the oven method are that jars can be processed at one

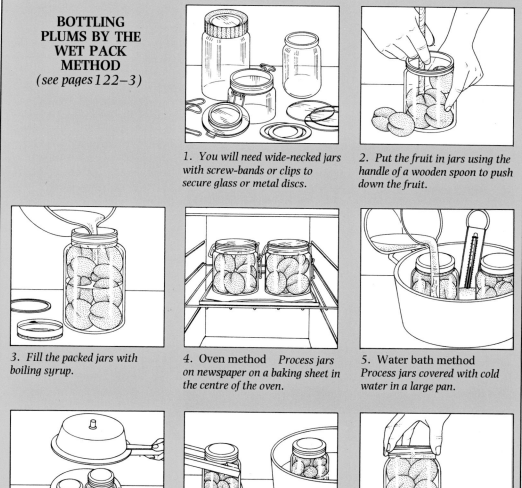

BOTTLING PLUMS BY THE WET PACK METHOD
(see pages 122–3)

1. You will need wide-necked jars with screw-bands or clips to secure glass or metal discs.

2. Put the fruit in jars using the handle of a wooden spoon to push down the fruit.

3. Fill the packed jars with boiling syrup.

4. Oven method Process jars on newspaper on a baking sheet in the centre of the oven.

5. Water bath method Process jars covered with cold water in a large pan.

6. Pressure cooker method Process jars in hot water in a pressure cooker.

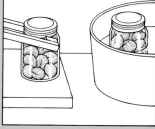

7. After processing, place jars on a wooden board and seal at once.

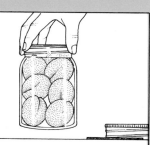

8. Leave the jars to cool, then test for a good seal (see page 126).

time and no special equipment is needed. It is, however, not quite so exact as the water bath method, as it is not easy to maintain a constant temperature throughout the oven and it is easier to over-cook the fruit. The oven method is not recommended for tall jars. If you use this method, use only one shelf of the oven, placed just below the centre. Don't crowd too many jars in the oven at one time or the heat will fail to penetrate the fruit evenly.

Wet pack oven method Heat the oven to 150°C (300°F) mark 2. Fill the packed jars with boiling syrup or water to within 2.5 cm (1 inch) of the top. Dispel all air bubbles by jarring each jar on the palm of the hand. Alternatively, pack the fruit and add the liquid alternately until the jar is full. Put on the rubber rings and glass caps or metal discs but not screw-bands or clips. Place the jars 5 cm (2 inches) apart on a solid baking sheet lined with newspaper to catch any liquid which may boil over. Put in the centre of the oven and process for the time stated in the table opposite. Remove jars one by one, placing them on a wooden surface, and put on clips or screw-bands, screwing the bands as tightly as possible. Hot jars should always be placed on a wooden surface after processing as a colder surface could cause them to crack. Allow to become quite cold before testing for a good seal (see page 126).

Dry pack oven method Heat the oven to 130°C (250°F) mark ½. Pack the bottling jars with fruit but do not add any liquid. Put on the caps but not rubber rings, discs with rings, screw-bands or clips. Place the jars 5 cm (2 inches) apart on a solid baking sheet lined with newspaper. Put in the centre of the oven and process for the time stated in the table opposite. Remove jars one at a time, placing them on a wooden surface. Use the contents of one jar to top up the others if the fruit has shrunk during the cooking. Fill up at once with boiling syrup.

When the jars have been filled with syrup, give each one a quick, vigorous twist to remove as many air bubbles as possible. Remember to use a cloth as the jars will be very hot. Fill the jars to the brim before putting on the fittings. Place the rubber bands (dipped first in boiling water), caps or metal discs in position and secure with clips or screw the bands on tightly. Leave to cool.

The dry pack oven method is not recommended for fruits which discolour in the air, such as apples, pears and peaches. From the chart, it will be seen that with both oven methods the time required varies not only with the type of fruit, but also with the tightness of the pack and the total load in the oven at any one time; the load is calculated according to the total capacity of the jars. Fruits such as strawberries and raspberries can be rolled in caster sugar before packing dry; the flavour will be delicious but the appearance less attractive.

Water bath method The water bath method is a more exact method of sterilisation, but needs special equipment—a large vessel about 5 cm (2 inches) deeper than the height of the bottling jars, a thermometer and bottling tongs. The vessel can be a very large saucepan, a zinc bath or a zinc bucket; it must have a false bottom such as a metal grid, strips of wood nailed together trellis-fashion, or even a folded coarse cloth. A sugar-boiling thermometer will be satisfactory. Bottling tongs are not essential, but they make it easier to remove the jars from the water bath.

Slow water bath Pack the jars with fruit, then fill up with cold syrup. Put the rubber bands and glass caps or metal discs and screw-bands or clips in place, then turn the screw-bands back a quarter-turn. Place the jars in the large vessel and cover with cold water, immersing them completely if possible, but at least up to the necks. Heat gently on top of the cooker, checking the temperature of the water regularly. Raise the temperature to 54°C (130°F) in 1 hour, then to the processing temperature given in the chart on page 124 within a further 30 minutes. Maintain the temperature for the length of time given in the chart.

Remove the jars with the tongs (or bale out enough water to remove them, with the aid of an oven cloth). Place the jars one at a time on a wooden surface, and tighten the screw-bands immediately. When cool, test for a seal (see page 126).

Quick water bath If you have no thermometer, this is a good alternative method. Fill the packed jars with hot (not boiling) syrup, cover and place in the vessel of warm water. Bring the water to simmering point in 25–30 minutes, and keep simmering for the time stated in the table.

Times for Oven Method

These are the temperatures and processing times recommended by the Long Ashton Research Station.

Type of fruit	Wet pack		Dry pack	
	Pre-heat oven to 150°C (300°F) mark 1. Process time varies with quantity in oven, as below.		Pre-heat oven to 130°C (250°F) mark ½. Process time varies with quantity in oven, as below.	
	Quantity	Time	Quantity	Time
Soft fruit, normal pack: blackberries, currants, loganberries, mulberries, raspberries;	500 g–2 kg (1–4 lb) 2.25–5 kg (4½–10 lb)	30–40 minutes 45–60 minutes	500 g–2 kg (1–4 lb) 2.25–5 kg (4½–10 lb)	45–55 minutes 60–75 minutes
Gooseberries and rhubarb (for made-up dishes)	As above	As above	As above	As above
Apples, sliced	500 g–2 kg (1–4 lb) 2.25–5 kg (4½–10 lb)	30–40 minutes 45–60 minutes	Not recommended	
Soft fruit, tight pack: As above, including Gooseberries and rhubarb (for stewed fruit)	500 g–2 kg (1–4 lb) 2.25–5 kg (4½–10 lb)	40–50 minutes 55–70 minutes	500 g–2 kg (1–4 lb) 2.25–5 kg (4½–10 lb)	55–70 minutes 75–90 minutes
Stone fruit, dark, whole: cherries, damsons, plums	As soft fruit (tight pack)		As soft fruit (tight pack)	
Stone fruit, light, whole: apricots, cherries, gages, plums	As above		Not recommended	
Apples, solid pack; Apricots, halved; Nectarines; Peaches; Pineapples; Plums, halved	500 g–2 kg (1–4 lb) 2.25–5 kg (4½–10 lb)	50–60 minutes 65–80 minutes	Not recommended	
Figs	500 g–2 kg (1–4 lb) 2.25–5 kg (4½–10 lb)	60–70 minutes 75–90 minutes	500 g–2 kg (1–4 lb) 2.25–5 kg (4½–10 lb)	80–100 minutes 105–125 minutes
Pears	As Figs		Not recommended	

Times for water bath method
These are the temperatures and processing methods recommended by Long Ashton Research Station.

Type of fruit	Slow method	Quick method
	Raise from cold in 90 minutes and maintain as below	Raise from warm 38°C (100°F) to simmering 88°C (190°F) in 25–30 minutes and maintain for:
Soft fruit normal pack: blackberries, currants, loganberries, mulberries, raspberries; Gooseberries and rhubarb (for made-up dishes); Apples, sliced	74°C (165°F) for 10 minutes	2 minutes
Soft fruit, tight pack: As above, including gooseberries and rhubarb (for stewed fruit) *Stone fruit, whole:* apricots, cherries, damsons, gages, plums	82°C (180°F) for 15 minutes	10 minutes
Apples, solid pack Apricots, halved; Nectarines; Peaches; Pineapple; Plums, halved	82°C (180°F) for 15 minutes	20 minutes
Figs Pears	88°C (190°F) for 30 minutes	40 minutes

Pulped Fruit
Soft and stone fruits can be bottled as pulp. Prepare as for stewing, then add only the minimum of water and stew until just cooked. If desired, the fruit can be sieved at this point. While still boiling, pour into hot jars and place the rubber bands and glass caps or metal discs and screw-bands in position.

Immerse the jars in a deep pan and add hot water up to the necks. Raise the temperature to boiling point and maintain for 5 minutes. Remove the jars and allow to cool. If preferred, the fruit can be sieved after stewing and before bottling.

Pressure Cooker Method
This method shortens the time and also ensures that the temperature is controlled exactly. The cooker must have a low (5-lb) pressure control. Any pressure cooker will take the 500-g (1-lb) bottling jars, but you will need a cooker with a domed lid when using larger bottling jars.

the chart below. Any change in pressure will cause liquid to be lost from the jars and under-processing may result.

Remove the pan carefully from the heat and reduce the pressure at room temperature for about 10 minutes before taking off the lid. Lift out the jars one by one, placing them on a wooden surface, and tighten the screw-bands. When cool, test for a seal (see page 126).

Times for pressure cooker method
Prepare the fruit as for ordinary fruit bottling, unless otherwise stated. Bring to pressure and process for the time given in the chart.

Fruit	Processing time in minutes at low (5-lb) pressure
Apples (quartered)	1
Apricots or plums (whole)	1
Blackberries	1
Loganberries	1
Raspberries	1
Cherries	1
Currants (red and black)	1
Damsons	1
Gooseberries	1
Pears, eating	5
Pears, cooking (very hard ones can be pressure-cooked for 3–5 minutes before packing in jars)	5
Plums or apricots (stoned and halved)	1
Rhubarb (in 5-cm (2-inch) lengths)	1
Strawberries	Not recommended
Soft fruit, solid pack: put the fruit in a large bowl, cover with boiling syrup— 175 g (6 oz) sugar to 600 ml (1 pint) water— and leave overnight. Drain, pack jars and cover with same syrup. Process as usual.	3
Pulped fruit, e.g. apples: prepare as for stewing. Pressure cook with 150 ml (¼ pint) water at high (15-lb) pressure for 2–3 minutes, then sieve. While still hot, fill jars and process.	1

Prepare the fruit as for ordinary bottling, but look at the additional notes in the following chart. Pack the fruit into clean, warm jars, filling them right to the top. Cover with boiling syrup or water to within 2.5 cm (1 inch) of the top of the jars. Put on the rubber bands, glass caps or metal discs, clips or screw-bands, screwing these tight, then turning them back a quarter-turn. Next, as an extra precaution, heat the jars by standing them in a bowl of boiling water.

Put the inverted trivet into the pressure cooker and add 900 ml (1½ pints) water, plus 15 ml (1 tbsp) vinegar to prevent the pan from becoming stained. Bring the water to the boil. Pack the bottles into the cooker, making sure they do not touch by packing newspaper between. Fix the lid in place, put the pan on the heat without weight and heat until steam comes steadily from the vent. Put on the low (5-lb) pressure control and bring to pressure on a medium heat. Reduce the heat and maintain the pressure for the time given in

Testing for a Good Seal

After processing, allow the jars to cool, then test for correct sealing by removing the screw-band or clip and trying to lift the jar by the cap or disc. If this holds firm, it shows that a vacuum has been formed as the jar cooled and it is hermetically sealed. If the cap or disc comes off, there is probably a flaw in the rim of the jar or on the cap. If, however, several bottles are unsealed, the processing procedure may have been faulty. Use the fruit from the jars at once; it can be re-processed but the result is loss of quality.

Storing

Store bottled fruits without clips or screw-bands as this can stretch them. If you do leave screw-bands on, smear each one with a little oil and screw on loosely. This helps to prevent rust and makes for ease of opening later. Label the bottles and store in a cool, dark place.

Bottling Tomatoes

Whole unskinned tomatoes (recommended for oven sterilising). The fruit must be small or medium, even in size, ripe yet firm. Remove the stalks and wash or wipe the tomatoes. Pack into jars and fill up with a brine solution made with 15 g ($\frac{1}{2}$ oz) salt per 1.2 litres (2 pints) water. Add 1.25 ml ($\frac{1}{4}$ level tsp) citric acid or 10 ml (2 tsp) lemon juice to each 500-g (1-lb) jar.

Solid pack, with no liquid added Any size of fruit may be used, but they must be firm. Skin the tomatoes. Small tomatoes may be left whole, but larger ones should be cut in halves or quarters, so that they may be packed really tightly with no air spaces, making it unnecessary to add water. The flavour is improved if about 5 ml (1 level tsp) salt and 2.5 ml ($\frac{1}{2}$ level tsp) sugar are added among the fruit in each 500-g (1-lb) jar. Add 1.25 ml ($\frac{1}{4}$ level tsp) citric acid or 10 ml (2 tsp) lemon juice to each 500-g (1-lb) jar.

In their own juice Skin the tomatoes and pack tightly into jars. Stew some extra tomatoes in a covered pan, with 5 ml (1 level tsp) salt to each 1 kg (2 lb) fruit, strain the juice and use to fill up the jars. Add 1.25 ml ($\frac{1}{4}$ level tsp) citric acid or 10 ml (2 tsp) lemon juice to each 500-g (1-lb) jar.

Bottling Tomato Purée

This method enables poorly shaped tomatoes to be used, though they must be sound and ripe. Wash, place in a covered pan with a little water and salt and cook until soft. Press the pulp through a nylon sieve and return it to the pan, then bring to the boil. Pour it at once into hot jars and put the rubber bands and glass caps or metal discs and screw-bands or clips in place. (It is very important that this process should be carried out quickly, as the pulp deteriorates if left exposed to the air.) Immerse the bottles in a pan of hot water (padded at the base and between the bottles with thick cloth or newspaper), bring to the boil and boil for 10 minutes. Finish and test for a seal as usual.

Bottling Tomato Juice

Simmer ripe tomatoes until soft and press them through a nylon sieve. To each 1.2 litres (2 pints) of pulp, add 300 ml ($\frac{1}{2}$ pint) water, 5 ml (1 level tsp) salt, 30 ml (2 level tbsp) sugar, 5 ml (1 level tsp) citric acid or 30 ml (2 tbsp) lemon juice and a pinch of pepper. Process the juice as for tomato purée.

Times for Sterilising Bottled Tomatoes

Oven method		
	Wet pack Pre-heat oven to 150°C (300°F) mark 1, process as below	*Dry pack* Pre-heat oven to 130°C (250°F) mark ½, process as below
Whole tomatoes	500 g–2 kg (1–4 lb) for 60–70 minutes 2.25–5 kg (4½–10 lb) for 75–90 minutes	500 g–2 kg (1–4 lb) for 80–100 minutes 2.25–5 kg (4½–10 lb) for 105–125 minutes
Solid pack tomatoes (halved or quartered)	500 g–2 kg (1–4 lb) for 70–80 minutes 2.25–5 kg (4½–10 lb) for 85–100 minutes	Not recommended

Water bath method		
	Slow method Raise from cold in 90 minutes and maintain as below	*Quick method* Raise from warm 38°C (100°F) to simmering 88°C (190°F) in 25–30 minutes and maintain for:
Whole tomatoes	88°C (190°F) for 30 minutes	40 minutes
Solid pack tomatoes (halved or quartered)	88°C (190°F) for 40 minutes	50 minutes

Pressure cooker method	
Whole or halved tomatoes in brine (prepare as for ordinary bottling)	Process for 5 minutes at low (5-lb) pressure
Solid pack	Process for 15 minutes at low (5-lb) pressure

Bottling Problems

When the seal fails   Check the neck of the jar for chips, cracks or other faults. Inspect the sealing disc to make sure that there are no faults or irregularities in the metal or the rubber rim. (You must use a new sealing disc every time.) The instructions for each method of sterilising must be followed exactly—it is very important to tighten tops at once.

When fruit rises in the jar   This does not affect the keeping qualities, but it does spoil the appearance. It is due to over-processing, too high a temperature during processing, loose packing, over-ripe fruit or a heavy syrup.

When mould appears or fermentation takes place   These are caused by poor-quality fruit, insufficient sterilising or a badly sealed bottle.

When fruit darkens   If only the top pieces are attacked, it can be due to their not being fully covered by liquid or to under-processing. If the contents are darkened throughout, this is probably due to using produce in poor condition, to over-processing or failure to store in a cool, dark place.

Preparing Fruit for Bottling

Fruit	Preparation
Apples	*Normal pack* Peel, core and cut into thick slices or rings; during preparation put into a brine solution made with 10 ml (2 level tsp) salt to 1.2 litres (2 pints) water. Rinse quickly in cold water before packing into jars. *Solid pack* Prepare slices as above, remove from brine and dip in small quantities in boiling water for 1½–3 minutes, until the fruit is just tender and pliable. Pack as tightly as possible into the jars.
Apricots (Illustrated in colour on page 148)	*Whole* Remove stalks and wash fruit. *Halves* Make a cut round each fruit up to the stone, twist the two halves apart and remove the stone. Crack some stones to obtain the kernels and include with the fruit. Pack quickly, to prevent browning.
Blackberries	Pick over, removing damaged fruits, and wash carefully.
Blackberries with apples	Prepare apples as for solid pack (see Apples) before mixing with the blackberries.
Blackcurrants	String, pick over and wash.
Cherries	*Whole* Remove stalks and wash fruit. *Stoned* Use a cherry stoner or small knife to remove stones. Collect any juice and include with the fruit. If liked, add 7 g (¼ oz) citric acid to each 4.8 litres (1 gallon) syrup (with either black or white cherries), to improve the colour and flavour.
Damsons	Remove stems and wash fruit.
Figs	Remove stems and peel, if liked. Add 2.5 ml (½ level tsp) citric acid to each 600 ml (1 pint) syrup, to give acidity and ensure good keeping. Pack with an equal amount of syrup.
Gooseberries	Small green fruit are used for pies and made-up dishes; larger, softer ones are served as stewed fruit. Top, tail and wash. To prevent shrivelling if fruit is preserved in syrup, the skins can be pricked.
Mulberries	Pick over, handling fruit carefully. Try to avoid washing it.

Fruit	Preparation
Peaches (Illustrated in colour on page 145)	Immerse the fruit in a saucepan of boiling water for 30 seconds then rinse in cold water and peel off the skin. Peaches can be bottled whole but are more usually cut in half (see Apricots). Bottle quickly before fruit discolours.
Pears (dessert)	Peel, halve, remove cores with a teaspoon. During preparation, keep in a solution of 15 g ($\frac{1}{2}$ oz) salt and 7 g ($\frac{1}{4}$ oz) citric acid per 1.2 litres (2 pints) water. Rinse quickly in cold water before packing. Add 1.25 ml ($\frac{1}{4}$ level tsp) citric acid or 10 ml (2 tsp) lemon juice to each 500-g (1-lb) jar.
Pears (cooking)	As these are very hard, prepare as for dessert pears but, before packing, stew gently in a sugar syrup—100–175 g (4–6 oz) sugar to 600 ml (1 pint) water—until just soft. Add 1.25 ml ($\frac{1}{4}$ level tsp) citric acid or 10 ml (2 tsp) lemon juice to each 500-g (1-lb) jar.
Pineapple	Peel, trim off leaves, remove central core and as many 'eyes' as possible. Cut into rings or chunks.
Plums and Greengages (Illustrated in colour on page 148)	*Whole* Remove stalks and wash fruit. *Halves* Make a cut round the middle of each fruit to the stone, twist the halves and remove the stone. Crack some stones to obtain the kernels and include with the fruit.
Quinces	Prepare as for pears. Always pack into small jars, as they are usually used in small quantities only, e.g. as flavouring in apple dishes.
Raspberries/Loganberries	Remove the hulls and pick over the fruit. Avoid washing if possible.
Redcurrants	String, pick over and wash.
Rhubarb	The thicker sticks are generally used for made-up dishes; the more delicate, forced rhubarb is used as stewed fruit. Cut rhubarb into 5-cm (2-inch) lengths. To make it pack more economically and taste sweeter when bottled, it may be soaked first; pour hot syrup over and leave overnight. Pack rhubarb in jars and use the syrup to top up the jars.
Strawberries	These do not bottle well.

Salting, Storing, Drying, Curing and

Salting, storing, drying, curing and smoking are the original methods of preservation. Except storing, they are all types of dry preserving—for without moisture, micro-organisms cannot grow and eventually spoil foods. Storing vegetables and fruits carefully under certain conditions enables them to be kept fresh for longer periods. Salting, storing and drying processes are economical and simple to carry out at home.

Curing

Curing is the method of salting and smoking fish or meat to preserve it. This method of preserving is not often carried out at home as few people now have the time or opportunity. The raw materials can be expensive and commercially cured foods are more convenient and safer to eat. Curing is therefore not recommended as a method of home preserving.

Smoking

Smoking is the method of preserving meat and fish by drying them in the smoke of a wood fire. The flavour of the food depends on the type of wood used, for example oak, beech and juniper, which give their own special flavour. Some old houses had chimneys specially constructed for smoking and in others a special outhouse was used. Since few homes now have these chimneys, and a wide variety of good quality commercially smoked foods is now available, lengthy home smoking is no longer necessary.

A type of home smoker is now on the market for use domestically. They are particularly suitable for fish, poultry and meat. Food

---

SALTING FISH
(see opposite)

1. Place the fish in a dish between layers of salt and leave overnight.

2. Drain the fish on absorbent kitchen paper.

3. Pack the fish between layers of salt in a wide-necked jar.

4. Use a bottle filled with water as a weight to press down the fish and salt in the jar.

5. Remove the oil that comes to the surface with a spoon. Cover the jars and store.

Smoking

smoked in this way is for immediate consumption and not for preservation.

Salting

This method of preserving fish and meat dates back to Roman times. It was widely used until the advent of refrigeration. For best results at home, salting is limited to certain fish, vegetables and nuts. Choose rock, kitchen or block, or sea salt; kitchen or block salt is cheaper and perfectly adequate. Do not use free-running table salt.

SALTED ALMONDS OR HAZELNUTS

This method of preserving nuts, by roasting in fat and then sprinkling with salt, produces a delicious result to serve with drinks.

25 g (1 oz) butter or margarine
375 g (12 oz) shelled almonds or hazelnuts
10 ml (2 level tsp) kitchen salt

If the almonds are not blanched, put them in a bowl, cover with boiling water and leave for 3–4 minutes. Plunge into cold water for 1 minute, then slide off the skins between your fingers. To skin hazelnuts, put them in a grill pan and grill for 2–3 minutes, shaking the pan occasionally. Rub off the skins between your fingers or in a clean cloth.

Melt the butter or margarine in a roasting tin and add the almonds or hazelnuts, tossing them until they are evenly coated. Roast in the oven at 150°C (300°F) mark 2 for 30 minutes, stirring occasionally. Add the salt and toss well. When cold, store in an airtight container.

SALTING BEANS

375 g (12 oz) kitchen salt for each 1 kg (2 lb)
French or runner beans

Choose small, young, fresh and tender French or runner beans; it isn't worth preserving old, stringy ones. Cut off the stalks, wash and string if necessary. French beans can be left whole, but runner beans should be sliced.

Place a layer of salt in a glass or stoneware jar, then a layer of beans. Fill the jar with alternate layers, pressing the beans down well and finishing with a layer of salt. Cover with a moisture-proof covering—cork or plastic material—and tie tightly. Leave for a few days to allow a strong brine solution to form. The beans will shrink considerably as the salt draws out the moisture from them, and so the jars can be filled up with more layers of beans and salt—always finishing with salt. Store in a cool, dry, dark place. Use within 6 months.

To cook, remove some beans from the jar. (Put a layer of salt on top of the remaining beans and re-cover the jar.) Wash thoroughly several times in cold water, then soak for 2 hours in warm water. Cook as for fresh beans, but in boiling *unsalted* water, until tender. Drain and serve in the usual way.

SALTING FISH
Illustrated in colour on page 135

1½ kg (3 lb) anchovies or sprats
1–1¼ kg (2–2½ lb) sea salt

Remove the heads and gut the fish. Place the fish in a dish between two layers of salt and leave for at least 12 hours or overnight. Drain the fish on absorbent kitchen paper.

Put a 1-cm (½-inch) layer of salt in the bottom of a wide-necked jar. Pack a layer of fish tightly together on top of the salt, head to tail. Add another layer of salt and then a layer of fish, crossways to the first layer. Repeat layering until the jar is full, finishing with a layer of salt. Leave about 1 cm (½ inch) between the salt and the rim of the jar. Continue until all the fish have been packed into jars. Place a non-metal weight inside each jar on top of the final layer of salt. A bottle filled with water is ideal. Leave in a cool place for 5–6 days, until an oily substance rises to the surface. Remove the oil with a spoon. Cover the jars and store in a cool place.

Fish preserved in this way will keep for up to 6 months. Before using the fish, soak them in cold water for about 15 minutes to remove excess salt.

SAUERKRAUT
Illustrated in colour on pages 146–7

15 g (½ oz) sea salt for each 500 g (1 lb) cabbage, trimmed and washed

Choose firm, white cabbages and finely shred them. Put layers of shredded cabbage in a large stoneware jar (or crock) or wooden tub and sprinkle each layer with salt. Toss the cabbage with your hands, then pack the cabbage down after each layer. When the container is filled, cover the cabbage with a large piece of cling film (not foil) and place an inverted plate or lid on top and press down with a heavy, non-metal weight, such as a jar filled with water. Make sure it is airtight. In a few days the lid should be under the surface of the brine. Leave at room temperature for about 3 weeks, for fermentation to take place, removing any scum every few days, as necessary. If the level of brine falls, top it up with a solution of 25 g (1 oz) salt in 1.2 litres (2 pints) water.

After about 3 weeks, when the salted cabbage has stopped frothing and fermentation is complete, the cabbage is ready to use.

For storage, the sauerkraut must be bottled. Drain the brine into a large saucepan and bring to the boil. Add the cabbage and bring back to the boil, stirring occasionally. If liked, add caraway seeds or juniper berries to flavour. Place at once into hot, clean jars, packing the sauerkraut down to remove any air pockets. Leave a headspace of 2.5 cm (1 inch) at the top of the jars. Cover and process for 25 minutes (see page 121). Test the seal, cover and store. Sauerkraut is generally cooked in its own liquid and served with bacon, smoked sausages or pork.

Storing
There are various methods and techniques of storing some root vegetables, hard fruits and nuts to keep them in good condition. (Green vegetables and soft fruits do not store well.) Select produce in prime condition for storing. Although storage life is fairly limited, it is well worth the effort if you have a suitable space. The ideal storage area should be cool, moist and dark. A cellar, shed or outbuilding with an earth, brick or concrete floor is ideal. It must be well ventilated and protected from frost and mice. It may be necessary to dampen the floor to keep the atmosphere moist. If kept in a warm, dry atmosphere—such as an upstairs room—the fruit and vegetables will quickly shrivel and dry up.

Storing Root Vegetables
There are many different methods and techniques of storing, ranging from racks and shelves, boxes, wire trays, sacks, sand, peat and nets to old-fashioned clamps and 'pies'. The method used depends on what is being stored.

Never store anything which is not in perfect condition, as rot or disease will spread quickly. Watch out for the following conditions which indicate that produce should not be stored.

Onions   Softness, especially round the neck, or black areas on the bulbs.
Carrots   Scored by fly maggots.
Parsnips   Soft, dark areas of canker.
Any root vegetables   Skin damaged on lifting: the skin is the insulation.

Making a Clamp or 'Pie'
This cheap and simple method gives complete protection to root vegetables through the winter, although the clamp cannot be opened during a frost without risk to the stored roots. Use a well protected, well drained part of the garden. Put down a layer of dry straw or clinker about 1.50 metres (5 feet) wide. Build the roots into a broad-based, tapering heap on the straw base. Cover the heap with a 15-cm (6-inch) thickness of straw and leave the root vegetables to sweat for a few days.

After a few days, cover the straw and the whole heap with a layer of packed soils of the same depth, made smooth and firm by patting with the back of a spade. The heap must be entirely soil-crusted apart from a tuft of straw at the peak to act as a chimney and ventilator. To cover the clamp, use soil dug from around the base, so forming a drainage trench. This will prevent the bottom of the clamp becoming waterlogged in wet weather.

Note   This system is best used where a large quantity of root vegetables have to be stored, and when a good number can be taken out at a time. A clamp should not be opened too regularly. To remove moderate quantities, plunge your hand down the 'chimney'. For large quantities, break the 'pie crust' and then replace after removing the vegetables.

Storing Vegetables

Vegetable	Condition and/or Preparation	Storing
BEETROOT	After lifting, remove any excess earth. Twist off the tops, leaving about 5 cm (2 inches) of leaf stalk. This reduces 'bleeding' which occurs if the leaves are cut from the root.	Line a deep box with 2 cm (1 inch) of slightly damp sand or peat, put in a single layer of the prepared beetroots, followed by a layer of sand, and so on. Keep the boxes in a cool, dry, frostproof place, and watch out for mice. The sand, peat or other strong material should not be over-wet; just sufficient to stop shrivelling but not enough to cause rotting or encourage fresh growth. Beetroot can also be stored in a clamp or 'pie' (see opposite).
CARROTS	As for beetroot, except tops are cut off close to the head.	As for beetroot, with the roots laid head to tail.
CELERIAC	Lift before the frost arrives. Remove excess earth.	Store in sand in an airy shed. In warmer parts of the country, they can be left in the ground covered with bracken or straw and dug up during winter as needed.
CUCUMBER	Select firm cucumbers.	Store in a cool place. Stack on racks, or on a stone floor.
KOHLRABI	As for beetroot.	Store for a short time as for beetroot. Late-sown ones can be left in the ground and used as wanted.
MARROW, pumpkin squash	The skins must be hard for storing purposes.	Store marrows, etc., hung up in netting, string bags or anything which will let the air circulate around them. Small ones can be stored on a shelf in a well-ventilated, frostproof place. Turn to prevent bruising or mould.
ONIONS	Lift when the leaves are yellow and drooping. Leave on the surface of the soil to dry off. In wet weather spread the onions in a single layer and dry under cover. They must be thoroughly dry before storing.	Store so the air can move freely between them. They can be placed on slatted, wooden trays, wire-based boxes, or strung up in ropes. Hang up stout lengths of thin rope or strong twine on a pole or beam in a shed or garage. Pull the roots off the onions and tie the necks round the cord. If necks are too short, use string or raffia. Stop before an onion 'rope' is too heavy to carry about. Keep one rope handy, in or near the kitchen, and the rest in a dry, ventilated, frostproof place. Alternatively, use old nylon stockings or tights (the ladders or holes will ensure better ventilation). Put the onions down the legs, tying a knot between each one. Cut them off as you want them, below a knot.
PARSNIPS, leeks celery Jerusalem artichokes	Remove any excess earth.	These are best left in the ground and lifted as required. If parsnips cannot be left in the ground, lift them and leave in a heap where the frost can touch and sweeten them, and the rain can wash them clean.
POTATOES	Remove any excess earth.	Large quantities can be stored in clamps (see opposite). Put small quantities in orange boxes lined with straw and topped with more straw or newspapers. Or keep in slatted trays topped with straw. Sacks of hessian, paper or polythene are other alternatives. The roots must be allowed to 'sweat' for a few days before being bagged, and must be inspected regularly for mice and rotting. Make small holes in polythene and paper sacks so the potatoes can breathe.

Storing Vegetables cont.

SALSIFY	Remove any excess earth.	If they cannot be left in the ground until needed, store in layers of sand or peat.
SHALLOTS	Leave to dry as for onions. Separate bulbs, take off the dried outer skin, leaves, etc.	Store as for onions on wire or wooden trays and racks. They are rather fiddley to 'rope'.
SWEDES	As for beetroot, carrots and potatoes.	As for beetroot, carrots and potatoes.
TOMATOES	Choose firm tomatoes with no skin blemishes or cuts.	Hang whole green trusses in a frostfree place which need not be dark. Alternatively, keep green tomatoes on trays under a bed, in a cupboard or in drawers lined with newspapers. Much depends on their condition when harvested. If you want them for Christmas, keep them cool but frostfree and bring a few at a time into the warmth. Place them in a wide fruit bowl in the living room; the ripe tomatoes will help to ripen the green ones among them.
TURNIPS	As for beetroot, carrots and potatoes.	As for beetroot, carrots and potatoes.

Salting sprats (page 131)

**STORING
ROOT
VEGETABLES**
(see pages 132–4)

1. Store beetroots in a deep box in layers of slightly damp sand or peat.

2. Store carrots as for beetroots.

3. Store onions in the legs of old nylon stockings, tying a knot between each one.

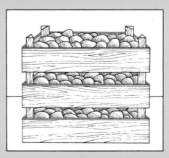

4. Store potatoes in slatted trays stacked on top of one another.

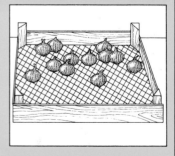

5. Store shallots on wire-based wooden trays.

Storing Apples and Pears

Usually the early varieties do not keep well and should be used quickly, but the later varieties can be stored for several months. Pick them only when they are fully matured and then only store perfectly sound fruit. Apples or pears with bruises, scars, bird pecks, missing stalks or other blemishes should be preserved by a different method. Handle the fruit very carefully. Pears need particularly careful handling as they are usually only at their best for a few days.

After picking, the fruit should be allowed to stand in a cool, airy place overnight. Store different varieties separately. Each fruit must then be individually wrapped. Use oiled paper preferably, or tissue paper or newspaper. Lay the fruit in single layers, not touching each other, in trays, racks or boxes or on the floor. Boxes can be stacked on top of each other as long as air can circulate underneath and between them. Store in a dark place. Covering with straw or paper will help if the store cannot be darkened. Examine and turn occasionally during storage to prevent mould.

Storing Nuts

You can store most nuts for several months, providing they are quite dry and in good condition when gathered. Discard any that appear diseased. Do not remove the shells.

Walnuts Gather the nuts when they are mature and fall to the ground. Remove the husk and then any fibrous material as this is where mould begins to grow. If necessary, quickly scrub the nuts in cold water using a soft brush, for only a few seconds as scrubbing may crack them. Then spread the nuts out to dry at room temperature, in a current of air if possible, turning them occasionally. When dry, store the nuts in a large jar or earthenware crock with alternate layers of a mixture of equal quantities of cooking salt and coconut-fibre refuse, or sawdust, bulb fibre or

Drying herbs (page 138)

DRYING FRUIT, VEGETABLES AND HERBS
(see pages 138–9)

1. Thread apple rings on sticks and dry in a warm place.

2. Spread stoned plum halves on a baking sheet or tray and dry in a warm place.

3. Separate onion slices into rings and slice mushrooms. Spread on trays to dry.

4. Lay sprigs of herbs on a wire rack and leave to dry in a warm place.

5. Tie sprigs of herbs in bunches and hang to dry from a rail in a warm place.

well dried hardwood shavings if coconut fibre residue is not available. Store in a cool, dry place. Store for up to 6 months.

Chestnuts Remove the husks, wipe and store the nuts in sacks or boxes in a cool, dry place.

Sweet almonds Store as for walnuts.

Hazelnuts, filberts and cobnuts Gather when the husks begin to dry and lay the nuts out thinly on wire trays in an airy room. Turn occasionally to prevent mildew.

Drying

Some foods, such as apples, pears, plums, mushrooms, herbs and onions, are more suitable than others for drying and can be dried at home using basic kitchen equipment.

Select good quality fruit that is just ripe. Avoid any with blemishes or bruises, or cut out the blemishes.

In the home, any source of heat can be utilised for drying, providing it is applied with ventilation. Unfortunately the average oven does not have a low enough temperature setting to dry foods slowly and instead tends to bake and shrivel the food. However, the heat left in the oven after cooking can be used to dry food. This method of using residual heat means the food has to be dried over a longer period. A warm airing cupboard or the area over a central heating boiler is ideal because there is a continuous supply of gentle heat and the air can circulate freely. The prepared food should be placed on an open rack—a wire rack or cooling tray is ideal.

If this method of preservation appeals to you, you may want to invest in an electrical 'food dehydrator' that dries larger quantities of foods in each batch.

Drying Fruit

Illustrated in colour on pages 146 and 147

Apples and pears Prepare by peeling and coring. Slice apples into rings about 0.5 cm ($\frac{1}{4}$ inch) thick, and cut pears in half or into quarters using a stainless steel knife. Put the prepared fruit in a solution of 50 g (2 oz) salt to 4.8 litres (1 gallon) water, to prevent discoloration. Leave in the solution for 5 minutes, then dry on a cloth.

Spread the fruit on baking sheets or trays, or thread rings of fruit on thin sticks and place across a roasting tin. Dry in a cooling oven, in an airing cupboard or over a central heating boiler until leathery in texture. This will take 6–8 hours. When dried, remove the fruit from the heat and allow to cool. Pack into jars, tins, or paper-lined boxes—they needn't be airtight containers—and store in a cool, dry, well-ventilated place.

Plums and apricots For best results, cut the fruit in half and remove the stones, although smaller fruit can be dried whole. Wash the fruit, dry carefully and arrange, cut sides up, on trays or baking sheets. Dry as for apples and pears.

To cook dried fruit Soak in cold water overnight or for several hours before use. Drain well before using for stewed fruit or in puddings and pies.

Drying Vegetables

Mushrooms Wipe with a damp cloth; do not wash. Leave whole or cut into slices or quarters. Dry as for apples etc. Add dried mushrooms to soups, stews and casseroles. Soak dried mushrooms in water for 30 minutes before frying or grilling.

Onions Remove the skins and cut into 0.5-cm ($\frac{1}{4}$-inch) slices. Separate into rings and dip each ring into boiling water for 30 seconds. Drain, dry and spread on trays or thread on to thin sticks. Dry as for apples etc. Soak dried onions in hot water for 30 minutes. Drain and dry on absorbent kitchen paper before frying or grilling.

Drying Herbs

Illustrated in colour on page 136

Herbs should be picked on a dry day, when the dew has lifted, before the sun dispels the volatile oils. The best time is shortly before they flower—usually June or July—when they contain the maximum amount of oil. Pick off any damaged leaves and rinse dusty stems and leaves quickly in cold water.

Herbs can be dried in the sun over a period of four to five days. However, this method tends to result in loss of the colour and aromatic properties of some herbs. It is much quicker and better to dry them in an airing cupboard or the oven on the lowest possible setting, both with the door left slightly ajar to allow air to circulate. The oven temperature should not exceed 32°C (90°F). Place the herbs on wire racks covered with muslin or cheesecloth which lets the air through. Herbs will dry in an airing cupboard in 3–5 days and in 2–3 hours in the oven. From time to time, turn the herbs gently to ensure quicker, more even drying.

Herbs can also be dried very successfully in a microwave oven. Place herbs on a paper towel, in a single layer, and cook at high for 2–3 minutes, depending on the quantity. When cool, crumble between your fingers and store.

Parsley and mint will keep green if dipped in boiling water for 1 minute and then dried fairly quickly.

Herbs are dry when the stem and leaves become brittle but remain green and will crumble easily when rubbed between the fingers. If you are not quite sure about this, check by putting the dried herbs into a glass jar, cover it and watch for a few days to see if moisture appears. If it does, turn them out and continue the drying process. If the leaves turn brown you know that they have been over-dried and are of no further use.

It is also possible to dry herbs by hanging bunches in a dry place. Pick the stems as long as possible, tie them loosely in small bunches and suspend them out of direct sunlight. If this is difficult, place them in brown paper bags and hang them up. Check at regular intervals after three days until they are dry.

Once dried, you can strip the leaves from the stems and crumble them for storage. Don't rub so hard that they turn to dust as some of the flavouring properties will be lost. The exception are bay leaves which should be left whole as they contain large amounts of oil and, if crushed, they will release it before it is required. Store dried herbs in small screw-topped jars.

When using dried herbs, remember that they have a more concentrated flavour than fresh. Use half the quantity if substituting dried herbs for fresh in a recipe. You can make your own bouquets garni by placing a bay leaf, a sprig of parsley and a sprig of thyme on a square of muslin cloth and tying into a small bag with string. Dry and add to soups, stews and casseroles.

SPICED BLACK PEPPER

15 g ($\frac{1}{2}$ oz) freshly ground black pepper
15 g ($\frac{1}{2}$ oz) dried marjoram
15 g ($\frac{1}{2}$ oz) dried thyme
15 g ($\frac{1}{2}$ oz) dried rosemary
15 g ($\frac{1}{2}$ oz) winter savory
15 g ($\frac{1}{2}$ oz) ground mace

Mix all the ingredients together well, sift them and store in a labelled jar.

HERB SPICE

25 g (1 oz) ground dried bay leaves
25 g (1 oz) dried thyme
25 g (1 oz) dried marjoram
25 g (1 oz) dried basil
22 ml (1$\frac{1}{2}$ level tbsp) ground mace
7.5 ml (1$\frac{1}{2}$ level tsp) nutmeg
7.5 ml (1$\frac{1}{2}$ level tsp) freshly ground pepper
7.5 ml (1$\frac{1}{2}$ level tsp) ground cloves

Mix and sift the herbs and spices together. Put into clean, dry glass jars and label. This herb spice may be used for flavouring meat or sausage dishes, stuffings etc.

MIXED DRIED HERBS

50 g (2 oz) parsley
25 g (1 oz) winter savory
25 g (1 oz) lemon-scented thyme
25 g (1 oz) sweet marjoram

Weigh the herbs before drying. When dry, crumble, mix well and sift. Store in a labelled screw-topped jar.

Short-term Preserves

Although salting and curing are no longer recommended as practical methods of preserving meat and fish in the home, it is possible to preserve some meat and fish for a limited length of time by other methods. This is particularly useful if you haven't got a freezer or when cooking ahead for a special occasion. Methods of short-term preserving allow foods to be stored for anything from a few days to 3 months, depending on the food and method of preservation.

Sealing with Fat or Clarified Butter

Cooked meat or fish will keep for a longer period if stored under a seal of fat or clarified butter. The seal excludes air and moisture which encourage the growth of bacteria. Once the seal has been broken, the meat or fish should be eaten within a week.

Meat can be prepared in the form of *Rillettes* and stored in the refrigerator for up to 2 months before serving. This method of preserving best suits meats that are naturally fatty, such as pork or duck. It is important to remove all moisture from the meat, so it is first salted and then cooked for a long time until it is very tender. After cooking, the fat is strained off the meat and reserved. The meat is then separated into strands with a fork and piled into small pots or a large dish before being covered with the reserved fat.

Potted beef or shrimps make useful starters for a dinner party as they can be made a few days in advance and sealed under clarified butter until required.

Preserving in Vinegar

Vinegar acts as a preservative and some fish can be stored in much the same way as fruit and vegetables are pickled (see pages 74–91). Fish prepared in this way will keep for about a month in the refrigerator.

RILLETTES DE PORC

1 kg (2 lb) belly or neck of pork, rinded and
  boned
salt
500 g (1 lb) back pork fat
1 garlic clove, skinned and bruised
bouquet garni
freshly ground black pepper

Rub the meat well with the salt and leave it to stand for 4–6 hours. Cut the meat into thin strips along the grooves left after the bones were removed. Cut the pork fat into thin strips and put the meat and fat into an ovenproof dish. Bury the garlic clove and bouquet garni in the centre, season with a little pepper and add 75 ml (5 tbsp) water. Cover and cook in the oven at 150°C (300°F) mark 2, for about 4 hours. Discard the bouquet garni and garlic and season well. Strain the fat from the meat and when well drained, pound it slightly with the back of a wooden spoon, then pull it into fine shreds with two forks. Pile lightly into a glazed earthenware or china jar and pour the fat over the top. Cover with foil and keep in a cool place or in the refrigerator.

Rillettes should be soft-textured, so allow to come to room temperature before serving. Serve with toast or French bread. Store for 1–2 months but use within a week once the seal of fat is broken.

Serves 4–6

POTTED BEEF

500 g (1 lb) stewing steak, cut into 1-cm
  ($\frac{1}{2}$-inch) cubes
150 ml ($\frac{1}{4}$ pint) beef stock
1 clove
1 blade of mace
salt and freshly ground pepper
50 g (2 oz) butter, melted
fresh bay leaves (optional)

Place the meat in a casserole with the stock, clove, mace and seasonings. Cover and cook in the oven at 180°C (350°F) mark 4 for $2\frac{1}{2}$–3 hours, until tender. Remove the clove and mace and drain off the stock, setting it aside. Mince the meat twice or place it in a blender and blend for several minutes, until smooth. Add half the melted butter and enough of the reserved stock to moisten. Press the mixture into small pots and cover with the remaining melted butter. Store in the refrigerator and use within a few days. Serve garnished with fresh bay leaves if possible.

POTTED SHRIMPS

150 g (5 oz) shrimps, peeled
250 g (8 oz) butter
pinch of ground mace
pinch of cayenne pepper
pinch of ground nutmeg

Melt half the butter in a saucepan. Add the shrimps and heat very gently without boiling. Add the seasonings, then pour the shrimps into small pots. Leave them to cool. Gently heat the remaining butter in a pan until it melts, then continue to heat slowly, without browning. Remove from the heat and leave to stand for a few minutes for the salt and sediment to settle, then carefully pour a little clarified butter over the shrimps to cover. Store in the refrigerator and use within a few days.

Unless the pots are really attractive, turn the shrimps out on to individual plates lined with a few lettuce leaves, but try to retain the shape of the pot. Before serving, remove from the refrigerator and leave at room temperature for about 30 minutes. Serve with lemon wedges, brown bread or melba toast and freshly ground pepper.

Serves 4

ROLLMOP HERRINGS

6 small herrings, cleaned and filleted
12 small pickled gherkins
2 medium onions, skinned and thinly sliced
2 bay leaves
2.5 ml ($\frac{1}{2}$ level tsp) mustard seeds
3 whole cloves
6 peppercorns
450 ml ($\frac{3}{4}$ pint) distilled vinegar
60 ml (4 tbsp) salad oil
5 ml (1 level tsp) salt

Roll each herring fillet, skin-side out, firmly around a gherkin and secure with wooden cocktail sticks. Place in a wide-necked jar in layers, alternating with layers of onions, bay leaves, mustard seeds, cloves and peppercorns. Heat the vinegar, oil and salt together and bring just to boiling point, then allow to cool slightly. Pour over the herrings. Cover the jars and leave in the refrigerator to marinate for 2–3 days before serving. The rollmops will keep, under refrigeration, for 3 weeks after they are ready. Serve as an appetiser or with salad.

Makes 12

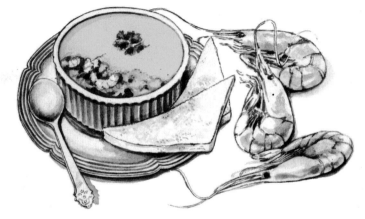

Conserves, Fruits in Alcohol and

Conserves, fruits in alcohol and mincemeats all preserve fruit with the minimum of cooking. Although they do not have the keeping qualities of jams etc. made by the traditional boiling method, the fruits retain a flavour which is very much closer to the original taste of the fruit. Use the same equipment as for jam making and cover and store in the same way (see pages 10 and 12). All these preserves make the most acceptable gifts.

Conserves

These are whole, sometimes chopped, fruits suspended in a thick syrup. In most cases, the fruit is layered with an equal quantity of sugar and left for 24 hours to extract the juices, before boiling for a short time. Fruits which make good conserves are strawberries, raspberries and loganberries.

Conserves make an excellent dessert when served with cream, custard or milk pudding.

Fruits in Alcohol

The flavour of brandy is the most compatible with fruits, although many spirits can be used, such as kirsch with pineapple, cherries or raspberries. These luxurious preserved fruits make delicious desserts.

Mincemeats

Mincemeat was originally a way of preserving meat without using the smoking or salting methods. Today, mincemeat is a mixture of fruits, mostly dried, preserved in alcohol and sugar. The only reminder of the past is the addition of suet.

If mincemeat becomes dry with keeping, stir in a little of the type of alcohol used in the original mixture.

BRANDIED CHERRIES
(*see page 149*)

1. Prick the cherries all over with a darning needle.

2. Put the cherries in a pan with the syrup and cinnamon and poach gently.

3. Drain and cool the cherries, then arrange them in small jars.

4. Dissolve the sugar in the syrup, cool, measure and add an equal quantity of brandy.

5. Pour the brandy syrup over the cherries.

Mincemeats

STRAWBERRY CONSERVE

1.5 kg (3 lb) strawberries, hulled and washed
1.5 kg (3 lb) granulated sugar

Place the strawberries in a large bowl in layers with the sugar. Cover and leave for 24 hours. Put into a saucepan and bring to the boil, stirring until the sugar dissolves. Boil rapidly for 5 minutes. Return the mixture to the bowl, cover and leave for a further 2 days. Return to the pan again and boil rapidly for 10 minutes. Leave to cool for 15 minutes, then pot and cover as for jam.

RASPBERRY LIQUEUR CONSERVE

500 g (1 lb) raspberries
500 g (1 lb) granulated sugar
15 ml (1 tbsp) kirsch or brandy

Place the raspberries and sugar in separate ovenproof containers in the oven at 180°C (350°F) mark 4 for 15 minutes. Mix them together in a large bowl and stir for a few minutes. Leave to stand for 20 minutes. Repeat the stirring and standing three times, then add the kirsch or brandy. Pot in 500-g (1-lb) jars and cover as for jam.

STRAWBERRY CONSERVE *(see above)*

1. Layer the strawberries in a bowl with the sugar. Cover and leave for 24 hours.

2. Pot and cover the conserve as for jam (see page 12).

RICH MINCEMEAT *(see page 150)*

1. Put the ingredients in a bowl, pour in the brandy, cover and leave for 2 days.

2. Stir the mincemeat well and spoon into jars. Cover as for jam (see page 12).

KUMQUAT CONSERVE

1 kg (2 lb) kumquats, washed
1 kg (2 lb) granulated sugar
90 ml (6 tbsp) brandy

Prick the kumquats all over with a needle. Place the fruit in a bowl in layers with the sugar. Cover and leave for 24 hours. Transfer to a saucepan, bring to the boil slowly, stirring until the sugar dissolves. Boil rapidly for 10 minutes. Remove any pips that have risen to the surface. Stir in the brandy. Leave to cool for 15 minutes, then pot and cover as for jam.

KIWI CONSERVE

1 kg (2 lb) kiwi fruit (Chinese gooseberries),
*   peeled*
1 kg (2 lb) granulated sugar

Slice the fruit thickly and place in a bowl in layers with the sugar. Cover and leave for 24 hours. Transfer to a saucepan and bring slowly to the boil, stirring until the sugar dissolves. Boil rapidly for 5 minutes. Leave to cool for 15 minutes, then pot and cover as for jam.

BAR-LE DUC

This famous French conserve originally came from Bar-le Duc in Lorraine. To make it correctly, the currants should be pricked individually so that they remain plump and do not shrivel. This takes a lot of patience and fortunately the conserve is still delicious if it is not done. Bar-le Duc can be made from white currants, if available, black or redcurrants, or a mixture of both.

1 kg (2 lb) black or redcurrants, washed and
*   strung*
1.5 kg (3 lb) granulated sugar

If time, gently prick each currant and place in a bowl with the sugar. Cover and leave overnight. Transfer to a saucepan, bring to the boil slowly and boil for 3 minutes. Remove from the heat and leave for about 30 minutes, until a skin begins to form. Stir gently to distribute the fruit, then pot and cover the conserve as for jam.

BRANDIED PEACHES

500 g (1 lb) fresh peaches or one 822-g (1 lb
*   13-oz) can peach halves*
250 g (8 oz) granulated sugar (if using fresh
*   peaches)*
about 150 ml ($\frac{1}{4}$ pint) brandy or orange
*   flavoured liqueur*

If using fresh peaches, skin the peaches by plunging them into boiling water, then gently peeling off the skins. Halve the peaches and remove the stones. Make a light syrup by dissolving 100 g (4 oz) of the sugar in 300 ml ($\frac{1}{2}$ pint) water. Add the peaches and poach gently for 4–5 minutes. Remove from the heat, drain and cool, then arrange the fruit in small jars. Add the remaining sugar to the reserved syrup and dissolve it slowly. Bring to the boil and boil to 110°C (230°F), then allow to cool. Measure the syrup and add an equal quantity of brandy or liqueur. Pour over the peaches. Cover as for pickles (see page 75).

If using canned peaches, drain the syrup from the peaches and put it in a saucepan (this size can yields about 450 ml ($\frac{3}{4}$ pint) syrup). Reduce the syrup to half the quantity by boiling gently, remove from the heat and cool. Prick the peaches with a fine skewer or darning needle and place in small jars. Add brandy or liqueur to the syrup and pour over the fruit. Cover as for pickles (see page 75).

Bottled peaches (page 129)
OVERLEAF: Top (from left): *Dried pears,*
Drying apple rings (page 138), Salting beans
(page 131)
Bottom (from left): *Sauerkraut (page 132),*
Storing walnuts, Storing apples (page 136)

BRANDIED CHERRIES

These are a good accompaniment to chicken.

500 g (1 lb) fresh cherries, washed
250 g (8 oz) granulated sugar
1 cinnamon stick
about 150 ml ($\frac{1}{4}$ pint) brandy

Prick the cherries all over with a darning needle. Make a light syrup by dissolving 100 g (4 oz) of the sugar in 300 ml ($\frac{1}{2}$ pint) water. Add the cherries and cinnamon stick and poach gently for 4–5 minutes. Remove from the heat and drain, reserving the syrup but removing the cinnamon stick. Cool, then arrange the fruit in small jars. Add the remaining sugar to the reserved syrup and dissolve it slowly. Bring to the boil and boil to 110°C (230°F), then allow to cool. Measure the syrup and add an equal quantity of brandy. Pour over the cherries. Cover as for pickles (see page 75).

ORANGE SLICES IN COINTREAU
Illustrated in colour on page 158

6 firm oranges, washed
1$\frac{1}{2}$ quantity sugar syrup (see page 120)
1 small cinnamon stick
5 ml (1 level tsp) whole cloves
150 ml ($\frac{1}{4}$ pint) Cointreau

Cut the oranges into 0.5 cm ($\frac{1}{4}$ inch) thick slices. Place in a saucepan with the sugar syrup. Add the spices and poach gently for about 45 minutes until tender. Remove from the heat and drain, reserving the syrup but removing the cinnamon stick. Cool, then arrange the fruit in jars, adding a few of the cloves. Add the liqueur to the remaining syrup and pour over the orange slices. Cover as for pickles (see page 75).

BRANDIED PINEAPPLE

1 small fresh pineapple or one 822-g (1 lb 13-oz) can pineapple pieces
250 g (8 oz) granulated sugar (if using fresh pineapple)
3 whole cloves
5 cm (2 inches) cinnamon stick
150 ml ($\frac{1}{4}$ pint) brandy or kirsch

If using fresh pineapple, peel and trim leaves, remove the central core and as many 'eyes' as possible. Cut into chunks. Make a light syrup by dissolving 100 g (4 oz) of the sugar in 300 ml ($\frac{1}{2}$ pint) water. Add the cloves, cinnamon and pineapple and poach gently for 10 minutes. Remove from the heat, drain and cool, then arrange the fruit in a wide-necked bottle. Add the remaining sugar to the reserved syrup and dissolve it slowly. Bring to the boil and boil to 110°C (230°F), then allow to cool. Measure the syrup and add an equal quantity of brandy or kirsch. Pour over the fruit. Cover as for pickles (see page 75).

If using canned pineapple, drain the juice from the pineapple and put it in a saucepan. Add the cloves and cinnamon and simmer gently until a syrupy consistency. Add the pineapple pieces and simmer for a further 10 minutes. Remove from the heat and add the brandy or kirsch. Cool, then place the fruit into a wide-necked bottle. Pour on the syrup and cover as for pickles (see page 75).

DRUNKARD'S PLUMS

1 kg (2 lb) ripe plums, washed
300 ml ($\frac{1}{2}$ pint) sugar syrup (see page 120)
300 ml ($\frac{1}{2}$ pint) sherry

Place the plums in a saucepan with the sugar syrup and poach gently for 4–5 minutes until the skins split. Remove from the heat and drain, reserving the syrup and allowing it to cool. While the plums are still warm, remove the skins, then leave to cool. Arrange the fruit in jars. Add the sherry to the reserved syrup and pour over the plums. Cover as for pickles (see page 75).

Clockwise from top: *Bottled plums, Bottled apricots, Bottled greengages (pages 120–129)*

RICH MINCEMEAT

500 g (1 lb) currants
500 g (1 lb) sultanas
500 g (1 lb) seedless raisins
250 g (8 oz) chopped mixed peel
250 g (8 oz) cooking apples, peeled, cored and
  grated
100 g (4 oz) blanched almonds, chopped
500 g (1 lb) soft dark brown sugar
175 g (6 oz) shredded suet
5 ml (1 level tsp) ground nutmeg
5 ml (1 level tsp) ground cinnamon
grated rind and juice of 1 lemon
grated rind and juice of 1 orange
300 ml ($\frac{1}{2}$ pint) brandy

Place the dried fruits, peel, apples and almonds in a large bowl. Add the sugar, suet, spices, lemon and orange rind and juice and brandy, and mix all the ingredients together thoroughly. Cover the mincemeat and leave to stand for 2 days. Stir well and put into jars. Cover as for jam (see page 12). Allow at least 2 weeks to mature before using.

Makes about 2.75 kg (5$\frac{1}{2}$ lb)

Note For mincemeat that will keep well, use a firm, hard type of apple, such as Wellington; a juicy apple, such as Bramley Seedling, may make the mixture too moist.

CHERRY AND NUT MINCEMEAT
Illustrated in colour on page 175

175 g (6 oz) currants
175 g (6 oz) seedless raisins
175 g (6 oz) sultanas
250 g (8 oz) glacé cherries
250 g (8 oz) cooking apples, peeled, cored and
  grated
100 g (4 oz) walnuts, chopped
100 g (4 oz) shredded suet
375 g (12 oz) demerara sugar
5 ml (1 level tsp) ground mixed spice
300 ml ($\frac{1}{2}$ pint) brandy or rum

Place all the ingredients in a large bowl. Mix well together, cover and leave for 2 days. Stir well and put into jars. Cover as for jam (see page 12). Allow at least 2 weeks to mature before using.

Makes about 1.5 kg (3 lb)

Note See Rich mincemeat note opposite about the choice of apples.

SPICY CARROT MINCEMEAT

250 g (8 oz) cooking apples, peeled and cored
100 g (4 oz) carrots, trimmed and peeled
500 g (1 lb) sultanas
250 g (8 oz) currants
grated rind and juice of 1 orange
100 g (4 oz) shredded suet
pinch of salt
100 g (4 oz) demerara sugar
60 ml (4 tbsp) sherry
5 ml (1 level tsp) ground nutmeg
5 ml (1 level tsp) ground cloves
5 ml (1 level tsp) ground cinnamon
5 ml (1 level tsp) ground allspice

Finely grate the apples and carrots. Place in a large bowl and add all the remaining ingredients. Mix well together. Put into jars and cover as for jam (see page 12). Allow 2 weeks to mature before using.

Makes about 1.3 kg (2$\frac{3}{4}$ lb)

ELIZA ACTON'S MINCEMEAT

4 lemons
375 g (12 oz) currants
375 g (12 oz) raisins
375 g (12 oz) chopped mixed peel
375 g (12 oz) apples, peeled and cored (prepared weight)
375 g (12 oz) shredded suet
500 g (1 lb) granulated sugar
5 ml (1 level tsp) ground mace
5 ml (1 level tsp) ground cloves
5 ml (1 level tsp) ground ginger
5 ml (1 level tsp) salt
300 ml ($\frac{1}{2}$ pint) rum or brandy

Place the lemons in a saucepan of water, bring to the boil and simmer until tender. Meanwhile, mince the fruit and suet and mix well together. When the lemons are soft, remove the pips and mince the rind and pulp. Add to the rest of the fruit with the sugar, spices, salt and rum or brandy (use more if liked). Mix well and put into jars. Cover as for jam (see page 12). Allow at least 2 weeks to mature before using.

This mincemeat improves with storing and keeps for 1 year. If necessary, add a little more rum or brandy to moisten.

Makes about 3 kg (6 lb)

APRICOT AND ORANGE MINCEMEAT

250 g (8 oz) dried apricots, soaked overnight
grated rind and juice of 2 large oranges
250 g (8 oz) raisins
250 g (8 oz) currants
250 g (8 oz) sultanas
100 g (4 oz) chopped mixed peel
500 g (1 lb) demerara sugar
100 g (4 oz) blanched almonds, chopped
250 g (8 oz) shredded suet
30 ml (2 level tbsp) marmalade
10 ml (2 level tbsp) ground mixed spice
2.5 ml ($\frac{1}{2}$ level tsp) salt
60 ml (4 tbsp) sherry
100 ml (4 fl oz) rum

Drain the apricots, pat dry with absorbent kitchen paper and chop. Mix the grated orange rind and juice, the dried fruit, mixed peel, sugar, almonds, suet, marmalade, spice and salt thoroughly together. Cover and leave for 24 hours. Add the sherry and rum and stir well to mix. Pot and cover as for jam (see page 12).

Makes about 2 kg (4 lb)

Drinks and Liqueurs

Fruit drinks such as fruit syrups, squashes, cordials and liqueurs are most rewarding to make at home. As well as tasting delicious, fruit syrups and squashes are economical to make and full of vitamins. Almost any fruit can be used. Autumn is an excellent time to prepare them as many of the fruits are ripe then and some can simply be gathered from the garden or the hedgerows. Home-made squashes and cordials are health giving drinks which are usually diluted before drinking. They will keep for about 6 weeks unopened. Making liqueurs during autumn is especially well timed as the liqueur has three months to mature before the Christmas season. Syrups, squashes and cordials need sterilising, liqueurs do not.

Note When using, rose-hip syrup, squash and cordial recipes, refer to the Fruit syrup method for detailed bottling and sterilising instructions (see page 153).

Liqueurs
Liqueurs are made by infusing fruits in spirits for several weeks or months and require no fermentation. After infusion and before bottling, the fruits can be eaten separately as a dessert. Liqueurs are surprisingly simple to prepare and keep well. Serve with coffee after dinner.

Fruit Syrups
These are made with soft berry fruits such as blackberries, blackcurrants, raspberries, bilberries, loganberries and strawberries etc. The fruit must be fresh and ripe; choose fruit that is too ripe for bottling or jam making. Use fruit syrups as a sauce with ice creams, steamed or baked puddings and desserts; or serve as a drink diluted with water or soda water, or with hot water for a winter drink.

No water is necessary when extracting the juice from fruit; except when using blackcurrants—300 ml ($\frac{1}{2}$ pint) per 500 g (1 lb), and blackberries—300 ml ($\frac{1}{2}$ pint) per 3 kg (6 lb). There are three methods of extracting the juice:

Method 1 Wash the fruit and drain thoroughly. Place in a bowl over a saucepan of boiling water. Break up the fruit with a wooden spoon or stainless steel masher, and leave for about 1 hour for 3 kg (6 lb) fruit until the juice flows freely, keeping the pan replenished with boiling water as it evaporates. This method ensures that the fruit is not overcooked, which tends to spoil both the colour and flavour.

Method 2 Wash the fruit and drain thoroughly. Place in a saucepan with the water (if used) and bring quickly to the boil, stirring continuously. Boil for 1 minute, crushing any whole fruit with a wooden spoon or stainless steel masher.

Method 3 There are various types of electric juice extractor on the market which can be used. Follow the manufacturer's instructions.

CHERRY BRANDY
(see page 160)

1. Prick the cherries all over with a darning needle.

2. Put the fruit and sugar in layers in a jar and cover with brandy.

Remove the fruit from the heat, if necessary, and strain overnight through a scalded jelly bag or cloth. Transfer the pulp to a clean linen cloth and fold over the ends. Twist them in opposite directions to squeeze out as much juice as possible. Measure the extracted juice, adding 375 g (12 oz) sugar to every 600 ml (1 pint) juice. Stir thoroughly until dissolved.

Pour into small sterilised bottles to within 4 cm (1½ inches) of the top for corks, or under 2.5 cm (1 inch) for screw type caps, to leave room for expansion on heating. Before use, bottles must be sterilised and corks, caps, stoppers, etc., must be submerged in boiling water for 15 minutes. Seal the bottles with a cork, which must be cut off level with the top of the bottle and covered by a metal or plastic screw cap; a screw stopper; or a cork alone which must be tied with wire or string to prevent being blown off during the sterilisation process.

To sterilise, place the bottles of fruit drink in a deep pan padded on the base and between the bottles with thick cloth or newspaper. Fill to the base of the corks, caps or stoppers with warm water, then raise to simmering point and maintain this temperature for 20 minutes. (If you have a thermometer, maintain at 77°C (170°F) for 30 minutes.) Remove the bottles. If using corks only, seal by brushing over with or dipping into melted sealing wax as soon as the bottles are cold and corks dry (see page 110).

Store in a cool dry place; the bottles may be wrapped in brown paper to preserve the colour of the syrup. Serve as a sauce or dilute with water or soda water to drink.

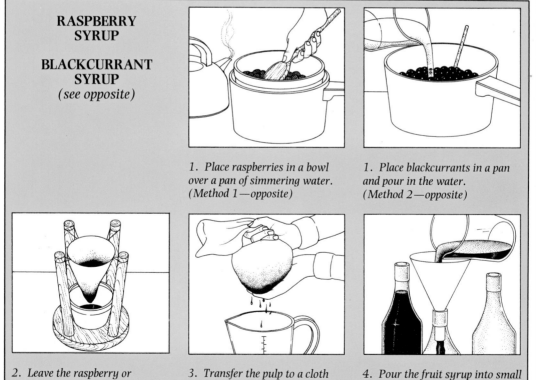

RASPBERRY SYRUP

BLACKCURRANT SYRUP
(see opposite)

1. Place raspberries in a bowl over a pan of simmering water. (Method 1—opposite)

1. Place blackcurrants in a pan and pour in the water. (Method 2—opposite)

2. Leave the raspberry or blackcurrant pulp to strain through a jelly bag overnight.

3. Transfer the pulp to a cloth and squeeze out as much juice as possible.

4. Pour the fruit syrup into small sterilised bottles and sterilise (see above).

RASPBERRY GIN

500 g (1 lb) raspberries
375 g (12 oz) granulated sugar
one 75-cl (26.4-fl oz) bottle of gin

Place all the ingredients in a jar and seal securely. Leave in a dark place for 3 months, shaking the jar every day for the first month, then occasionally. Strain the liqueur through muslin, then bottle. Serve as a liqueur.

Makes about 1.3 litres (2¼ pints)

PRUNE LIQUEUR

500 g (1 lb) prunes
one 70-cl bottle of red wine
150 g (5 oz) granulated sugar
150 ml (¼ pint) rum

Pierce the prunes right through using a skewer but do not remove the stones. Place them in a large glass jar. Pour the wine into a large saucepan, add the sugar and heat gently until just beginning to boil. Remove from the heat and stir in the rum. Pour the wine and rum mixture over the prunes to cover. Leave until cold, then seal the jar. Leave in a dark place for at least 1 month before drinking. To serve, place a prune on a cocktail stick in a small glass and pour in enough liqueur to cover the fruit.

Makes about 750 ml (1¼ pints)

ORANGE LIQUEUR

peel of 6 thin-skinned oranges
600 ml (1 pint) white wine
150 g (5 oz) caster sugar
150 ml (¼ pint) white rum

Cut the orange peel into quarters, then cut into strips as fine as possible. Leave the wine in the wine bottle and add as many strips of peel as possible by pushing them down the neck of the bottle with a wooden spoon. Cork the bottle and leave in a dark place for at least 2 months, shaking the bottle several times a week. Strain the peel and wine through a nylon sieve, pressing the peel lightly with the back of a wooden spoon. Add the sugar to the wine and stir until dissolved. Add the rum and mix well together, then strain through muslin. Bottle and leave for 1 month before using. Serve as a liqueur.

Makes about 600 ml (1 pint)

APRICOT LIQUEUR

500 g (1 lb) apricots, washed
500 g (1 lb) granulated sugar
one 70-cl bottle of dry white wine
300 ml ($\frac{1}{2}$ pint) gin

Cut the apricots in half and remove the stones. Crack the stones in a nutcracker and remove the kernels from inside, then blanch the kernels in boiling water for 1 minute. Place the apricots, sugar and wine in a saucepan and heat gently, stirring, until the sugar has dissolved. Bring to the boil, then remove from the heat and stir in the gin and apricot kernels. Pour into a large bowl or jug, cover tightly and leave for 5–6 days. Strain through muslin, then bottle the liqueur. Leave for at least 1 month before using.

Makes about 1.5 litres ($2\frac{1}{2}$ pints)

ORANGE GIN

peel of 10 medium oranges
one 75-cl (26.4-fl oz) bottle of gin
250 g (8 oz) granulated sugar
300 ml ($\frac{1}{2}$ pint) water

Cut the peel of each orange into eight sections and place on a baking sheet. Heat in the oven at the lowest setting for several hours until they are hard and brittle. Place the peel in a wide-necked glass jar and pour in the gin to cover. If necessary, remove some of the peel or add more gin to ensure that the gin covers the peel. Seal the jar and leave in a dark place for 6 weeks, shaking the jar several times a week.

Put the sugar and water in a pan and heat gently, stirring until the sugar has dissolved, then bring to the boil and boil for 3 minutes. Remove from the heat and leave until cold. Strain the peel and gin through a nylon sieve, pressing the peel lightly with the back of a wooden spoon. Add the syrup to the orange gin, then strain through muslin. Pour into small bottles and seal. Store in a cool place for 2 months before using. Serve as a liqueur.

Makes about 1.2 litres (2 pints)

155

ROSE-HIP SYRUP

Rose-hips give a syrup which is very rich in vitamin C compared to other fruit syrups, so a different method is used when making it to ensure that the highest possible amount of the vitamin is retained.

2.7 litres (4½ pints) water
1 kg (2 lb) ripe rose-hips
500 g (1 lb) granulated sugar

Have ready 1.8 litres (3 pints) boiling water, preferably in an aluminium or unchipped enamel saucepan. Press the rose-hips through the coarse blade of a mincer and place immediately in the boiling water. Bring to the boil again. As soon as the mixture boils, remove the pan from the heat and leave for 15 minutes. Pour into a scalded jelly bag and allow the bulk of the juice to drip through. Return the pulp to the saucepan, add 900 ml (1¼ pints) boiling water, re-boil and allow to stand without further heating for another 10 minutes, then strain as before. Pour the juice into a clean saucepan and simmer to reduce until it measures about 900 ml (1½ pints), then add 500 g (1 lb) sugar, stir until dissolved and boil for a further 5 minutes.

Pour the hot syrup into hot bottles and seal at once (see Fruit syrups on pages 152–3). Sterilise for 5 minutes. If using corks only, seal with melted paraffin or sealing wax (see page 110).

Note It is advisable to use small bottles, as the syrup will not keep for more than a week or two once it is opened. About 10 ml (2 tsp) of this syrup each day is recommended as a pleasant way to improve a diet lacking in vitamin C.

LEMON SQUASH

about 4 lemons, washed
750 g (1½ lb) granulated sugar
450 ml (¾ pint) water
1.25 ml (¼ level tsp) citric acid (optional)

Grate the rind of 2 lemons and squeeze out the juice from all the fruit to make 300 ml (½ pint) juice. Place the lemon rind, sugar and water in a saucepan and heat slowly until boiling, stirring until the sugar has dissolved. Strain into a jug, add the lemon juice and citric acid, if used, and stir well. Pour into bottles, seal and sterilise (see Fruit syrups on pages 152–3).

To serve, dilute with water or soda water—allow 1 part squash to 2–3 parts water, according to taste. Do not store for longer than 1–2 months, as the colour and flavour deteriorate.

Makes about 900 ml (1½ pints)

Making kir with Cassis (page 161)

ORANGE SQUASH

about 3 oranges, washed
750 g (1½ lb) granulated sugar
450 ml (¾ pint) water
15 g (½ oz) citric acid

Grate the rind of the oranges, squeeze out the juice and measure 300 ml (½ pint) juice. Place the orange rind, sugar and water in a saucepan and heat slowly until boiling, stirring until the sugar has dissolved. Strain into a jug, add the orange juice and citric acid, and stir well. Pour into bottles, seal and sterilise (see Fruit syrups on pages 152–3).

To serve, dilute with water or soda water—allow 1 part squash to 2–3 parts water, according to taste. Do not store for longer than 1–2 months, as the colour and flavour deteriorate.

Makes about 900 ml (1½ pints)

GINGER CORDIAL

25 g (1 oz) root ginger, bruised
500–750 g (1–1½ lb) granulated sugar
7.5 ml (1½ level tsp) tartaric acid
½ a lemon, washed and sliced
4.8 litres (8 pints) boiling water

Place the ginger, sugar (use the larger amount if you like sweet ginger cordial), tartaric acid and lemon into a large bowl. Cover with the boiling water. Stir until the sugar has dissolved, then leave for 3–4 days. Strain through muslin. Pour into bottles, seal and sterilise (see Fruit syrups on pages 152–3).

This cordial is ready to drink, undiluted, after a few days.

Makes about 4.8 litres (8 pints)

ELDERFLOWER CORDIAL

10 large elderflower heads
1 kg (2 lb) granulated sugar
2 lemons, washed and sliced
25 g (1 oz) tartaric acid
2.4 litres (4 pints) boiling water

Place all the ingredients in a bowl. Cover and leave for 24 hours, stirring occasionally. Strain through muslin. Pour into bottles, seal and sterilise (see Fruit syrups on pages 152–3). To serve, dilute to taste.

Makes about 2.1 litres (3½ pints)

Orange slices in Cointreau (page 149)

APRICOT BRANDY

12 apricots, washed
600 ml (1 pint) brandy
225 g (8 oz) caster sugar

Cut the fruit into small pieces, reserving the stones. Crack open the stones to obtain the kernels, crush the kernels and place in a jar with the fruit. Add the brandy and sugar, seal the jar and shake to dissolve the sugar. Leave in a dark place for 1 month, shaking the jar several times a week. Strain off the fruit and eat separately. Bottle the liqueur and store until required.

Makes about 750 ml (1¼ pints)

VARIATION
Peach brandy
Follow the recipe above using peaches instead of apricots.

CHERRY BRANDY

500 g (1 lb) Morello cherries, washed
75 g (3 oz) caster sugar
600 ml (1 pint) brandy

Either remove the stalks from the cherries or cut them within 0.5 cm (¼ inch) of the fruit. Dry the cherries and prick all over with a darning needle. Put the fruit and sugar in alternate layers into a wide-necked jar. Cover with the brandy, then seal the jar. Leave in a dark place for at least 3 months, shaking the jar 2 or 3 times a week until the brandy is a rich cherry colour. Strain off the fruit and eat separately. Bottle the liqueur and store until required.

Makes about 750 ml (1¼ pints)

SLOE GIN

500 g (1 lb) sloes, washed and stripped
75–100 g (3–4 oz) granulated sugar
a few drops of almond essence
75-cl (26.4-fl oz) bottle of gin

Prick the sloes all over with a darning needle and put them into a screw-topped jar. Add the sugar and almond essence. Cover with gin, then screw down tightly. Leave in a dark place for 3 months, shaking occasionally. Strain the gin through muslin until clear. Bottle the gin and leave until required.

Makes about 900 ml (1½ pints)

PINEAPPLE LIQUEUR

1 fresh pineapple
granulated sugar
brandy

Remove the skin and 'eyes' from the pineapple and slice very thinly. Place in a large bowl, sprinkle with a little sugar, cover and leave for 24 hours. Strain off the juice, measure it and add an equal amount of brandy. With each 300 ml (½ pint) brandy, add 50 g (2 oz) sugar. Pour into a screw-topped jar with a few slices of the fresh pineapple, then screw down tightly. Leave in a dark place for 3 weeks. Strain off the fruit and eat separately. Bottle the liqueur and store until required.

CASSIS
Illustrated in colour on page 157

Cassis, drunk with chilled dry white wine, is known as kir. Put a dash of cassis and a twist of lemon rind into a wine glass and fill with white wine.

500 g (1 lb) blackcurrants, washed and strung
600 ml (1 pint) gin or brandy
granulated sugar

Crush the blackcurrants. Place with the gin or brandy in screw-topped jars, then screw down tightly. Leave in a dark place for about 2 months. Strain, then add 175 g (6 oz) sugar to each 600 ml (1 pint) liquid. Pour into a jug, cover and leave for 2 days, stirring at intervals to dissolve the sugar. Strain through muslin. Bottle the liqueur and store for 6 months.

ORANGE WHISKY

2 oranges
100 g (4 oz) granulated sugar
1 cinnamon stick
600 ml (1 pint) whisky

Thinly pare the rind from the oranges. Cut the rind into thin strips and place in a jar. Squeeze out the juice from the fruit and add to the rind with the sugar and cinnamon stick. Pour in the whisky, then seal the jar. Shake to dissolve the sugar. Leave in a cool, dark place for 1 month, shaking the jar occasionally. Strain off the fruit and bottle the whisky. Store until required.

Makes about 750 ml (1¼ pints)

BLACKBERRY LIQUEUR

2 kg (4 lb) blackberries, washed
600 ml (1 pint) water
15 ml (1 level tbsp) whole cloves
15 ml (1 level tbsp) grated nutmeg
about 500 g (1 lb) granulated sugar
300 ml (½ pint) brandy

Place the blackberries, water, cloves and nutmeg in a saucepan. Bring to the boil, then simmer gently for about 15 minutes until the blackberries are soft. Leave until cold.

Strain the blackberries through a piece of muslin. Measure the juice and add 500 g (1 lb) sugar for every 600 ml (1 pint) juice. Pour into a saucepan and heat gently until the sugar has dissolved. Remove from the heat and stir in the brandy. Pour into bottles and store until required.

Makes about 2.1 litres (3½ pints)

Candying and Crystallising

Candying and crystallising are methods of preserving by the use of sugar. Candied fruits are served as a dessert or eaten as sweets. The peel of such citrus fruits as oranges, lemons and citrons can also be candied and is widely used in making cakes, cookies, puddings and in mincemeats, etc. Crystallised flowers, petals or leaves are used as cake or dessert decorations.

Candying

Candying essentially consists of soaking the fruit in a syrup, the sugar content of which is increased daily over a stated period of time until the fruits are completely impregnated with sugar. They can be left plain or be given a crystallised or glacé finish.

Candied fruits are expensive to buy because of the labour involved and the amount of sugar used. The process is possible to do in the home provided certain basic rules are followed. The most suitable fruits to treat are those with a really distinctive flavour—pineapples (illustrated in colour on page 176), peaches, plums, apricots, oranges, cherries, crab-apples and pears. Both fresh and canned fruits may be used, but different types should not be candied in the same sugar syrup.

Fruit and Syrup for Candying

Fresh fruit   The fruits must be ripe, but firm and free from blemishes. Prepare them according to kind. Small whole crab-apples, apricots and plums should be pricked all over with a stainless fork; cherries must be stoned and peaches and pears peeled and halved or cut into quarters. Fruits which are peeled and cut up need not be pricked.

Place the prepared fruits in sufficient boiling water to cover them and cook gently

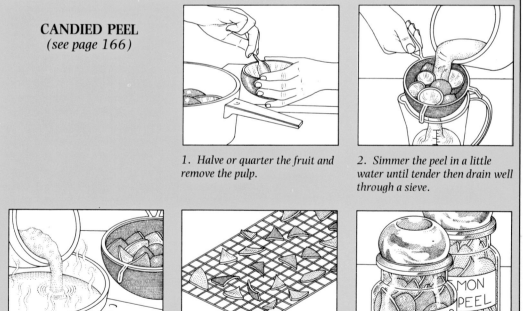

CANDIED PEEL
(see page 166)

1. Halve or quarter the fruit and remove the pulp.

2. Simmer the peel in a little water until tender then drain well through a sieve.

3. Pour the liquid into a pan, add the sugar, boil, add the peel and leave for 2 days.

4. After boiling and soaking the peel for the stated times, leave on a wire rack to dry.

5. Store in labelled, airtight jars.

until just tender. Tough fruits such as apricots may take 10–15 minutes, soft ones need only 2–4 minutes. Overcooking spoils the shape and texture, while undercooking results in slow penetration of the syrup and causes dark colour and toughness.

Canned fruits Use good quality fruit. Pineapple chunks or small rings, plums, sliced and halved peaches and halved apricots are all suitable for candying.

The syrup Granulated sugar is generally recommended for the preparation of the syrup. Part of the sugar may be replaced by glucose—see the chart which gives full details of the proportion of sugar to liquid at the different stages.

Processing Chart for Candied Fruit
Using 500 g (1 lb) prepared fruit (see Notes on page 164).

CANNED FRUIT		
Day	Syrup	Soaking time
1	Drain off canning syrup and make up to 300 ml ($\frac{1}{2}$ pint); add 225 g (8 oz) sugar [or 100 g (4 oz) sugar and 100 g (4 oz) glucose]. Dissolve, bring to the boil and pour over fruit.	24 hours
2	Drain off syrup, add 50 g (2 oz) sugar, dissolve, bring to the boil and pour over fruit.	24 hours
3	Repeat Day 2	24 hours
4	Repeat Day 2	24 hours
5	Repeat Day 2, using 75 g (3 oz) sugar.	48 hours
6	—	—
7	Repeat Day 2, using 75 g (3 oz) sugar.	4 days
8	—	—
9	—	—
10	—	—
11	Dry in the oven at lowest setting or cover lightly and leave in a warm place until quite dry (this may take from a few hours to 2–3 days), turn them 2–3 times.	—

FRESH FRUIT		
Day	Syrup	Soaking time
1	Drain 300 ml ($\frac{1}{2}$ pint) cooking liquid from fruit, add 175 g (6 oz) sugar [or 50 g (2 oz) sugar and 100 g (4 oz) glucose]. Dissolve, bring to the boil and pour over fruit.	24 hours
2	Drain off syrup, add 50 g (2 oz) sugar, dissolve, bring to the boil and pour over fruit.	24 hours
3	Repeat Day 2	24 hours
4	Repeat Day 2	24 hours
5	Repeat Day 2	24 hours
6	Repeat Day 2	24 hours
7	Repeat Day 2	24 hours
8	Repeat Day 2, using a further 75 g (3 oz) sugar.	48 hours
9	—	—
10	Repeat Day 8	4 days
11	—	—
12	—	—
13	—	—
14	Dry as for canned fruit.	—

Notes on Candying Fruit

Amount of syrup If the syrup is not sufficient to cover the fruit, make up more of the same strength, but remember that the amount of sugar to add later must be increased accordingly. For example, if you increase the amount used for fresh fruit on Day 1 to 450 ml ($\frac{3}{4}$ pint) liquid and 250 g (9 oz) sugar, on Day 2 you must add 75 g (3 oz) sugar and on Day 8 add a further 125 g ($4\frac{1}{2}$ oz) sugar.

Soaking time It is important that the fruit should soak for a full 24 hours (or as specified) before the next amount of sugar is added.

Days 5, 7, 8, 10 When the added sugar is increased to 75 g (3 oz), first dissolve the sugar in the strained syrup, then add the fruit and boil it in the syrup for 3–4 minutes.

Day 11 or 14 Once the syrup has reached the consistency of honey, the fruit may be left to soak for as little as 3 days or up to 2–3 weeks, depending on how sweet you like the candied fruit to be.

Finishing the Candied Fruit

When the fruits are thoroughly dried, pack them as described opposite, or give them one of the following finishes before packing.

Crystallised finish Take the pieces of candied fruit and dip each quickly into boiling water. Drain off excess moisture, then roll each piece in caster sugar.

Glacé finish Prepare a fresh syrup, using 500 g (1 lb) sugar and 150 ml ($\frac{1}{4}$ pint) water, bring to the boil and boil for 1 minute. Pour a little of the syrup into a cup. Dip the candied fruit into boiling water for 20 seconds, then dip them one at a time in the syrup, using a skewer. Place the fruit on a wire rack to dry. Cover the rest of the syrup in the pan with a damp cloth and keep it warm (a double pan is useful for this purpose). As the syrup in the cup becomes cloudy, replace it with fresh. Dry the fruit as before, turning it occasionally.

Using the Surplus Syrup

After the fruit has been removed, the surplus syrup can be used in several different ways. It has a delicious fruity flavour and is the consistency of honey. Add to fruit salads and sauces or use to sweeten puddings or stewed fruit.

Packing the Candied Fruit

Pack the fruits in cardboard or wooden boxes, keeping each piece separate between layers of waxed paper. If preferred, they may be stored in jars covered with a piece of paper or cloth over the top. Containers must not be sealed or airtight as the fruit may become mouldy under these conditions.

Crystallising

Flowers, petals and leaves crystallised at home usually look more attractive than the commercially prepared ones and are quite easy to make. The flowers or leaves are simply painted with lightly beaten egg white and then sprinkled with caster sugar.

Most flowers are suitable to use, except those grown from bulbs as they are poisonous. The best results are obtained from flattish flowers with a small number of petals, e.g. violets, primroses, rose petals, fruit blossoms—apple, pear or cherry. Choose

CRYSTALLISED LEAVES
(see page 167)

1. *Paint both sides of the leaves with lightly whisked egg white.*

2. *Dip the wet leaves in caster sugar, shake off any surplus and leave to dry.*

whole flowers that are fresh and free from damage, bruises or brown marks. Pick them in the morning once the dew has lifted and the petals are completely dry. The most popular leaves to crystallise are mint because of their pleasant taste. Be just as selective when picking leaves, making sure they are blemish free.

CARAMELLED FRUITS

about 500 g (1 lb) mixed prepared fruits
250 g (8 oz) preserving sugar
60 ml (4 tbsp) water
5 ml (1 level tsp) powdered glucose
a large pinch of cream of tartar

Suitable fruits are orange or mandarin segments, small pieces of pineapple, black or white grapes, cherries or strawberries. Select only perfect fruit without bruises or defects.

Wash and dry the fruit carefully and drain any canned fruit used thoroughly. Skewer each piece of fruit on a fork or cocktail stick.

Make a syrup of the sugar and water in a small, deep, heavy-based saucepan. When the sugar has dissolved, add the glucose and cream of tartar. Boil gently until it is golden brown and has reached a temperature of 143°C (290°F). Dip the prepared fruit, one piece at a time, into the syrup. Drain well by tapping the fork or stick gently on the edge of the saucepan and place on an oiled marble slab or an oiled plate, and leave, without touching, until quite dry. Then place in paper cases. Serve as petits fours.

FRUIT SWEETMEATS

Unusual and attractive sweets can be made from sweetened fruit pulp. Choose fully ripe fruit, chop roughly and put in a saucepan with a very little water. Simmer until soft, then sieve to remove pips and skin. Add sugar to taste (except in the case of ripe dessert pears). Simmer the sweetened pulp gently, stirring constantly until it is really thick. Spread it out on a baking sheet or on muslin stretched over a wire cooling tray and dry slowly at a low temperature as for candied fruit (see page 163). This may take from a few hours to 2–3 days. When firm enough to handle, cut the fruit into small bars, squares or rounds and roll the pieces in caster sugar.

To vary the sweets, add suitable spices or flavourings, or a little food colouring.

CANDIED PEEL
Illustrated in colour on page 176

oranges, lemons or grapefruit
350 g (12 oz) granulated sugar

Wash or scrub the fruit thoroughly, halve or quarter it and remove the pulp. Simmer the peel in a little water for 1–2 hours until tender. (Change the water 2–3 times when cooking grapefruit peel.) Drain well. Make the liquid up to 300 ml ($\frac{1}{2}$ pint) with water. Add 250 g (8 oz) of the sugar, dissolve over a low heat, then bring to the boil. Add the peel and leave for 2 days.

Drain off the syrup, dissolve another 100 g (4 oz) sugar in it and simmer the peel in this syrup until semi-transparent. The peel can be left in this thick syrup for 2–3 weeks. Drain off the syrup and place the peel on a wire rack to dry. Put the rack in a warm place such as an airing cupboard, in the oven at the lowest setting with the door slightly ajar, or in the residual heat of the oven after cooking. The temperature should not exceed 50°C (120°F) or the fruit may brown and the flavour spoil. The drying will take several hours and is completed when the peel is no longer sticky. If liked, finish the fruit with a glacé or crystallised finish (see page 164). Store in airtight jars or containers.

CANDIED ANGELICA
Pick angelica shoots in April or May.

angelica
salt
granulated sugar

Drop the angelica shoots immediately into brine—7 g ($\frac{1}{4}$ oz) salt to 2.4 litres (4 pints) water—and leave to soak for 10 minutes, to preserve the green colour. Rinse in cold water. Cook the angelica in boiling water for about 5 minutes until quite tender. Drain, retaining the liquid, and scrape the angelica to remove the outer skin.

Using the angelica cooking liquid, make a syrup of 175 g (6 oz) sugar to 300 ml ($\frac{1}{2}$ pint) of the liquid. Place the angelica in a bowl, add the syrup, cover and leave for 24 hours. Drain off the syrup, add 50 g (2 oz) sugar to every 300 ml ($\frac{1}{2}$ pint) and bring to the boil. Pour back into the bowl over the angelica, cover and leave for 24 hours. Repeat this process a further five times until the syrup is of the consistency of runny honey. Boil the angelica for 2–3 minutes at the last addition of the sugar, then leave for 2 days. Dry off on a wire rack in a warm place or in the oven at 110°C (225°F) mark $\frac{1}{4}$. Store in screw-topped jars.

Quick method   Choose tender shoots and cut into 7.5–10-cm (3–4-inch) pieces. Place in a pan with 500 g (1 lb) sugar to each 500 g (1 lb) shoots, cover and leave to stand for 2 days. Bring slowly to the boil and boil until the angelica is clear and green, then drain in a colander. Toss the shoots in caster sugar and dry them off in the oven at 110°C (225°F) mark $\frac{1}{4}$ before storing.

166

CRYSTALLISED FLOWERS, PETALS OR LEAVES

Once crystallised, the flowers, petals or leaves can be stored for 1–2 months in an airtight container in a cool, dry place.

1 egg white
flowers, petals or leaves (see page 164)
caster sugar

Whisk the egg white lightly. Divide the flowers, petals or leaves, leaving a short piece of stalk if possible. Paint both sides of each flower, petal or leaf with egg white and then sprinkle both sides with caster sugar. Shake off surplus sugar and leave to dry. If necessary, sprinkle a second time with sugar to ensure they are evenly coated. Leave to dry completely before storing in a screw-topped jar. Use to decorate cakes or desserts.

CHESTNUTS IN SYRUP

This recipe gives a delicious result, but the chestnuts are not exactly like commercially prepared Marrons glacés, which cannot be reproduced under home conditions.

225 g (8 oz) granulated sugar
225 g (8 oz) glucose or dextrose
180 ml ($\frac{1}{4}$ pint plus 2 tbsp) water
375 g (12 oz) whole chestnuts, peeled and
  skinned (weight after preparation) or one
  439-g (15$\frac{1}{2}$-oz) can chestnuts, drained
a few drops of vanilla essence

Put the granulated sugar, glucose or dextrose and water in a saucepan and heat gently together until the sugars dissolve; bring to the boil. Remove from the heat, add the chestnuts and bring to the boil again. Remove from the heat, cover and leave overnight, preferably in a warm place. On the second day, re-boil the chestnuts and syrup in the pan without the lid. Remove from the heat, cover and again leave overnight. On the third day, add 6–8 drops of vanilla essence and repeat the boiling process as above. Warm some 500-g (1-lb) bottling jars in the oven, fill with the chestnuts and cover with syrup. Seal the jars to make them airtight.

Freezing

Preserving fruits and vegetables by freezing enables you to make good use of an abundant cheap supply or to enjoy the luxury of out-of-season fruit desserts and vegetable dishes. Select fruits and vegetables carefully for freezing, choosing only those which are really fresh and in prime condition, as freezing cannot improve quality. Fruits should be just ripe and vegetables young and tender. Slightly over-ripe fruit can be made into purées before freezing and used for sauces or fool-type desserts. Vegetables need to be blanched before freezing to reduce the micro-organisms and preserve the colour, flavour and nutritive value.

Packaging

Pack fruits and vegetables carefully, for faulty packaging results in loss of quality. Allow 1 cm ($\frac{1}{2}$ inch) headspace for expansion with purées, etc., and with any fruits or vegetables packed in liquid. Exclude as much air as possible before sealing. Special moisture-proof and vapour-proof packaging materials should be used. Some of the most useful are:

Polythene bags These should be of fairly heavy-gauge polythene unless they are to be used for over-wrapping, when thin bags will do. They must be sealed by special covered metal strips or by heat-sealing with an iron. (When using the latter method, shield the polythene with a piece of paper before applying the iron.) Have an assortment of sizes on hand. A self-sealing bag is obtainable.

Polythene sheeting Very useful for covering pies, tarts, cakes, etc. Seal with freezer tape.

Cling film (Use freezer quality.) Ideal as an inner wrapping.

Foil Use standard thickness foil, rather than thinner brands. Ideal as an inner wrapping to exclude all air from the food. Overwrap with a polythene bag.

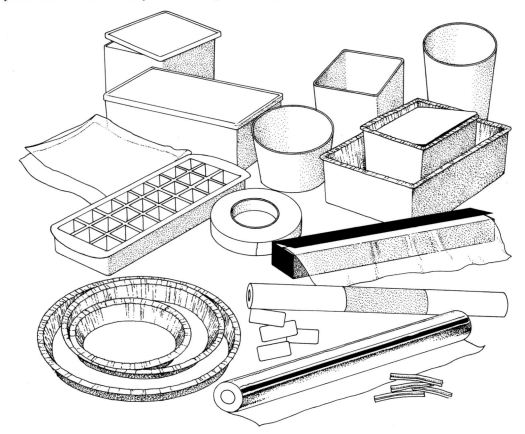

Foil dishes and bowls   Good freezer-to-oven containers for pies, tarts, puddings and vegetable dishes which are to be frozen and re-heated.

Polythene boxes   Have a supply of storage boxes with airtight lids in various sizes. Choose the size carefully, so that there is not too much air space round the food. If necessary, seal the lid with freezer tape.

Waxed tubs   Firm, round, waxed tubs with airtight lids stack well and are suitable for liquids and for soft, squashable foods, e.g. sauces, fruits in syrup and purées. Let the food cool before putting it in the tubs.

Waxed cartons   Box-shaped cartons are usually of a waxed material slightly thinner than that used for tubs. They are used for fruits and vegetables which might squash. The edge of the lid should be sealed with freezer tape.

Waxed paper   Useful for separating asparagus, aubergine slices, etc. within a larger pack.

Freezer tape   Ordinary adhesive tape will not stick at freezer temperatures. Use the special freezer tape to make packages airtight.

Labelling

Label all packages carefully with the date of freezing, contents, weight, number of servings, any special processing, etc. Keep

**FREEZING PINEAPPLE—
DRY SUGAR PACK**
(*see pages 170 and 173*)

1. Core pineapple slices with a plain round biscuit cutter.

2. Pack in rigid containers, sprinkling each pineapple ring with sugar.

**OPEN
FREEZING
RASPBERRIES**
(*see pages 170 and 171*)

1. Spreading raspberries out on a tray before freezing.

2. Packing frozen raspberries into polythene freezer bags to store.

account in a notebook of what is in the freezer and cross off each item as it is used. Use items in rotation. Special adhesive freezer labels can be obtained, but ordinary labels fixed on with freezer tape are equally satisfactory. Tie-on luggage labels can also be used. Waxed containers and foil dishes can be marked with a wax pencil or a waterproof felt-tipped pen. (These markings cannot be removed, so avoid them if you wish to re-use the containers.)

Storing
Once frozen, fruits and vegetables should be stored at a maximum temperature of −18°C (0°F), to prevent any increase in the micro-organisms present. Fluctuating temperatures, or storing at a higher temperature, will cause gradual deterioration, with conditions conducive to growth of spoilage agents.

Freezing Fruit
Preparation Rinse all but soft fruits (such as raspberries) in ice-cold water, a few at a time to prevent undue handling. Drain very thoroughly, as wet fruit dilutes the sugar syrup. Avoid using chipped enamel or iron utensils, which may give the fruit a metallic taste. To prevent fruits such as apricots, peaches, pears and yellow plums from discolouring, keep them covered with water and lemon juice [the juice of 1 large lemon to 1 litre ($1\frac{1}{4}$ pints) water] during preparation.

Packing—Dry pack Suitable for fruit that is to be used for pies or preserves and for small whole fruits (so long as the skins are undamaged) and for those not likely to discolour, e.g. currants, blackberries, strawberries, gooseberries. Pick over, wash, dry on absorbent kitchen paper and use a rigid container to prevent damage during handling and storage.

Packing—Open freezing (dry pack) This method is suitable for small fruit (or pieces of fruit), e.g. raspberries, strawberries, cherries, grapefruit segments. Pick the fruit over, prepare as necessary, spread out on a baking sheet and freeze until firm, then pack for storage (see pages 168–9).

Packing—Dry sugar pack Particularly suitable for soft fruits. Pick over the fruit but don't wash it unless really necessary. The sugar (caster sugar is best) and fruit can be put into the containers in layers or they can be well mixed together before being put in. The fruit is more likely to retain its shape if layered, for when mixed with the sugar, the juice is drawn out, leaving the fruit almost in purée form when thawed.

Packing—In syrup Best for non-juicy fruits or for those which discolour during preparation and storage.

The strength of the syrup used varies with the fruit being treated.

To make the syrup (for quantities, see individual fruit in the following chart), dissolve the sugar in the water by heating gently and bringing to the boil; cover and allow to become quite cold before using.

Use approximately 300 ml ($\frac{1}{2}$ pint) syrup to each 500 g (1 lb) fruit—this is normally enough to cover the fruit. Leave 1–2 cm ($\frac{1}{2}$–$\frac{3}{4}$ inch) headspace for expansion during the freezing. If the fruit tends to float above the level of the syrup in the container, hold it down with a crumpled piece of non-absorbent kitchen paper.

Storage Times for Fruit
Packed in sugar or syrup:	9–12 months
Whole fruits:	6–8 months
Fruit purées:	6–8 months
Fruit juices:	4–6 months

Thawing and Cooking Fruit
If the fruit is to be served raw, thaw it slowly in the unopened container and eat while still slightly chilled; transfer to a serving dish only just before serving. Fruits which tend to discolour, e.g. peaches, benefit from being thawed more rapidly. Stone fruits which tend to discolour should be kept submerged in the syrup while thawing. The times to allow per 500 g (1 lb) fruit are as follows (remembering that dry sugar packs thaw rather more quickly than fruit in syrup):

In a refrigerator	allow 6–8 hours
At room temperature	allow 2–4 hours

For quick thawing, place the container in slightly warm water for 30 minutes–1 hour.

If the fruit is to be cooked, thaw it until the pieces are just loosened. Cook as for fresh fruit, but do not forget when adding sugar that the fruit will already be sweet if it has been packed in sugar or syrup.

Fruit Freezing Chart

Fruit	Preparation
APPLES, sliced	Peel, core and drop into cold water. Cut into 0.5-cm ($\frac{1}{4}$-inch) slices. Blanch for 2–3 minutes and cool in ice-cold water before packing. Useful for pies and flans.
purée	Peel, core and stew in the minimum amount of water—sweetened or unsweetened. Sieve or liquidise. Leave to cool before packing.
APRICOTS	Plunge into boiling water for 30 seconds to loosen the skins, then peel. Pack (a) cut in half or sliced in cold syrup—500 g (1 lb) sugar to 1 litre ($1\frac{3}{4}$ pints) water with some lemon juice added to prevent browning (for each 1 litre ($1\frac{3}{4}$ pints) syrup, allow the juice of 1 lemon). Immerse the apricots by placing a crumpled piece of non-absorbent paper on the fruit, under the lid. (b) Leave whole and freeze in cold syrup (as above). After long storage, an almond flavour may develop round the stone.
BERRIES	All may be frozen by the dry pack method, but the dry sugar pack method is suitable for soft fruits, e.g. raspberries. *Open freeze* Sort the fruit; some whole berries may be left on their sprigs or stems for use as decoration. Spread the fruit on paper-lined trays or baking sheets, put into the freezer until frozen, then pack. *Dry sugar pack* Pack dried whole fruit with 100–175 g (4–6 oz) sugar to 500 g (1 lb) fruit; mix together or layer in rigid containers and seal.
Blackberries	Dry pack or dry sugar pack—250 g (8 oz) sugar to 1 kg (2 lb) fruit. Leave a headspace and pack in rigid containers.
Blueberries	Wash in chilled water and drain thoroughly. Pack (a) dry pack; (b) dry sugar pack—100 g (4 oz) sugar to 500–750 g (1–$1\frac{1}{2}$ lb) fruit; slightly crush berries, mix with sugar until dissolved and then pack in rigid containers; (c) in cold syrup—1 kg (2 lb) sugar dissolved in 1 litre ($1\frac{3}{4}$ pints) water.
Gooseberries	Wash, top and tail and thoroughly dry fruit. Pack (a) dry pack in polythene bags, without sugar; use for pie fillings; (b) in cold syrup, using 1 kg (2 lb) sugar to 1 litre ($1\frac{3}{4}$ pints) water; (c) as purée—stew fruit in a very little water, press through a nylon sieve and sweeten to taste; useful for fools and mousses.
Loganberries	Choose firm, clean fruit. Remove stalks and dry pack in rigid containers or dry sugar pack—see Blackberries.
Strawberries and raspberries	Choose firm, clean dry fruit; remove stalks. Pack (a) dry pack; (b) dry sugar pack—100 g (4 oz) sugar to each 500 g (1 lb) fruit; (c) as purée—press through a nylon sieve or liquidise. Sweeten to taste—about 50 g (2 oz) sugar to each 250 g (8 oz) purée—and freeze in small containers; useful for ice creams, sorbets, sauces or mousses.
Blackcurrants	Wash, dry and string. Pack (a) dry pack for whole fruit; (b) purée—cook to a purée with very little water and brown sugar, according to taste.
Redcurrants	Wash, dry and string, then open freeze on a paper-lined tray or a baking sheet in a single layer until frozen. Pack in rigid containers.

CHERRIES	Remove stalks, wash and dry. Use any of these methods: (a) dry pack; (b) dry sugar pack—250 g (8 oz) sugar to 1 kg (2 lb) stoned cherries, pack in containers; best used stewed for pie fillings; (c) with cold syrup—500 g (1 lb) sugar to 1 litre (1¾ pints) water, mixed with 2.5 ml (½ tsp) ascorbic acid per 1 litre (1¾ pints) syrup; leave headspace. Do not open pack until required as fruit loses colour rapidly on exposure to air.
DAMSONS	Wash in cold water. The skins are inclined to toughen during freezing. Pack (a) as cooked purée, to be used later in pies; (b) halve, remove the stones and pack in cold syrup—500 g (1 lb) sugar to 1 litre (1¾ pints) water. They will need cooking after freezing, then can be used as stewed fruit; (c) poached and sweetened.
FIGS	Wash gently to avoid bruising and remove stems. Pack (a) freeze unsweetened, either whole or peeled, in polythene bags; (b) peel and pack in cold syrup—500 g (1 lb) sugar to 1 litre (1¾ pints) water; (c) leave whole and wrap in foil—suitable for dessert figs.
GRAPEFRUIT	Peel fruit, removing all pith, and segment. Pack (a) in cold syrup—equal quantities of sugar and water; use any juice from the fruit to make up the syrup; (b) dry sugar pack—allowing 250 g (8 oz) sugar to each 500 g (1 lb) fruit, sprinkled over fruit; when juices start to run, pack in rigid containers.
GRAPES	The seedless variety can be packed whole; others should be skinned, pipped and halved. Pack in cold syrup—500 g (1 lb) sugar to 1 litre (1¾ pints) water.
GREENGAGES	Wash in cold water, halve, remove stones and pack in syrup—500 g (1 lb) sugar to 1 litre (1¾ pints) water, with ascorbic acid added (see Apricots). Place in rigid containers. Do not open pack until required, as fruit loses colour rapidly. Skins tend to toughen during freezing.
LEMONS AND LIMES	There are various methods. (a) Squeeze out juice and freeze in ice-cube trays; remove frozen cubes to polythene bags for storage. (b) Leave whole, slice or segment before freezing. (c) Remove all pith from the peel, cut into julienne strips, blanch for 1 minute, cool and pack; use for garnishing dishes. (d) Mix grated lemon rind and a little sugar to serve with pancakes. (e) Remove slivers of peel, free of pith, and freeze in foil packs to add to drinks.
MANGOES	Peel and slice ripe fruit into cold syrup—500 g (1 lb) sugar to 1 litre (1¾ pints) water; add 30 ml (2 tbsp) lemon juice to each 1 litre (1¾ pints) syrup. Serve with additional lemon juice.
MELONS	Cantaloup and honeydew melons freeze quite well (though they lose their crispness when thawed), but the seeds of watermelon make it more difficult to prepare. Cut in half and seed, then cut flesh into balls, cubes or slices and put straight into cold syrup—500 g (1 lb) sugar to 1 litre (1¾ pints) water. Alternatively, use dry pack method, with a little sugar sprinkled over. Pack in polythene bags.

ORANGES	Prepare and pack as for Grapefruit or squeeze and freeze the juice; add sugar, if liked, and freeze in small quantities in containers or as frozen orange cubes. Grate rind for orange sugar as for lemon sugar. Seville oranges may be scrubbed, packed in suitable quantities and frozen whole until required for making marmalade. (Thawing whole frozen fruit in order to cut it up before cooking is not recommended as some discoloration often occurs—use whole fruit method for marmalade. It is advisable to add one eighth extra weight of Sevilles, bitter oranges or tangerines when freezing for subsequent marmalade-making in order to offset pectin loss.)
PEACHES	Really ripe peaches are best skinned and stoned under running water, as scalding them to ease skinning will soften and slightly discolour the flesh. Firm peaches are treated in the usual way. Brush over with lemon juice. Pack (a) halves or slices in cold syrup—500 g (1 lb) sugar to 1 litre (1¾ pints) water, with ascorbic acid added (see Apricots); pack in rigid containers, leaving 1 cm (½ inch) headspace. (b) Purée peeled and stoned peaches by pressing through a nylon sieve or liquidising; mix 15 ml (1 tbsp) lemon juice and 100 g (4 oz) sugar into each 500 g (1 lb) fruit—suitable for sorbets and soufflé-type desserts.
PEARS	It is really only worthwhile freezing pears if you have a large crop from your garden, as they discolour rapidly, and the texture of thawed pears can be unattractively soft. Peel, quarter, core and dip in lemon juice immediately. Poach in syrup—500 g (1 lb) sugar to 1 litre (1¾ pints) water for 1½ minutes. Drain, cool and pack in the cold syrup.
PINEAPPLE	Peel and core, then slice, dice, crush or cut into wedges. Pack (a) unsweetened in boxes, separated by non-stick paper; (b) in cold syrup—500 g (1 lb) sugar to 1 litre (1¾ pints) water—in rigid containers, including any pineapple juice from the preparation; (c) crushed pineapple in rigid containers, allowing 100 g (4 oz) sugar to about 375 g (12 oz) fruit.
PLUMS	Wash, halve and discard stones. Freeze in syrup with ascorbic acid (see Apricots); use 500 g (1 lb) sugar to 1 litre (1¾ pints) water. Pack in rigid containers. Do not open pack until required, as the fruit loses colour rapidly.
RHUBARB	Wash, trim and cut into 1–2.5-cm (½–1-inch) lengths. Heat in boiling water for 1 minute and cool quickly. Pack (a) in cold syrup, using equal quantities of sugar and water; (b) dry pack, to be used later for pies and crumbles.

Fruits not suitable for freezing   Bananas, pomegranates.

Note   Chestnuts can be frozen. Wash the nuts, cover with water and bring to the boil. Drain and peel. Pack in rigid containers. Can be used to supplement raw chestnuts in recipes, or can be cooked and frozen as purée for soups and sweets.

Freezing Vegetables

It is advisable to blanch vegetables before freezing to destroy and reduce the micro-organisms and so that the colour, flavour and nutritive value of the vegetables can be preserved during storage.

When dealing with a glut of vegetables, they can be frozen without blanching, but the storage time is about one quarter of the storage time of blanched vegetables.

Blanching Use a saucepan large enough to hold a colander or wire basket. Place the prepared vegetables in the basket and immerse this in boiling water using about 3.6 litres (6 pints) to 500 g (1 lb) vegetables. Bring the water back to the boil within 1 minute of adding the vegetables. Blanch the vegetables for the recommended length of time (see chart). Blanching times should be timed from the moment when the water returns to the boil. After blanching, quickly remove the vegetables from the boiling water and immediately plunge them into ice-cold water to cool. Drain, dry and pack at once.

Do not add salt until the frozen vegetables are cooked for serving. Do not blanch more than 500 g–1 kg (1–2 lb) vegetables at a time; the same water may be used for blanching successive batches of the same kind of vegetable.

Packing Cool, drain and dry thoroughly. Pack into rigid containers, leaving a little space for expansion for those vegetables that pack tightly, e.g. peas and sweetcorn kernels. If freeflow packs are required, e.g. for peas or beans, open freeze on a paper-lined tray or baking sheet until just firm before packing.

Storage Times for Vegetables

Whole or prepared vegetables:	10–12 months
Vegetable purées:	6–8 months
Mushrooms:	6 months

Thawing and Cooking Vegetables

Put the frozen vegetables in a minimum amount of boiling salted water, about 300 ml ($\frac{1}{2}$ pint) water and 2.5 ml ($\frac{1}{2}$ level tsp) salt to each 500-g (1-lb) pack. Cover the saucepan and simmer until the vegetables are tender.

Alternatively, frozen vegetables can be cooked in a covered pan with just a knob of butter and a little seasoning or herbs; or added to soups or stews without prior cooking. The final cooking should be very short so that the vegetables retain their texture.

**BLANCHING
FRENCH BEANS**
(*see above and page 177*)

1. *Place the beans in a wire basket and dip in boiling water. Blanch for the stated time.*

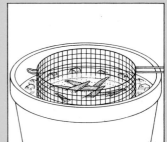

2. *Quickly remove from the boiling water and plunge at once into ice-cold water.*

Cherry and nut mincemeat (page 150)

Vegetable Freezing Chart

Vegetable	Preparation and Packing	Blanching Time
ARTICHOKES, globe	Remove all coarse, outer leaves and stalks and trim tops and stems. Wash well in cold water. Blanch a few at a time, adding a little lemon juice to the blanching water. Cool and drain upside-down. Pack in rigid boxes.	7–10 minutes
ASPARAGUS	Grade into thick and thin stems. Wash in cold water, blanch, cool and drain. Tie into small bundles, packed tips to stalks, separated by non-stick paper.	Thin stems—2 minutes Thick stems—4 minutes
AUBERGINES	Peel and cut roughly into 2.5-cm (1-inch) slices. Blanch, cool, drain and dry on absorbent kitchen paper. Pack in layers, separated by non-stick paper.	4 minutes
AVOCADOS	Prepare in pulp form. Peel and mash, allowing 15 ml (1 tbsp) lemon juice to each avocado. Pack in small polythene containers.	
BEANS	Select young beans. Wash thoroughly. Broad—shell and blanch. French—trim ends and blanch. Runner—slice thickly and blanch. Cool, drain and pack in polythene bags.	Broad—3 minutes French—2–3 minutes Runner—2 minutes
BEETROOT	Choose small beetroots. Wash well and rub skins off after blanching. Beetroot under 2.5 cm (1 inch) in diameter may be frozen whole; large ones should be sliced or diced. Cool, drain and pack in cartons. *Note* Short blanching and long storage can make beetroot rubbery.	Small whole—5–10 minutes Large—45–50 minutes (until tender)
BROCCOLI	Trim off any woody parts and large leaves. Wash in salted water and cut into small sprigs. Blanch, cool and drain well. Pack in boxes in 1–2 layers, tips to stalks, or in polythene bags.	Thin stems—3 minutes Medium stems—4 minutes Thick stems—5 minutes
BRUSSELS SPROUTS	Use small compact heads. Remove outer leaves and wash. Blanch, cool and drain well before packing in polythene bags.	Small—3 minutes Medium—4 minutes
CABBAGE, green and red	Use only young, crisp cabbage. Wash thoroughly and shred finely. Blanch, cool and drain. Pack in small quantities in polythene bags.	$1\frac{1}{2}$ minutes

Candied peel (page 166),
Candied pineapple (page 162)

CARROTS	Scrape, then slice or cut into small dice. Blanch, cool, drain and pack in polythene bags.	3–5 minutes
CAULIFLOWER	Heads should be firm, compact and white. Wash and break into small sprigs, about 5 cm (2 inches) in diameter. Add the juice of a lemon to the blanching water to keep them white. Cool, drain and pack in polythene bags.	3 minutes
CELERY	Trim, removing any strings, and scrub well. Cut into 2.5-cm (1-inch) lengths. Blanch, cool, drain and pack in polythene bags.	3 minutes
CORN ON THE COB	Select young cobs with fresh yellow kernels, not starchy, over-ripe or shrunken. Remove husks and 'silks'. Blanch, cool, drain and pack in polythene bags. *Note* There may be loss of flavour and tenderness after freezing. Thaw before cooking.	Small—4 minutes Medium—6 minutes Large—8 minutes
COURGETTES	Choose young courgettes. Wash and cut into 1-cm ($\frac{1}{2}$-inch) slices. Either blanch and cool, or sauté in a little butter and drain. Pack in polythene bags.	1 minute
FENNEL	Trim and cut into short lengths. Blanch, cool, drain and pack in polythene bags.	3 minutes
KOHLRABI	Use small roots, 5–7 cm (2–3 inches) in diameter. Cut off tops, peel and dice. Blanch, cool, drain and pack in polythene bags.	$1\frac{1}{2}$ minutes
LEEKS	Cut off tops and roots; remove coarse outside leaves. Slice into 1-cm ($\frac{1}{2}$-inch) slices and wash well. Sauté in butter or oil for 4 minutes. Drain, cool and pack in polythene bags.	
MARROW	Choose young marrows. Peel and cut into 1–2.5-cm ($\frac{1}{2}$–1-inch) slices. Blanch, cool, drain and pack in polythene bags.	3 minutes
MUSHROOMS	Choose small button mushrooms and leave whole; wipe clean but do not peel. Sauté in butter for 1 minute. Drain, cool and pack in polythene bags. Mushrooms larger than 2.5 cm (1 inch) in diameter are only suitable for slicing and using in cooked dishes after freezing.	

PARSNIPS	Trim and peel young parsnips and cut into narrow strips. Blanch, cool, drain and pack in polythene bags.	2 minutes
PEAS	Use young, sweet green peas, not old or starchy. Shell and blanch, shaking the blanching basket from time to time to distribute the heat evenly. Cool, drain and pack in polythene bags.	1–2 minutes
MANGE-TOUT	Trim the ends. Blanch, cool, drain and pack in polythene bags.	2–3 minutes
PEPPERS	Freeze red and green peppers separately. Wash well, remove stems, seeds and membranes. Can be blanched as halves for stuffed peppers, or in thin slices for stews and casseroles. Cool, drain and pack halves in containers and slices in polythene bags.	3 minutes
SPINACH	Select young leaves. Wash very thoroughly under running water; drain. Blanch in small quantities, cool quickly and press out excess moisture. Pack in rigid polythene containers or polythene bags, leaving 1 cm ($\frac{1}{2}$ inch) headspace.	2 minutes
TOMATOES	Tomatoes are most useful if frozen as purée or as juice, although whole ones can be used in casseroles. *Purée*—Skin and core tomatoes, then simmer in their own juice for 5 minutes until soft. Press through a nylon sieve or liquidise, cool and pack in small polythene containers. *Juice*—Trim, quarter and simmer tomatoes for about 10 minutes. Press through a nylon sieve and season with salt—5 ml (1 level tsp) salt to every 1 litre ($1\frac{3}{4}$ pints). Cool and pack in small polythene containers.	

Vegetables not suitable for freezing Chicory, cucumber, endive, kale, lettuce, radishes, Jerusalem artichokes (suitable only as soups and purées).

Note Herbs, such as thyme, sage, rosemary, parsley and mint can be frozen for up to 6 months. Wash and dry the herbs. Either chop before freezing, or crumble when frozen. Prepare bouquet garni, if required. Wrap in small bundles and place in moisture-proof bags. Make individual foil-wrapped packs of chopped herbs. If kept accessible, frozen herbs are as useful as dried, for they can be popped into stews, etc., while still frozen.

Vegetable Preserving Chart

Vegetable	Prime Condition	Time for Seasonal Glut	Methods of Preserving
ARTICHOKES, Globe	Leaves should be closely folded, without dry edges, and have a slight bloom. There should be no swelling at the base of the globe.	July–September	Freezing
Jerusalem	Use as fresh as possible as they become wrinkly and soft.	October–March	Pickling
ASPARAGUS	The heads should be well-formed and tightly packed. Avoid woody or wilting stems.	May–June	Bottling Freezing
AUBERGINES	Skin should be shiny and un-wrinkled. Fruit should feel firm when gently squeezed. Avoid any with blemishes.	November–December	Chutney Freezing
AVOCADOS	Skin will be smooth or knobbly according to variety—avoid wrinkled skin. Buy fruit that is firm rather than soft.	November–December	Freezing
BEANS, broad	The smaller pods will contain sweeter beans. Avoid any pods with blemishes.	June–August	Drying Freezing
French and runner	The beans should be bright green in colour and crisp. Avoid over-grown and stringy beans.	July–August	Freezing Pickling Salting
BEETROOT	Uncooked—avoid beetroot with damaged or wrinkled skin. Cooked—the skin should look fresh and moist.	December–January	Chutney Freezing Pickling Storing
BROCCOLI	Select small, tightly packed heads or curds. The stalks should be crisp when snapped.	Purple: November–December Green or Calabrese: July–August	Freezing
BRUSSELS SPROUTS	Select even-sized, bright green sprouts, with no wilting leaves.	November–March	Freezing
CABBAGE	Select firm, crisp heads without wilting or damaged outer leaves.	Spring cabbage: April–May Spring greens: November–April Summer cabbage: June–October White cabbage: October–February Savoy cabbage: August–May Red cabbage: August–January	Freezing Pickling Relish Salting

Vegetable	Prime Condition	Time for Seasonal Glut	Methods of Preserving
CARROTS	Select fresh-looking carrots without bruises or blemishes.	November–March	Chutney Freezing Jam Mincemeat Pickling Storing
CAULIFLOWER	Select white, tightly packed curds without yellow blemishes. Leaves should also look fresh.	August–November	Chutney Freezing Pickling Relish
CELERY	Select thick stalks with fresh leaves. English celery is usually covered with soil—avoid any broken or blemished stalks.	July–March	Freezing Pickling Relish
COURGETTES	Select smooth-skinned even-sized courgettes about 7.5–10 cm (3–4 inches) long.	August–September	Freezing
CUCUMBERS	Select even-shaped, smooth-skinned cucumbers which are firm to the touch.	July–August	Chutney Pickling Relish Storing
FENNEL	Select pale green or white coloured fennel, avoiding any that are dark green.	All year	Freezing
KOHLRABI	Select small, young, tender kohlrabi, avoiding large, coarse ones with decaying leaves.	July–March	Freezing Storing
LEEKS	Select even-sized, straight leeks. The tops should be trimmed but are a guidance to freshness.	October–January	Freezing
MANGE-TOUT	Select young, crisp, bright green mange-tout which will have a sweet taste.	April–June	Freezing
MARROW	Select smaller marrows weighing about 1 kg (2 lb).	August–October	Chutney Jam Freezing Pickling Storing
MUSHROOMS	Select mushrooms that are clean and white. Avoid those that are discoloured or limp.	All year	Drying Freezing Ketchup Pickling

Vegetable Preserving Chart cont.

Vegetable	Prime Condition	Time for Seasonal Glut	Methods of Preserving
ONIONS	Select firm onions with a dry paper skin. Press onions at the neck to test for softness and decay.	October–March	Chutney Drying Pickling Relish Sauces Storing
PARSNIPS	Select clean, pale-coloured roots. Avoid those that are split or have brown blemishes.	October–March	Freezing Storing
PEPPERS	Select shiny even-shaped peppers. Avoid split or blemished peppers.	Red: March Green: July–August	Chutney Drying Freezing Pickling Relish
POTATOES	Select clean, even-sized, even-shaped potatoes free from eyes, splits and blemishes.	Main crop: October–March New: July–September	Storing
SALSIFY	Avoid damaged roots.	October–April	Storing
SHALLOTS	Select firm shallots with no soft spots. The skin should be fine and papery without blemishes.	September–January	Chutney Pickling Sauces Storing
SPINACH	Select crisp, unwilted leaves.	May and September–December	Freezing
SWEDES	Select small swedes, avoiding any that have been forked when lifted.	September–March	Storing
SWEETCORN	Select cobs with stiff bright green leaves with a dark brown 'silk' at the tip. The corn should be pale golden and extrude milky coloured liquid when squeezed.	September–November	Freezing Relish
TOMATOES	Select firm, bright red/orange fruits. Buy under- rather than over-ripe fruit. Avoid squashy or damaged fruit.	August–September	Bottling Chutney Freezing Jam Marmalade Pickling Relish Sauce Storing
TURNIPS	Select small, even-sized turnips. Avoid any that are blemished or have soft patches.	October–March	Storing

Fruit Preserving Chart

Fruit	Prime Condition	Time for Seasonal Glut	Methods of Preserving
APPLES, cooking	Fresh looking and sweet smelling. Firm to the touch. Without bruises or marks on the skin.	September–October	Bottling Butter Cheese Chutney Curd Drying Freezing Jam Jelly Marmalade Mincemeat Pickling Sauce Storing
APPLES, eating	Fresh looking and sweet smelling. Firm to the touch. Without bruises or marks on the skin.	September–October	Butter Drying Freezing Storing
APRICOTS	Fruits should be firm. Skin should be unwrinkled and without bruises and blemishes.	May–August December–February	Bottling Butter Candying Chutney Drying Freezing Jam Liqueur Pickling
BANANAS	Buy when slightly green. Avoid marked skins or squashy fruits.	All year	Chutney Pickling
BILBERRIES	Choose firm, well shaped fruits, avoiding any that are squashed or damaged.	July–September	Jam
BLACKBERRIES	Berries should be glossy and a dark colour. Avoid squashed or damaged fruit.	August–October	Bottling Cheese Freezing Jam Jelly Liqueur Pickling Vinegar
BLACKCURRANTS	Select dark ripe berries. Avoid damaged or moist fruit.	July–August	Bottling Conserve Freezing Jam Jelly Liqueur Vinegar

Fruit Preserving Chart cont.

Fruit	Prime Condition	Time for Seasonal Glut	Methods of Preserving
CHERRIES	Select fruit that is firm and dry, whether black, red or white.	June–July	Bottling Brandy Candying Conserve Freezing Jam Jelly Pickling
CRAB-APPLES	Select firm, shiny, unblemished fruits.	September	Candying Jelly Pickling
CRANBERRIES	These berries vary in colour but should be bought bright, dry and unshrivelled.	October–February	Cheese Chutney Jam Jelly
DAMSONS	Select dark fruits with a bloom on the skins. Avoid marked or blemished fruits.	August–September	Bottling Cheese Chutney Freezing Jam Jelly Pickling
DATES	Choose plump, shiny dates with a smooth skin.	September–March	Chutney Pickling
ELDERBERRIES	Select firm, purplish-black berries.	September–October	Jelly Sauces
FIGS	Select figs that are soft to the touch with a bloom on the skins.	July–October	Bottling Chutney Freezing Jam
GOOSEBERRIES	Select the berries that have a slight yellow tinge. Avoid split or damaged fruit.	July–August	Bottling Chutney Curd Freezing Jam Jelly Pickling
GRAPEFRUIT	Select fruit that is bright yellow in colour with an undamaged or un-blemished skin. Avoid squashy skin—usually means dry fruit.	January–March	Candying Curd Freezing Marmalade
GRAPES	Buy grapes in bunches, avoiding any with shrivelled, split or squashed fruits on them.	August	Freezing Jelly

Fruit	Prime Condition	Time for Seasonal Glut	Methods of Preserving
GREENGAGES	Select fruit that is firm to the touch with a yellow tinge. Avoid wrinkled skins and damaged fruit.	August	Bottling Freezing Jam
GUAVAS	Guavas vary in size and are light yellow in colour when ripe.	May–July	Jelly
JAPONICAS	Select firm, pale green fruit.	September	Jelly
KIWI FRUIT (Chinese gooseberries)	Avoid fruit with shrivelled skins.	January and May–November	Conserve
KUMQUATS	Choose even-sized fruits with bright yellow skin.	October–March	Conserve
LEMONS AND LIMES	Smooth-skinned lemons will usually produce more juice and have thin skins.	All year	Candying Chutney Curd Freezing Jelly Marmalade Pickling Squash
LOGANBERRIES	Choose firm, undamaged fruits.	July–August	Bottling Freezing Jam
MANGOES	Choose mangoes that are just soft and have a good perfume. Avoid under-ripe or blemished fruits.	January and September	Chutney Freezing
MELONS	Test for ripeness by gently pressing the top of the fruit—it should yield.	April–June	Freezing Jam Pickling
MULBERRIES	Choose firm, sweet-scented mulberries.	August–September	Bottling Jam Jelly
NECTARINES	Select only perfect and ripe fruits.	July–September	Bottling
ORANGES	Select fruit that is light rather than dark orange in colour. Buy under-ripe with green tinge rather than over-ripe.	Seville: January–February	Candying Chutney Conserve Curd Drink Freezing Jelly Liqueur Marmalade Pickling

Fruit Preserving Chart cont.

Fruit	Prime Condition	Time for Seasonal Glut	Methods of Preserving
PEACHES	Select peach-coloured fruit rather than yellow for ripeness. Avoid split or blemished fruit.	July–August	Bottling Candying Chutney Conserve Freezing Jam Liqueur Pickling
PEARS	Select under- rather than over-ripe fruits and store for 1–2 days at room temperature. Avoid split or blemished fruit.	Cooking: October–December Eating: August–November	Bottling Candying Chutney Drying Freezing Jam Pickling Sauce Storing
PINEAPPLES	Select fruit that yield to slight pressure, with stiff leaves. Avoid bruised or blemished fruit.	April–May	Bottling Conserve Freezing Jam Liqueur
PLUMS	Select fruit with a bloom on the skin. Buy firm, slightly under-ripe fruit and store for 1–2 days.	September	Bottling Butter Candying Chutney Conserve Drying Freezing Jam Pickling
QUINCES	Select firm, yellow, unmarked fruits. Quinces turn pink when cooked.	October–November	Bottling Cheese Jam Jelly
RASPBERRIES	Select deep-coloured, firm fruits. Pale-coloured fruits will not be so ripe or juicy.	July–August	Bottling Conserves Curd Freezing Jam Jelly Liqueur Vinegar
REDCURRANTS	Select firm, dry fruit. Avoid damp or blemished fruit which will rot quickly.	July–August	Bottling Conserve Freezing Jam Jelly

Fruit	Prime Condition	Time for Seasonal Glut	Methods of Preserving
RHUBARB	Select firm, crisp stalks with clean, fresh ends. Avoid split or blemished stalks or those with brown ends.	March–June	Bottling Chutney Freezing Jam
ROSE HIPS	Select hard, shiny, bright red fruits.	September	Jelly Syrup
ROWAN-BERRIES	These berries are red-orange in colour and are the fruit of the mountain ash tree.	September–October	Jelly
SLOES	These berries are small and dark in colour.	September–October	Jelly Liqueur
STRAWBERRIES	Select fruit that is bright red in colour and firm to the touch. Avoid over- or under-ripe fruit.	June–July	Bottling Conserve Freezing Jam Jelly
TANGERINES	Buy tangerines that have a bright orange to red, loose skin.	October–March	Curd Marmalade

Index